ALSO BY JAMES ROMM

Ghost on the Throne:
The Death of Alexander the Great and the War for Crown and Empire

The Edges of the Earth in Ancient Thought

The Landmark Arrian: The Campaigns of Alexander

Dying Every Day

Dying Every Day

Seneca at the Court of Nero

JAMES ROMM

ALFRED A. KNOPF   NEW YORK   2014

THIS IS A BORZOI BOOK
PUBLISHED BY ALFRED A. KNOPF

www.aaknopf.com

Library of Congress Cataloging-in-Publication Data
Romm, James S.
Dying every day : Seneca at the court of Nero / by James Romm. —
First Edition.
pages cm
Includes bibliographical references.
ISBN 978-0-307-59687-1 (hardcover)
ISBN 978-0-385-35172-0 (eBook)
1. Seneca, Lucius Annaeus, approximately 4 B.C.–65 A.D.
2. Statesmen—Rome—Biography.   3. Philosophers—
Rome—Biography.   4. Nero, Emperor of Rome, 37–68.
5. Rome—History—Nero, 54–68.   I. Title.
B618.R64 2014
188—dc23
[B]
2013020720

Jacket images (left) Seneca, bpk, Berlin. Antikensammlung,
Staatliche Museen, Berlin, Germany; (right) Nero
© RMN-Grand Palais / (both) Art Resource, NY

Front-of-jacket photo montage by Markley Boyer

Jacket design by Jason Booher

Manufactured in the United States of America
First Edition

for Tanya
meae deliciae, mei lepores

Renaissance medallion, "Nero Watching the Dying Seneca."

Contents

Amici vitia si feras, facias tua.

If you put up with the crimes of a friend,
you make them your own.

—ROMAN PROVERB

Introduction

The Two Senecas

Here is one way to describe the career of Seneca, writer, thinker, poet, moralist, and for many years, top adviser and close companion of the emperor Nero:

By a strange twist of fate, a man who cherished sobriety, reason, and moral virtue found himself at the center of Roman politics. He did his best to temper the whims of a deluded despot, while continuing to publish the ethical treatises that were his true calling. When he could no longer exert influence in the palace, he withdrew and in solitude produced his most stirring meditations on virtue, nature, and death. Enraged by his departure, the emperor he had once advised seized on a pretext to force him to kill himself. His adoring wife tried to join him in his sober, courageous suicide, but imperial troops intervened to save her.

And here is another way to describe the same life:

A clever manipulator of undistinguished origin connived his way into the center of Roman power. He used verbal brilliance to represent himself as a sage. He exploited his vast influence to enrich himself and touched off a rebellion in Britain by lending usuriously to its inhabitants. After conspiring in, or even instigating, the palace's darkest crimes, he tried to rescue his reputation with carefully crafted literary self-fashionings. When it was clear that the emperor's enmity posed a threat, he sought refuge at the altar of philosophy even while leading an assassination plot. His final bid for esteem was his histrionic suicide, which he browbeat his unwilling wife into sharing.

These are the opposing ways in which Romans of the late first century A.D. regarded Seneca, the most eloquent, enigmatic, and politically engaged man of their times. The first is taken largely from the pages of *Octavia,* a historical drama written in the late decades of that century, by whom we do not know. The second is preserved by Cassius Dio, a Roman chronicler who lived more than a century after Seneca's death but relied on earlier writers for information. Those writers, it is clear, deeply mistrusted Seneca's motives. They believed the rumors that attributed to Seneca a debauched and gluttonous personal life, a Machiavellian political career, and a central role in a conspiracy to assassinate Nero in A.D. 65.

Between these extremes stands Tacitus, the greatest of Roman historians and by far the best source we have today for Nero's era. Tacitus, a shrewd student of human nature, was fascinated by the sage who extolled a simple, studious life even while amassing wealth and power. But ultimately Seneca posed a riddle he could not solve.

Tacitus made Seneca the principal character in the last three surviving books of his *Annals,* creating a portrait of great richness and complexity. But the tone of that portrait is hard to discern. Tacitus wavered, withheld judgment, or became ironic and elusive. Strangely, though aware of Seneca's philosophic writings, Tacitus made no mention of them, as though they had no bearing on the meaning of his life. And he passed no explicit judgment on Seneca's character, as he often did elsewhere. Our most detailed account of Seneca, in the end, is ambivalent and sometimes ambiguous.

One other ancient portraitist has left us his image of Seneca. In 1813 excavations in Rome unearthed a double-sided portrait bust created in the third century A.D. One side shows Socrates, the other Seneca, the two sages joined at the back of the head like Siamese twins sharing a single brain. The discovery gave the modern world its first glimpse of the real Seneca, identified by a label carved on his chest. The bust shows a full-fleshed man, beardless and bald, who wears a bland, self-satisfied mien. It seems the face of a businessman or bourgeois, a man of means who ate at a well-laden table.

Before the 1813 discovery, a different bust, now known as Pseudo-

Seneca, had been thought to show Seneca's face. It was gaunt, haggard, and haunted, its eyes seemingly staring into eternity. Its features had served as a model for painters depicting Seneca's death scene on canvas, among them Giordano, Rubens, and David.

Once again there were two Senecas. Pseudo-Seneca corresponded to what the Western world wanted to imagine about an ancient Stoic philosopher. Its leanness seemed to represent a hunger for truth and a rejection of wealth and material comfort. The discovery of the true Seneca in 1813 dispelled that fantasy. The world that gazed into that fleshy face realized that Seneca was not who he was thought to be.

The recovery of the 1813 bust parallels, for many, the experience of learning about Seneca's role in the history of Nero's Rome. The man we meet in the pages of Tacitus, still more in Dio, is not the man we imagine Seneca to be, if we know him through his moral treatises, letters, or tragedies. He does not seem to match up well with those writings, especially in his relationship to wealth. The two Senecas stand side by side, with no label of authenticity assuring us that one is the true visage, the other an illusion.

What follows is an effort to bring those two Senecas together into a single personality. It is a task that I had long believed impossible, and perhaps I was right to do so. Seneca wrote much but made few clear mentions of his political career, and he played a role in politics that often ignored the principles of his writings. My goal has been to hold both the writer and the courtier in view at all times, despite their nonacknowledgment of each other.

The resulting book is part biography, part narrative history, and part an exploration of Seneca's writings, both prose and verse. It does not give a comprehensive account of those writings, nor of the history of the Neronian era. My pursuit of a unified Seneca has forced me to be selective in both arenas.

I have focused on those Senecan texts, and passages of texts, that connect most clearly with Seneca's life at court. That has meant passing in silence over much of what a student of philosophy would look for. Indeed, it has meant omitting completely those works that cannot be

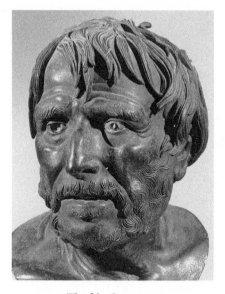

The false Seneca . . .

dated either before or after the accession of Nero. The reader will thus find no mention here of four important treatises—for the record, they are *De Otio, De Providentia, De Constantia Sapientis,* and *De Tranquilitate Animi*—that fall into this category.

Similarly, I have dealt with only the portion of Nero's life and reign in which Seneca was involved. I follow Nero's story only up to early A.D. 66, omitting the final two and a half years of his reign. By a happy coincidence, that is exactly the point at which our surviving text of Tacitus' *Annals* leaves off (if the loss of that work's final segment can be in any way called happy). I deal very little with the foreign affairs of Nero's regime, or even its domestic achievements. Instead, I have put the personal relations of Seneca and Nero at the forefront, as well as the interactions of both with Agrippina, Nero's mother. My story is thus in large part a family drama, to the extent that this threesome formed a peculiar sort of nuclear family.

Family dramas are always compelling, but the turbulence within Nero's palace also held huge historical importance. The future of a dynasty,

. . . and the real one. Roman portrait busts
of the first century B.C. and the
third century A.D.

even of Rome itself, hinged on whether a mother could get along with a son, whether a husband could stay married to his wife, and whether a tutor could get his student to respect and heed him. Nero's extreme youth at the time of accession, and his growing derangements afterward, made the task of managing him, or the failure to do so, critical to the fortunes of the empire and of the world—for the empire, as Romans liked to believe, had by Nero's era nearly reached the confines of the world that contained it.

My sources of information include the three works already mentioned, the *Annals* of Tacitus, the anonymous play *Octavia,* and Cassius Dio's *Roman History* (preserved only in fragments and summaries in the segments that cover the Neronian era). Additionally I have relied on Suetonius' *Lives of the Caesars,* various texts by Plutarch, Josephus, and Pliny the Elder, and the anonymous ancient biographies of Lucan. My most important and richest resource, naturally, has been the writings of Seneca himself—though these have also posed immense problems, as they do for all ancient historians.

Seneca wrote voluminously throughout Nero's reign but hardly ever discussed that reign in print. He rarely mentioned the people with whom he worked hand in glove for years—Claudius, Nero, Agrippina, Burrus, and Tigellinus. Perhaps a code of honor explains his reticence, or perhaps a sense that any disclosure would imperil his safety. In either case, he created a body of work filled with yawning chasms of silence. Even the great fire of 64, an event that destroyed much of Rome and caused massive upheaval, goes unmentioned.

Yet in the case of a writer so reflective, so alive to the world around him, the thought that the life had no influence on the work is implausible. Scholars have long tried to "feel out" that influence, some investing great effort in this inquiry, others willing only to raise a speculative question or two. I have borrowed from their insights in this book and also, I hope, contributed a few of my own. I do not claim Seneca's texts should be read as coded historical documents. But they do, I believe, reflect history, if only in the distorting mirrors of myth, metaphor, and analogy.

The debate begun in antiquity over who Seneca was, and whether to admire him, has never been resolved. In the year that this book was written, a scathing paragraph appeared in a popular history of Rome. The author, the art historian Robert Hughes, suggests that Seneca's contemporaries despised him as a patent fraud. "Seneca was a hypocrite almost without equal in the ancient world," Hughes claims. "Few can have mourned him." In the same year, a news item appeared about a man in his fifties, an immigrant from Eastern Europe who, while pushing a broom as a janitor at Columbia University, also managed to earn his degree there. In an interview, this man said that Seneca's letters had inspired him to pursue this rigorous path. To him, Seneca was no humbug.

My greatest challenge in writing this book has been how, or whether, to judge its central figure. I oscillated many times between opposing assessments, sometimes in the course of a single day. I did not feel, even as I completed the book, that I had settled in my own mind its central questions. I only hope that I have presented the problem of Seneca's character in some of its depth and complexity, and that I have not been unfair.

Seneca admitted in various ways that he had not lived up to his own ideals. He can be faulted for envisioning a better self than the one he was willing to settle for. Yet his vision is nonetheless beautiful, compelling, and humane. It has inspired great writers and thinkers through the ages, and janitors as well.

In the end, Seneca was human, all too human, with the flaws and shortcomings that the human condition entails. As he himself implied in one of his several *apologias,* he was not equal to the best, but better than the bad. And that, for many readers, will be good enough.

Dying Every Day

CHAPTER I

Suicide (I)

(A.D. 49 AND BEFORE)

How does one prepare a preteen for the task of ruling the world?

That question confronted imperial Rome at the midpoint of the first century A.D., as the reigning emperor, Claudius, grew increasingly infirm. It seemed likely then that supreme power would pass, for the first time, to an heir who was not fully grown. The most likely candidate was then twelve years old: Claudius' stepson, Domitius, whom he had recently adopted and given the name Nero. A natural son, Britannicus, was also waiting in the wings, but he was three years younger.

Given that the entire Roman empire, stretching from southern Britain to the Euphrates, a world-state of fantastic power and complexity, would rest on the shoulders of whichever boy succeeded, those three years might make a huge difference. At least, that was the hope of Nero's mother, Agrippina, the most powerful woman of her times, now Claudius' newly wedded wife.

Rome had no handbooks, no courses of study, to prepare a young man to be princeps—the executive office founded eight decades earlier by Augustus Caesar and still poorly defined. Four successive "first men" had imposed their own stamps on the job, with varying degrees of success.

Nero as a young boy.

Young Nero, in line to become the fifth princeps, would need to learn from their examples—and that task required no ordinary teacher.

Agrippina, doting mother of the new heir apparent, was awake to the demands of the situation—and the opportunities. Not only must her son—her only child—receive the best instruction on offer, but official Rome must *see* him receive it. The quality of Nero's tutor would reflect, as did every staffing change in the imperial household, the odds of his succeeding his adoptive father. Many Romans still hoped that Britannicus, the *natural* son of Claudius, would take his father's place; but Agrippina had dismissed her stepson's tutors and replaced them with nonentities, to discourage such expectations.

With a deft instinct for image making, Agrippina knew where to turn. A master speaker and writer, a man whose high repute as a moralist would shed its glow on her son, was then in exile on the island of Corsica, longing to return to Rome. This man would be forever in Agrippina's debt—or so she hoped—if she arranged his pardon and return; he would do whatever she required to elevate young Nero. Claudius had banished this man from Rome eight years earlier, but the charge—adultery—was pardonable. Claudius, worked on by Agrippina, could be persuaded to change his mind.

Thus was arranged the recall of Lucius Annaeus Seneca, the man known to us simply as Seneca or as Seneca the Younger. (His father, a literary figure of some repute, had the same name.) From his rocky island home on Corsica, where he had passed his time observing comets, stars, and planets, Seneca made his way to the imperial palace at Rome—an observatory of the dark recesses of the human heart.

> *I was better off hidden away, far from the crimes wrought by envy,*
> *shunted off from it all, on the cliffs of the Corsican sea. . . .*
> *How glad I was there, my eyes on Nature's masterwork—*
> *the sky, and the sacred paths of the sun,*
> *the cosmos' motions, the allotments of night and day,*
> *the sphere of the Moon, that glory of upper air,*
> *spreading its light to a ring of unanchored stars.*

With these words, the author of *Octavia,* a Roman play written by one of Seneca's admirers, introduces the character "Seneca" onto his stage. This unknown author has left us a mythicized, but nonetheless fascinating, account of Nero's inner circle, a self-enclosed group whose twisted relationships and psychic torments were already legendary in their own day. Tragic drama, this author felt, was the best way to understand these people, even if historical facts had to be bent. Many modern playwrights and operatic composers, including Racine, Monteverdi, and Handel, have concurred.

Seneca never commented, in any of his extant works, on whether he regretted his departure from Corsica, by far the most consequential of the many turns his life took. Some later claimed that he hoped to go to Athens, not Rome, when he left, to study the works of great Greek thinkers in the city where they had lived. But the claim might well have arisen as an effort at image repair. There were many supporters of Seneca, including *Octavia*'s author, who portrayed him as what he strove to be—a moral philosopher of the Stoic school—and sought to counter the charges, brought by others, that he was a politician, a greedy business-man, and a corrupt power-monger who used philosophy to cloak his motives. The divide between these views continues to this day.

By his own account, Seneca had been won over to Stoicism in boy-hood, at the feet of Attalus, a Greek who taught at Rome around the turn of the millennium.

Seneca, with his father and brothers, had moved to Rome from Cor-duba, in what is now Spain, at a time when Greek sages were thronging to the world's new imperial city. Attalus impressed young Seneca with his abstemious way of life, an asceticism that, he said, made him a king; by needing nothing—neither wealth, nor position, nor fine dress and food—he gained as much power and freedom as any monarch. "To me, he seemed even greater than a king, in that he was entitled to pass judg-ment on kings," wrote Seneca many decades later—after he himself had tasted the same privilege.

Attalus was only one of several whose wares young Seneca sampled in Rome's bustling marketplace of ideas. Cynics preached an even sterner ascetic code than the Stoics, ranting against wealth and power while wear-ing threadbare cloaks and gnawing crusts of bread. Pythagoreans taught the mystical doctrine of transmigration of souls and avoided the eating of meat, which they regarded as cannibalism. Seneca briefly adopted their practice, but his father made him desist. In that year, A.D. 19, a surge of xenophobia had gotten Jewish rites banned from Rome, and a vegetarian diet looked uncomfortably similar to a kosher one.

Most of the philosophers whom young Seneca heard were imports from Greece, but a native Roman school had also sprung up, and Seneca took a strong interest in it. Its founder, Quintus Sextius, had famously declined appointment to the Senate, a high privilege that had been offered to him by Julius Caesar. Sextius preferred to devote himself full-time to philosophy, though he at first found the work so difficult that he almost hurled himself out a window in frustration.

Seneca liked the way Sextius, in his writings, used tough, vigorous Roman language to express Greek moral ideas, which in their native tongue often felt flaccid and effeminate. A passage from Sextius that he admired contained a military analogy, comparing a virtuous man's resistance to evil to an infantry hollow square—a defensive formation that brought spearpoints to bear in four directions at once. The muscular image held for Seneca the appeal of the unattainable, for he suffered from respiratory ailments and never saw a day's military service. In his own later writings, of the countless metaphors he employed, among his favorite and most frequent would be that of moral effort, or human life itself, as armed combat.

In his writings, Seneca praised Sextius' choice, to practice philosophy and forsake politics, but in his own career, he did not follow it. Somehow, by a thought process he never revealed to his readers, Seneca decided, in his thirties, to pursue *both* paths. Still practicing ascetic habits that he learned from Attalus—sleeping only on hard pillows, and avoiding mushrooms and oysters, Rome's favorite delicacies—and studying natural phenomena, he nonetheless embarked on the *cursus honorum* that led, ladderlike, to ever higher offices. In his late thirties, after a sojourn in Egypt with a powerful uncle, Seneca, along with his older brother Novatus, entered the Senate—the very move Sextius had disdained.

By family status, Seneca had no right to a seat in the Senate house. His clan, the Annaei, were *equites,* "knights," well off but neither rich nor noble, and under Rome's class-stratified constitution, they were excluded from high office. Seneca's father—a tough-minded, rock-ribbed man of letters, still sharp as a tack in his late eighties—had once hoped for adlection, the magical process by which the princeps could elevate a knight to the Senate, if only so that he might hear Cicero declaim. His two elder sons would finally gain the rank that eluded him.

As he neared the end of a long life, back in the family seat of Corduba, the elder Seneca gave a qualified blessing to the path on which these two had set out, while praising his cherished third son—young Mela, the quiet and studious brother—for avoiding it. "I see your soul shrinks back from public office and disdains all ambition, and desires only one thing: to desire nothing," the crusty old man of letters wrote, urging Mela toward his own specialty, the study of rhetoric. "You were always more intelligent than your brothers. . . . *They* are all about ambition and are now preparing themselves for the Forum and for political office. In *those* pursuits," he remarked, as though issuing a warning, "the things one hopes for are also the things one must fear."

At around the time those words were written, just after Seneca had made his start in the Senate, Agrippina the Younger (so known because her mother was also named Agrippina) gave birth to a son. The event had political meaning, for this Agrippina was great-granddaughter of Augustus and sister to the reigning princeps, Caligula, who was as yet childless himself. Official Rome marked the arrival of a promising heir—for every male who shared Augustus' blood had promise, and young Domitius had a greater share than most.

If Seneca joined his colleagues in hailing the birth, as he must have done, he could have little guessed how much his own fate hung on this boy's future. There was as yet no clue that their two lives would, for

A digital reconstruction of the interior of the Roman Senate,
with benches on which senators sat.

almost two decades, be intertwined in a strange and tortuous partnership on which much of Rome's destiny hung. Nor could Agrippina have divined from the portent she saw at her son's birth—the rays of the rising sun falling full on the baby's face—that someday he would seek to have her murdered, and seek Seneca's help.

Agrippina was a spirited, beautiful twenty-two-year-old when her son was born, already well versed in the perils of dynastic politics. Her father, Germanicus, an adored war hero whom many had hoped would be princeps, died under mysterious circumstances in her childhood; his ashes, escorted home from abroad by her mother, had produced a national outpouring of grief. Over the next fifteen years, she lost that mother, and two of her three brothers, to political murders. The reigning princeps, Tiberius, resented the cultlike reverence the public felt for Germanicus, and looked with suspicion on the orphaned children who shared in it. But he nonetheless spared Agrippina and her sisters, as well as Germanicus' last surviving son, Gaius—known to us by his nickname, Caligula—whom in the end he adopted.

Tiberius had just died, and the four siblings had just come into their own, when Agrippina became a mother. Caligula was officially coruler, along with Tiberius' grandson, but he quickly eliminated his partner and assumed sole rule. A dashing twenty-five-year-old, sound of body and—for the moment—of mind, Caligula was hailed as the bringer of a new golden age, and his three charming sisters added to his luster. Caligula even made his sisters sharers of his power, adding their names to the oath of loyalty sworn annually to the princeps. Agrippina, one of the cherished children of Germanicus, had gained stature unprecedented for a Roman woman; and she had wealth as well, thanks to her marriage, since age thirteen, to a rich aristocrat, Domitius Ahenobarbus, Nero's father.

Agrippina could not attend meetings of the Senate (though one day she would try to fix that), but she heard much about what went on in that fervid chamber, the Curia. An orator who had recently arrived there, Lucius Annaeus Seneca, was attracting notice for his unique verbal style—seductive prose with short, punchy clauses and pithy epigrams. Agrippina formed a bond of friendship with Seneca, a man almost two decades older but, as an *eques,* well below her (and his fellow senators) in rank. So too did Agrippina's sister Livilla—and *that* bond was said, by some, to go beyond friendship.

Agrippina's brother did not care for Seneca, nor for the epigrammatic style in which he spoke. "Sand without lime," Caligula called those words, drawing an analogy from the building trade, where sand and lime were mixed to make mortar. Seneca's speeches, to Caligula, seemed to lack solidity—ear-catching phrases strung together without binder to firm them up. (That critique has been repeated, in various forms, ever since. Lord Macaulay echoed it in the 1830s when he wrote: "There is hardly a sentence [in Seneca] which might not be quoted; but to read him straightforward is like dining on nothing but anchovy sauce.") Or else they were "nothing but *commissiones,*" showy declamations like those put on for prizes at the start of public games.

Senators like Seneca were, at the outset of Caligula's reign, welcome visitors in the imperial household, for the Senate had cheered the new princeps and rushed to grant him supreme power. But the lessons of Roman history suggested that amity would not last. The Senate, still cherishing memories of its central role under the republic, had never reconciled itself to the principate, even though the attempt to prevent it— the killing of Julius Caesar—had failed. A bloody civil war had decided the question, and Augustus had taken over. But both he and his successor, Tiberius, had struggled to find a modus vivendi with stiff-necked senators. When that effort failed, those necks often went under the sword.

Over seven decades, the Senate had tried to assert its ancient prerogatives. But the princeps always had the final say, thanks to his personal army corps, the Praetorian Guard. These elite soldiers, encamped at the northeastern edge of the city, alone had the right to bear arms within Rome's boundaries. Each emperor had been careful to ensure that these troops, and in particular their prefects or commanding officers, were well fed, well paid, and loyal to his cause. Though it was bad taste for a princeps to deploy Praetorians against the Senate, all parties were certain that, if so ordered, the troops would obey.

The Praetorians were thus the ultimate weapon of a princeps. Calig-

The Praetorian Guard, depicted in a relief of
the first century A.D.

ula, as his sanity deteriorated and his hostility to the Senate grew, would test that weapon's limits—and finally exceed them.

No one quite knows how the downturn began, but Seneca, an eyewitness, attests to the terrifying depths it reached. Caligula stalks through Seneca's later writings like a monster in recurring nightmares, arresting, torturing, and killing senators, or raping their wives for sport and then taunting them with salacious descriptions of the encounters. "It seems that Nature produced him as an experiment, to show what absolute vice could accomplish when paired with absolute power," Seneca said of Caligula's madness.

Among the first whom Caligula victimized, after his mind began to turn, were his sisters, Agrippina and Livilla. They had been his closest companions, along with a third sister, Drusilla, who was thought by some to have been his lover. Drusilla died of illness in A.D. 38, plunging Caligula into deep grief; he emerged from the catastrophe a changed man. Without warning, while passing time with his surviving sisters at a posh estate, he accused them of having affairs—both at once—with their widowed brother-in-law, Lepidus, and conspiring to put *him* on the throne.

The Senate, asked to pass judgment, acceded to what the princeps desired. Agrippina and Livilla were branded state enemies and banished to the Pontine Islands, tiny patches of volcanic rock in the Tyrrhenian Sea. Probably Caligula meant for them never to return.

At age twenty-three, leaving her infant son in the care of her husband and sister-in-law, Agrippina went into exile. Before she left, Caligula added degradation (his signature touch) to her sentence. He forced Agrippina to carry the ashes of her alleged lover Lepidus, now executed, in a public burial procession. It was a cruel parody of their mother's heroic march, two decades earlier, with the ashes of their father, Germanicus. Ingenious in his sadism, Caligula had found a way to debase his sister, his dead brother-in-law, and the memory of his parents, all in a single spectacle. Then he auctioned off Agrippina's property to bearded Germans, leaving his sister destitute.

Exile to the Pontines had spelled death for most descendants of Augustus, and in this case, too, it seemed to be only a prelude. "I have swords as well as islands," Caligula quipped as he sent his sisters away. But somehow, as the weary months wore on, no Praetorians arrived at the prison of either Agrippina or Livilla, and the food allotments were not stopped. For whatever reason, Caligula, for the moment anyway, let his sisters live on.

Many Romans fell in the wake of the Lepidus conspiracy, among them aristocrats who had backed a different coup a generation earlier—that of a Praetorian prefect named Sejanus. Caligula had been but a boy when his adoptive father, Tiberius, put that plot down. But Caligula somehow grew suspicious that the remaining *Seianiani*, the supporters of Sejanus, were against him; the two plots, separated by fifteen years, seemed linked in his disordered mind. And that suspicion fell also on

Seneca, whose family was linked to the *Seianiani* in ways that could not have escaped notice.

Perhaps Seneca feared that the odor of the Sejanus conspiracy still clung to him, fifteen years later, and that Caligula would scent it out. That, at least, is one conclusion that has been drawn from a treatise he published at this time, his first extant philosophic work.

Consolation to Marcia, written about A.D. 40, takes the form of a letter addressed to a mother grieving for a dead son, but it was meant to be read widely. Seneca would play the same rhetorical trick his entire life, allowing his readers to listen in on what seemed to be an intimate exchange. His addressee was often a family member—his elder brother Novatus on several occasions—or a close friend. In this case, Marcia, a middle-aged woman of senatorial rank, was not connected with Seneca in any recoverable way. She was, however, the daughter of a man who had been persecuted by Sejanus, Cremutius Cordus.

In A.D. 25, Sejanus had deemed that Cordus, a senator and part-time historian, had committed treason by portraying Brutus and Cassius, Julius Caesar's assassins, as valiant men. Cordus defended himself in the Senate, claiming that freedom of speech had never before been so harshly repressed. But the mood in the Senate chamber, and the frowning countenance of the princeps as he sat in on the trial, foretold what the sentence would be. Cordus went home, shuttered himself in his room, and began fasting to death.

The sequel is related by Seneca in *Consolation to Marcia.* After her father had been locked away for four days, Marcia entered his room and discovered he was starving himself. He begged her not to prevent him. Meanwhile, in the Senate, word had gotten out that Cordus was trying to cheat Sejanus of his prey. Sejanus' partisans argued that a defendant on trial could not evade judgment in this way and pressed for an arrest and execution. While the debate proceeded, Cordus managed to achieve the death he sought. Angry officials ordered the burning of his histories, but a copy survived, and Marcia helped bring the work back into circulation twelve years later, after both Tiberius and Sejanus were dead.

It is an odd ploy Seneca uses—reminding Marcia of these painful details of her father's arrest and suicide, in a letter meant to offer her consolation. Perhaps he was merely maladroit. But perhaps, as one modern scholar suggests, he was pointedly putting himself on the right side of a political fault line. If to be friends with the friends of Sejanus was dangerous, then safety lay in being friends with his enemies—and in displaying that friendship to the world. On this reading, Seneca chose to console Marcia out of savvy self-interest.

Nothing can be proven, but the theory fits with a pattern of opportunism in much of Seneca's work. His command of the written word was so deft, his rhetorical skills so subtle, that it was easy for him to help himself while also helping others. The challenge for modern readers is deciding which motive is foremost in any given work. Perhaps Seneca himself often did not know.

In its larger goals, *Consolation to Marcia* uses Stoic ideas and methods to deal with the greatest of human griefs, the loss of a child. Seneca portrays himself as a doctor cleansing a patient's wounds. Those wounds have begun to fester: Marcia is still grieving more than two years after the death of her son Metistius. In Stoic terms, she has dangerously lost touch with Reason, the element that makes her fully a person. The Divine enthroned this element within the human soul, just as surely as it put a thinking brain atop the human body. If Reason cannot be restored to its proper primacy, Marcia will lose her personhood and any hope of happiness.

Seneca does not deny Marcia the right to grieve, for that would be cold—and coldness was often charged against the Stoics, as he was well aware. Seneca's version of Stoicism was softer, more adaptable to human frailties. Mourning is natural for a bereft parent, Seneca allows, but Marcia's grief has surpassed the bounds of Nature. Nature, for him as for all Stoics, was the master guide and template; it was allied with Reason and with God. Indeed these three terms, for Stoics, were close to synonymous.

Marcia's grief, for Seneca, exemplifies a universal human blindness. We assume that we *own* things—family, wealth, position—whereas we have only borrowed them from Fortune. We take for granted that they will be with us forever, and we grieve at their loss; but loss is the more normal event—it is what we should have expected all along. Our condition, could we see it aright, is that of an army assaulting a well-defended town: every moment might bring the bite of a barbed arrow. Then, shifting metaphors, Seneca compares our lot to that of a condemned criminal: "If you lament a dead son, his crime belongs to the hour in which he was born. A death sentence was passed on him then."

Is life on a battlefield, or on death row, worth living? Seneca seems to be of two minds. At one point, he extols the beauty of the world, the joys that outweigh all suffering. At another, he reckons up the pains of mortal life and claims that, were we offered it as a gift instead of being thrust into it, we would decline. In either case, life, properly regarded, is only a journey toward death. We wrongly say that the old and sick are "dying," when infants and youths are doing so just as certainly. We are dying every day, all of us. To finish the job early on, as Marcia's son did, is a fate to be envied.

Some of Seneca's comforts ring hollow or seem in dubious taste. When he tells Marcia to be grateful that she had joy of rearing her son, just as a breeder has joy of raising a puppy but then parts with the adult dog, we hear him reaching too far for analogies. Throughout his career, Seneca would struggle with the curse of the facile writer—not knowing when to stop. But his *Consolation to Marcia* is on the whole an inspiring work, impassioned in its tone and grand in the scope of its goals. Seneca aims, as he would do throughout the next quarter-century, to change the way humanity thinks about our greatest crisis, death.

Consolation to Marcia ends with a bizarre flourish, Stoic in origin but crafted into something all Seneca's own. Greek Stoicism held that the world would be burned away, then created afresh, in a recurring cycle. The doctrine was largely obsolete by Roman times, but Seneca gave it new life, in this work and others. He asks Marcia to picture her father, the heroic suicide Cordus, now dwelling in a place very much like Heaven (though Christianity had just begun at this time, half a world away in Jerusalem, and had only barely reached Roman ears). From his all-seeing seat in the sky, Cordus foresees what is to come:

Nothing will remain where it now stands. The old age of the world will level all, carry all away with itself. Not just mankind, but places, regions, continents—all these will be its sport. It will push down the mountains and toss new peaks to the sky. It will suck up the seas, turn rivers aside, and dissolve the congress of peoples that binds the social order of man. Cities will it drag down into deep chasms, shatter with earthquakes, infect with plague-bearing winds summoned up from its depths. It will swallow up with floods every inhabited place; it will kill every living thing on the submerged earth; it will burn and destroy mortal life with immense tongues of flame. And when the time comes for the earth to snuff itself out, in order to make itself new, all this will destroy itself by its own power; stars will crash into stars, and whatever now shines in an ordered array will burn up in a single flame in which all matter is consumed.

He offers all this to comfort Marcia, showing her that individual losses—like the death of Metistius—will soon be insignificant. But the ecstatic intensity of the passage goes well beyond this goal. It appears that Seneca, as he endured the horrors of Caligula, found something deeply stirring in the nearness of the world's end.

It was not apocalypse but redemption that arrived, soon after Seneca published his *Consolation.*

One day in early 41, when he was in his fourth year as princeps, Caligula awoke from a strange dream. He had been sitting at the feet of Jupiter on Mount Olympus, when the god pushed him with his big toe and sent him hurtling downward. It was a prophetic image, for before the next day ended, Caligula was dead.

His mad behavior had gone so far as to turn even his Praetorians against him. If they let him continue in power, he would destroy the principate itself, the institution that was their sinecure and raison d'être. They made common cause with the senators, his principal victims. A squad of soldiers cut him off in a tunnel leading out of a theater and stabbed him to death. His body was cremated unceremoniously, and his ashes were buried beneath a low mound of earth.

As the fatal strokes fell, they changed forever the unwritten definition of the principate. Caligula's experiment in absolute power had proved that there was, finally, a check. The Praetorians had imposed it. And in the hours that followed the murder, they also seized a central role in the question of succession. While the Senate dithered vaguely over a hoped-for return of the republic, soldiers collected Caligula's sickly paternal uncle, Claudius—found trembling behind a curtain, according to legend, though more likely well briefed on what was to happen—and brought him to the Praetorian camp, where he was hailed with cries of "Imperator!"

Claudius, in turn, thanked the guard with a huge bequest of five years' salary per man. Setting a precedent that was to endure for centuries, the Praetorians had dispatched one emperor and installed another—and got rich for their efforts. They had transformed themselves from honor guard and security force to Rome's behind-the-scenes kingmakers. Except that Claudius was not a king, but something vaguer and less substantial. Rome had abjured hereditary monarchy centuries before and could not admit to itself that a *rex*—even the word was considered toxic—was once again head of state.

The Senate, which had formally acclaimed three previous emperors, took no part in this transfer of power. The swiftness with which Caligula had imploded had allowed them no time to align behind the new ruler. Claudius, aware that the Senate mistrusted him, did not enter the Curia for a solid month—and then only with a bodyguard. He was a creature of the Praetorians, selected by none but them. He acknowledged it candidly on his coins, some of which depicted the gates to the Praetorian barracks or a soldier taking Claudius by the hand.

Seneca watched the bloody fall of Caligula from near at hand but seems to have taken no part. In his writings, at least, he kept a cool distance from the conspiracy. Regicide was a sensitive matter to discuss in print, for every princeps was threatened by it, and none could allow it to be praised. In one hypothetical discussion, Seneca advocated a final solu-

An early coin of Claudius, showing his own image on one side and the Praetorian camp on the other. The abbreviated words *Imperatore recepto,* "The commander received," recall the moment of Claudius' accession.

tion for a princeps who was incurably insane, but then went on to say—prudently, for a minister of state—that such freaks of nature were as rare as chasms gaping in the solid earth, or underwater volcanoes. Not even the case of Caligula, perhaps, would qualify under such strict guidelines.

Though he could not write openly about Caligula's fall, Seneca could at least survey the wreckage of the Roman political class. Victims of torture and rape stirred his pity, but also, perhaps more so, onlookers forced to accept those crimes without protest—the regime's moral casualties. The harrowing stories of *De Ira* ("On Anger"), probably written soon after Caligula's fall, show the young senator reckoning up the spiritual cost of despotism: the psychic wounds suffered by those forced to capitulate. It was the defining problem of Seneca's age, and he was to grapple with it as no one else did, both in his writings and in his own life.

De Ira is Seneca's first in a string of treatises, each dealing with a single ethical topic announced in the title (*De Clementia* or "On Mercy," *De Brevitate Vitae* or "On the Shortness of Life," and so on). Anger leads the series of topics because anger poses such an immense threat to Reason. Seneca shows first why *ira* must be avoided, then how it can be. If we exert strenuous effort—Seneca uses the analogy of a sponge diver learning to hold his breath for ever-longer intervals—we can master anger and prevent it from infecting our souls. Along the way, Seneca discusses some disturbing cases in point.

De Ira, for instance, tells of Pastor, a wealthy *eques,* whose son Caligula had marked as an enemy merely because he had nice hair. (The princeps himself was going bald.) Pastor begged the princeps to spare his son, prompting the peeved Caligula to immediately have the boy killed. After the murder, Caligula brought Pastor to the palace and ordered him to drink wine and put on festive garlands; a soldier stood nearby, watching for signs of discontent. Pastor steeled himself and cheerfully drank the health of his son's killer. How could he bring himself to do it? asks Seneca, then gives the answer: Pastor had *another* son (and Caligula knew it).

Not only in Rome, but everywhere and in all times, good men have knuckled under to despots. Elsewhere in *De Ira* Seneca calls to mind the sufferings of Asian viziers in old Greek legends. Harpagus served as chief minister to a Persian king but offended his master by disregarding an order. The king took a gory revenge: he served Harpagus a stew of his own children's flesh, then showed him the severed heads to reveal what he had eaten. How did Harpagus like his dinner? the king asked, with Caligulan cruelty. Harpagus' choking reply was "At a king's table, every meal is pleasant." The flattery at least gained him this, Seneca says grimly: he did not have to finish his meal.

De Ira teaches its readers to avoid anger by disregarding injuries. But the cases of Harpagus and Pastor test the limits of this doctrine. It is one thing for a great Stoic to ignore a man who jostled him in the public bath, or even one who spat in his face (two other tales told in *De Ira*). To accept the murder of one's children goes beyond anger management, into the realm of moral self-annihilation. Yet Seneca suggests, initially, that this is indeed what his teaching requires. "That's how one eats and drinks at the tables of kings, and that's how one replies," he comments on the tale of Harpagus. "One must smile at the slaughter of one's kin."

Then abruptly, as though shocked at where his own argument has led him, he changes track:

But is life really worth so much? Let us examine this; it's a different inquiry. We will offer no solace for so desolate a prison house; we will encourage no one to endure the overlordship of butchers. We shall rather show that in every kind of slavery, the road of freedom lies open. I will say to the man whom it befell to have a king shoot arrows at his dear ones, and to him whose master makes fathers banquet on their sons' guts: "What are you groaning for, fool? . . . Everywhere you look you find an end to your sufferings. You see that steep drop-off? It leads down to freedom. You see that ocean, that river, that well? Freedom lies at its bottom. You see that short, shriveled, bare tree? Freedom hangs from it. . . . You ask, what is the path to freedom? Any vein in your body."

This rhapsodic hymn to suicide stands as a second landmark in Seneca's thought, like the equally fervent apocalypse scene in *Consolation to Marcia*. Stoics had long considered suicide to be a remedy for inescapable ills, including abuse by a cruel despot. But what had been a minor topic among the Greek Stoics became all too central in Rome in the age of the Caesars. Indeed, for Seneca, it became a kind of fixation. In writings throughout his career, he recurs again and again to agonizing questions of how, why, whether, and when to take one's own life. Later ages decided he had been aptly named, deriving *Seneca* from the Latin phrase *se necare*, "to kill oneself."

The template for Roman political suicide had been set in the previous century, by a man named Marcus Porcius Cato. The last in a long line of famous Catos, an ascetic who trained himself to endure hunger and cold, Cato found himself ranged against Julius Caesar in a civil war of the 40s B.C. The city he governed, Utica in North Africa, was one of the last anti-Caesar strongholds, and after it fell, no hope was left. Cato and a small band of followers fled and took refuge in a friend's villa, where Cato—who had been reading a serene account of Socrates' death, Plato's *Phaedo*—retired to a private room and fell upon his sword. His companions heard his struggles and rushed to help him; a doctor among

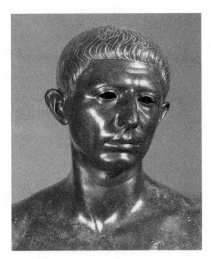

Bronze portrait bust of Marcus Cato,
the legendary Stoic suicide.

them tried to reinsert his viscera and sew up the wound. But Cato, briefly regaining consciousness, ripped out stitches and organs with his own hands and expired.

The gruesome self-disemboweling came to be seen as an exemplary act of lived philosophy. It showed a heroic devotion to autonomy—the personal freedom that Caesar's victory had threatened—and a superhuman defiance of pain and fear. As the Caesarean system took hold, Cato's suicide took on new meaning to those who mourned loss of liberty, shining ever brighter as a moral exemplum. In Seneca's works, it glows incandescent—as does nearly everything Cato did or said.

But political suicide in Seneca's day was a different gesture than it was in Cato's. Often it signaled acquiescence to autocracy rather than defiance. A bizarre compact had been struck between aristocracy and ruler: the princeps would allow his victims to pass on their wealth to their heirs, rather than forfeiting it to the state, if they executed *themselves* rather than force him to use his Praetorians. They could save self-respect, and avoid the horror of decapitation, if they took their own lives. Their bodies would be accorded due rites of burial. The princeps could then present their death to the public as evidence of guilt, or at least of surrender.

The system had become formalized by the time of Caligula, who kept two notebooks of enemies' names, titled "Sword" and "Dagger." The first listed those whom the soldiers would behead; those on the second would open their own veins (an operation requiring a much shorter blade). The state had a vital interest in keeping these categories distinct. In at least one case, a man attempting suicide and on the point of succeeding was rushed as he expired to a place of execution. He managed to die en route, cheating the princeps of an estate.

Even as their lifeblood ebbed away, political suicides knew that the princeps held the power to harm their wives and children. Their last words and gestures were carefully restrained. Wills were altered to give the princeps a sizable share of the property, lest he concoct a pretext to seize it all. The prudent might even insert flattery of the emperor into their suicide notes.

Seneca's hymn to suicide is thus very much of its time. By his day, suicide had come to signify, for aristocratic victims of the emperors, an inability to fight back; the best one could hope for was to embarrass the princeps by a highly public exit. In *De Ira*, accordingly, Seneca portrays suicide as an escape route, a way to gain release from the power of kings. What he doesn't acknowledge, or isn't aware of, is that suicide can also be a *means* of fighting back—even though an example was right before his eyes.

Prexaspes was another vizier like Harpagus, a right-hand man to a Persian monarch. His master, Cambyses, a notorious drunk, set out one day to prove to his court that wine did not affect him. He set up an archery course, with Prexaspes' son as the target; then, good as his word, he shot the boy through the heart. The story is related in *De Ira* just before the hymn to suicide above (in which Prexaspes is recalled as "the man whom it befell to have a king shoot arrows at his dear ones"). But Seneca leaves the sequel to the story curiously untold.

Years later Prexaspes found himself in possession of dangerous information. He knew that a group of plotters had murdered Cambyses' heir and put an impostor on the throne. He had colluded with the plot's leaders, who valued his high standing among the Persian people. When the people became uneasy about their king's legitimacy, the plotters asked Prexaspes to reassure them.

Prexaspes climbed a high tower in a central square of the capital. From a window at the top, he called out to the populace below—but not as instructed. He denounced the impostor and revealed the plot, confessing that he himself had killed the true heir to the throne, on Cambyses' orders. Then he launched himself off the tower and fell to his death. Inspired by his deed, the Persians rallied against the conspirators and soon overthrew them and their false king.

Prexaspes' model was one Seneca never contemplated, though he examined suicide in many forms. In *De Ira*, he configures the act as something private, passive, nonpolitical. He takes as implicit that regime change cannot happen at Rome, even if good men are willing to die.

That premise would govern the choices Seneca made in his own life and his own political career—which was soon to follow that of Prexaspes all too closely.

The fall of Caligula meant that Agrippina and Livilla, the two exiled sisters of the princeps, could return to Rome. Both now in their twenties, adored by the public as children of Germanicus and victims of their hated brother, these women enjoyed a stature that had never been higher. For some, it was too high.

Both women were beautiful, and one—Agrippina—was known to be fertile. Both were therefore suspected of using sex to gain power. Caligula, when getting them exiled, had accused them not just of backing the usurper Lepidus but of sleeping with him—a charge that played on the entrenched fears of Roman men. For decades, the women of the Caesars had held them in a cathectic spell, appearing to their mind's eyes as sexual sirens, manipulators, incestuous monsters, or some mixture of these frightening roles.

The sexuality of this sisterly pair was the special worry of Valeria

Messalina holding her infant son, Britannicus.

Messalina, the sixteen-year-old wife of the newly installed Claudius (soon to become herself a huge source of male anxiety). From the moment they returned, she regarded the daughters of Germanicus as rivals, even though they were her husband's nieces. She had already borne Claudius two children, including a son, Britannicus, but she feared the lineage of these two trophy women. Either one could solve a grave problem facing Claudius' regime, a problem that could be traced back decades earlier to Augustus, the principate's founder.

Rome's first princeps had been unlucky in the engendering of sons. Augustus' line had been carried forward through his sister Octavia, and through his only natural child, his daughter Julia. Claudius, and Messalina as well—she was his cousin, for the family was narrowly inbred—were descended from Augustus' sister, as they emphasized by naming their firstborn child Octavia. But Agrippina and Livilla were descended from his daughter. Their direct lineage trumped that of all collaterals.

The principate was not a monarchy—Rome had rejected that institution five centuries earlier and still officially reviled it—and so had no guidelines for succession. Nonetheless, a blood link to the holy figure of Augustus conferred innate legitimacy. The reign of Augustus' successor, his stepson Tiberius, had taken the throne outside that bloodline, while that of Caligula had restored it. With the accession of Claudius—who had not even been adopted by his predecessor, as Tiberius was adopted by Augustus—the office of princeps and the "royal" line had again parted ways, a situation that made all Rome uneasy.

Messalina had wed Claudius before he became princeps, when it seemed there was no chance he would be one. She had acceptable dynastic stature, but Claudius, significantly, had not allowed her to take the title *Augusta,* the ultimate mark of female dominion. Her lack of that title meant that Messalina was dispensable. In the imperial family, as she well knew, inconvenient marriages were easily broken so that new ones could be contracted. And the children of such broken unions, especially the males, had a peculiar habit of dying young.

Messalina had two assets with which to defend her place in the palace. The first was her youth, beauty, and warmth, which had a powerful hold on her husband (even if they did not enslave him as our sources represent). The second was her alliance with a canny Greek ex-slave, Narcissus, Claudius' private secretary. This highly placed staffer knew every trick in the political playbook. Messalina and Narcissus had discovered that if they worked on Claudius in tandem, she in the bedroom and he in offices of state, they could accomplish almost any goal. Their primary goal, in A.D. 41, was to get Livilla and Agrippina off the scene.

Livilla was married, so it was an easy matter to charge her with adultery, a criminal offense. No hard evidence was needed, only a demonstrably close tie to a man other than her spouse. Livilla had such a tie—to

Seneca. She was charged, tried, convicted, and sent back to the Pontine Islands, less than a year after leaving them. She had survived most of Caligula's reign on those obscure rocks, but this time her persecutors were more diligent. Within a few months, she was dead.

As her alleged partner in crime, Seneca was tried in the Senate, and one would give a lot to read the speech he made there. Perhaps Tacitus, that great chronicler of noble futility, recorded it in the now-lost portion of the *Annals;* he recorded many other speeches made by senators forced to defend themselves before colleagues forced to convict them. Seneca's case was particularly hopeless. The Senate not only condemned him but voted a death sentence, a harsh measure showing that someone, perhaps Messalina, considered him a threat. Claudius, however, wary of going too far, stepped in and commuted the sentence to exile, on Corsica.

Agrippina somehow escaped Messalina's wrath. It perhaps helped her cause that she was related to the empress; her sister-in-law Domitia was Messalina's mother. But aid from that quarter ended in 42, when Domitia's rich husband, Passienus Crispus, divorced her to marry Agrippina instead.

Probably Agrippina survived because her sister had died before her. She was now the last of a revered line, and she had borne a son. Domitius, now five years old, was a precious dynastic asset, the only male alive descended from *both* Germanicus and Augustus. Claudius and Messalina, sprung from a collateral line, thrust into power without support of the Senate or the people, reliant on the Guard and on Greek freedmen staffers whose loyalty was born of total dependence, were too weak to kill this mother and son—much though Messalina might have wished to.

Stripped of half his property, drummed out of the Senate, and having just buried an infant son—the only child he and his wife would ever have—Seneca made his weary way to Corsica.

The island on which he landed was no barren Pontine crag. Corsica had two Roman towns and many smaller settlements; among its diverse population, which included Ligurians, Spaniards, and Greeks, Seneca could find cultured countrymen. But in his first essay written there, a consolatory letter to his mother Helvia, Seneca transformed the place into an island fit for a Crusoe. He gloried in the role of unaccommodated man, living happily on what Nature provided.

"It is the mind that makes us rich," he told his mother, to dissuade her from mourning his fate. "The mind enjoys a wealth of its own goods, even in the harshest wilderness, so long as it finds what is enough to keep the body alive." These words might have been written by Thoreau at Walden Pond, although the terms of Seneca's exile, which allowed him to keep half his estate, gave him access to ready cash.

Corsica, as Seneca conjured it in *Consolation to Helvia,* was an ideal proving ground for the main Stoic tenet: true happiness comes from Reason, a force allied with Nature and with God. All that Seneca had left behind—senatorial rank, half his property, and what he called *gratia,* the public esteem he had won as a writer, a thinker, and a decent, fair-minded man—were "indifferents" in Stoic terms, inconsequential to the search for a good life. Of far greater consequence were the beauties that now surrounded him, especially the clear sky above—the sacred source from which, for the Stoics, the reasoning mind was sprung.

In his open letter to his mother, Seneca described in rapturous terms his observations of that sky, especially at night. He tracked carefully the phases of the moon and the motions of stars and planets. "So long as I can dwell with these, and lose myself—to the degree allowed to humans—in celestial things, what does it matter where I set my feet?" Closeness to the night sky was a kind of union with the Divine.

Rome, the city that had blocked the sky with walls and ceilings, appears in this letter as a monster of arrogance, ransacking the world to satisfy its gluttony. *Edunt ut vomant, vomunt ut edant* ("They eat to vomit, and vomit to eat"), writes Seneca in *Consolation to Helvia.* He describes the case of Apicius, Rome's greatest gourmand, who squandered a fortune on exotic shellfish, game birds, and delicacies. When his money began to run out, Apicius drank poison and killed himself. "His last draught was the most healthful he ever took," Seneca says, combining one favorite theme, overconsumption, with a second, suicide.

Why would any devoted Stoic, having found a paradise of Reason beneath a benign firmament, ever return to the cesspool called Rome?

The question goes to the heart of the enigma of Seneca's life. Seneca's friends and supporters recognized its importance, for they suggested, in the play *Octavia* and elsewhere, that his return to Rome from Corsica, eight years after leaving the city, was not voluntary. But Seneca gives them the lie in his own writings. In a second open letter from exile, probably written a year or two after the first, Seneca showed, obliquely but urgently, that he was desperate to be recalled by the emperor Claudius.

Claudius had firmed up his rule in those years, especially with an important military victory, the conquest of southern Britain. The princeps himself had symbolically led the final assault on Camulodunum, the center of resistance, though he spent only sixteen days on the other side of the Channel. It was enough for the Senate to grant him a triumphal parade in 44 and to dub him *Britannicus,* a title he humbly handed down to his son. As the date of his celebration approached, Claudius felt strong enough to pardon a few of his enemies. Seneca, who was no doubt following events from Corsica, hoped to be one of them.

The poet Ovid, banished from Rome decades earlier, had tried to win recall by barraging Augustus with groveling, flattering poems. Seneca took a different route. He addressed not the princeps himself but one of his highly placed staffers, a freedman named Polybius. Polybius had recently lost a brother, and Seneca seized the opportunity to send him a consolation, as he had earlier done with Marcia. His *Consolation to Polybius* survives nearly intact—though Seneca might wish it had not.

The shining Arcadia of the soul that Seneca had described in his first letter from Corsica has collapsed into dust in the second. His island is no longer a healthful bounty of Nature but a brutal, sterile rock. Seneca suggests, without saying so directly, that a man of refined mind must not be left to rot in such a place. Borrowing a trick from Ovid, he apologizes for the clumsiness of his style, claiming that hearing only the rude clamor of barbarian speech has damaged his ear for Latin.

Seneca's letter to Polybius repeats Stoic remedies for grief that he earlier preached to Marcia. But he has added a new one, tailored to the needs of a courtier. "When you wish to forget all your cares, think of Caesar," he wrote, referring to Claudius. "So long as he is safe, your family is well and you are in no way harmed . . . . He is your everything." A courtier's joy flows from the princeps he serves; and this particular princeps, Seneca goes on to say, brings joy supreme. "Whenever tears well up in your eyes, turn them toward Caesar; they will be dried by the sight of his greatest, most glorious godhead. His radiance will dull them so that they can behold nothing else, but will keep them fixed on himself."

Repugnant though this flattery might be, one can still be impressed by the ingenious way it is framed. Seneca could have fawned like Ovid, but instead he cleverly wove his plea into a high-minded work of philosophy. He measured out his obsequies with an expert eye. The right amount might do the trick yet not destroy his image or his self-esteem, should Claudius turn a deaf ear. Literary art, that supremely supple tool of which he was a supremely subtle master, could advance him in two ways at once, both as a political player and as a moral thinker.

But in this case, he failed on both scores. The effusions of *Consolation to Polybius* proved such an embarrassment that later, according to Dio, Seneca sought to have them suppressed. Nor was the work effective in winning him favor at court. Whatever Polybius made of it, Claudius passed Seneca by when inviting back other exiles to share his British triumph. For the next five years, he showed no concern for the Stoic languishing on Corsica. Seneca, to our knowledge, did not try again to beseech him.

Thus things might have remained, except that *impotens Fortuna*— Fortune that cannot be resisted, in the phrasing of the play *Octavia*— played its hand. A bizarre series of events in the year 48 put Agrippina into Messalina's place as empress and gave her the means to return Seneca, her old friend and ally, to Rome.

For almost seven years, Messalina continued as Claudius' wife but without the title *Augusta* that would have sealed her dynastic position. During those seven years, Agrippina, an attractive woman with a better lineage, had haunted the palace, and at some point she became a widow for a second time, inheriting a second fortune. Perhaps because of Agrippina's availability, or her own mental instability, Messalina felt her position deteriorating. In 48 she elected to try a new tack.

In a strangely unconcealed ritual, Messalina "married" a handsome, aristocratic lover, Gaius Silius, while her real husband, Claudius, was away from Rome. Silius had vowed to adopt Britannicus, son and heir of Claudius, as his own son. It was a kind of marital coup d'état. But without strong military backing, which Messalina seems not to have secured, it was doomed to fail. Soldiers confined Messalina in her private estate, the Lucullan gardens—today the grounds of the Villa Borghese—and, on orders issued by the palace, forced her to take her own life.

For the first time in eight decades of the principate, a widower with young children occupied the throne. The question of remarriage was a thorny one. Claudius wanted a new wife, but did he want a new heir? The public and the army had hailed Britannicus, but all were aware of his lack of Julian blood, and perhaps some also knew he had epilepsy. Descended through a collateral line going back only to Augustus' sister, he fell short of full legitimacy. Would not Britannicus forever struggle, as Claudius himself had struggled, with rivals who could claim descent from Augustus himself?

At some point, Claudius decided to scrap all previous dynastic assumptions and start his family over. He would marry Agrippina, daughter of Germanicus and great-granddaughter of Augustus. And even more significantly, he would betroth his daughter Octavia to Agrippina's son, Domitius. His own son Britannicus might thereby lose his chance at succession. But the chance that he himself could hold on to rule, and that his future grandsons would enjoy it, would be greatly enhanced. As had often been true in the Julian clan, what the male side lacked in legitimacy could be made up by the female.

Obstacles, however, stood in the way of this scheme. First, Agrippina, though widowed, available, and wealthy to boot, was, inopportunely, Claudius' *niece*. A decree had to be obtained from the Senate to allow the incestuous union. Second, Octavia, the emperor's daughter, now perhaps eight years old, was not free to marry Domitius. For years, she had been promised to Lucius Junius Silanus, who was, like Domitius himself, a direct descendant of the mighty Augustus.

Claudius had already built up high expectations for Silanus' future. He had put on a set of gladiatorial games in the man's honor and allowed him to wear a gold coronet and the *toga picta,* a purple-dyed garment suggesting royalty. Getting such an esteemed man dismissed from the imperial family would not be easy. Claudius and Agrippina called on Vitellius, their most trusted senatorial lackey, for help in blackening Silanus' name. Vitellius was father-in-law to Silanus' sister, giving him access to inside information—or at least, the right to pretend so.

Vitellius told the Senate that Silanus had been sexually intimate with his sister Junia. The allegation of incest must have struck many as ironic, under a regime headed by an uncle who was going to marry his niece. But the charge was nonetheless scandalous and damning. Silanus was thrown out of the Senate, and his sister was banished. His engagement with Octavia was null and void.

Rome watched the disbanding of one union and the forging of another—and registered the new course that the palace had set out on. To highlight this fresh start, Claudius set his wedding for New Year's Day, of the year we know as A.D. 49. For Romans, January 1 was inauguration day, when high officials began their term of office. Agrippina made ready to take the highest office available to a Roman woman, that of *Augusta*— the title that was long withheld from Messalina but that Claudius would confer on her soon after their marriage.

On December 29, Lucius Junius Silanus was removed from his praetorship by senatorial decree. He had but two days left in his term, but Claudius meant to make a point. A man polluted by incest could not be left in office even a moment longer than necessary, lest he contaminate the state.

Lucius had joined what would be a long line of victims from the doomed clan of the Junii Silani. Another Junius Silanus, Appius, had preceded him. Afraid of Appius' popularity, Claudius had had him executed on no more pretext than a bad dream reported by Messalina and one of his freedmen. When justifying his act to the Senate, Claudius, apparently without irony, thanked these two for keeping watch over the state even while asleep.

Was life under such arbitrary power worth living? It was the question Seneca had posed in *De Ira* and, in a different way, in *Consolation to Marcia*. For Lucius Junius Silanus, the answer—no—was clear enough. Three days after his dismissal, on the same day Claudius wed Agrippina, he took his own life.

It was about this time that Agrippina brought about Seneca's recall from Corsica. The Stoic sage returned to a Rome that had been shaken by yet another high-level suicide of a political victim. Some things had changed while he had been away, notably the regime's attitude toward him. But the powerlessness of those oppressed by the princeps, leaving only one avenue of escape, had not.

CHAPTER 2

Regicide

(A.D. 49–54)

Some said the world would end in fire; some said, in water.

Seneca's Stoic masters had taught that fire would bring to a close the present age of the world. Tongues of flame arising from the outer cosmos would rise in intensity until they scorched away all living things and all traces of humanity. Then, like a phoenix rising from its predecessor's ashes, life, and civilization, would begin again. Seneca adapted the cyclical scheme in *Consolation to Marcia* by making water, not fire, the agent of destruction. This made the apocalypse more imminent, for the fatal waters could arise from beneath our very feet, at any moment.

The Stoic cycle of death and rebirth was a purely natural event; it was not caused by an angry or punishing god. Yet because it always set human development back to zero, it raised the implicit question of how far that development could go. As in the biblical tale of the Tower of Babel, the very complexity of civilization seemed to carry the seeds of its own destruction—or at least to have a fixed terminus, reached at a regular point every few thousand years.

To Seneca, who lived in a city that had reached unimagined levels of sophistication, that terminus seemed not far off. Wealthy Romans could not only obtain snow and ice from mountain summits to cool their drinks and bathing pools—a practice Seneca deplored—they could dine on rare birds and shellfish and watch the combats of wild animals brought from all corners of the world. The reach and scope of the empire in the mid-first century A.D., its ability even to cross the English Channel and seize territory beyond, struck Seneca's mind not merely as a triumph of power and technology but as a sign that apocalypse was near.

That, at least, seems to be the message of his play *Medea,* written perhaps not long after Claudius conquered southern Britain in A.D. 43.

The story of Medea, as told by Seneca—retooling the more famous Greek drama by Euripides—was a parable about the perils of progress. Before Jason's voyage to Colchis (modern Armenia), there had been no ships and no seafaring. Earth's peoples had simply stayed in the lands where they were born. Then the *Argo* was built, a ship with supernatural powers. Jason crossed the Black Sea, seeking the golden fleece, and brought Medea home to Corinth along with that treasure. A fiery barbarian princess landed in a Greek city, and years later, when Jason's affections turned, a royal line was destroyed in a savage killing spree.

The breakthrough wrought by Jason's voyage had since increased a thousandfold, Seneca observes in his play's most famous passage. Where once a single ship had disturbed the natural order, Rome had now filled the seas with traffic, scrambling the races and dissolving global boundaries. Because of Rome, the Persians, dwellers on the river Euphrates, now drank the Rhine instead, while the sun-baked Indian sipped the frozen streams of Siberia. "The all-traveled earth leaves nothing in the place it once was," laments the chorus of Corinthians, speaking, as their obvious anachronisms reveal, with Seneca's own voice.

At the climax of this rush toward chaos, Seneca places the Roman invasion of Britain, an event he refers to obliquely by invoking the legendary island of Thule. Thule was thought to lie in the icy waters west of Britain—some have identified it with Ireland, the Hebrides, or even Iceland—and to form a natural limit to human travel. Attempts to reach it by Roman fleets had been blocked, according to one writer, by the slushiness of northern seas. Vergil, in the epic poem *Aeneid,* completed about 19 B.C., had given Thule its famous epithet *ultima,* implying it could never be surpassed.

But in *Medea,* Seneca imagined that it would be:

> *An age will come, in later years,*
> *when Ocean will loose the bonds of things,*
> *and earth's great breadth will stand revealed;*
> *Tethys will disclose new worlds,*
> *and Thule no longer be last among lands.*

These lines close the ode in which Seneca charts the parabolic progress of seafaring. That arc will end with Ocean and his wife Tethys—gods who represent the waters surrounding the world—bringing an epoch of history to a close. The smashing of the barrier formed by Thule, Seneca predicts, will bring a revelation of *novos orbes,* "new worlds," a phrase that has rung with unintended meaning since 1492. (Renaissance scholars quoted these lines as a prophecy of the discovery of America, and Columbus' own son scrawled a memo to that effect in the family copy of Seneca's plays.)

But the story of human progress does not end there. In the next ode of *Medea,* the chorus resumes its ruminations on seafaring, this time in a gloomier register. By now it is clear that Medea will kill her children and destroy her husband, undoing Corinth's political order. This horror is traced straight back to the primal sin of the voyage of *Argo.* An angry Neptune, god of the sea, has already destroyed most of the ship's crewmen, as the chorus reveals, and will soon finish off those few who remain. The ocean will exact a terrible vengeance on those who have penetrated its secrets.

It is not known when Seneca wrote *Medea* or any of his tragedies for that matter. But it's a fair guess that Claudius' invasion of Britain was much on his mind at the time. Romans celebrated the feat, and Claudius himself led a triumphal procession of conquered Britons through the capital's streets. In Seneca's view, however—a view that perhaps anticipates the thinking of modern environmentalists—the ceaseless advance of empire would turn the cosmos itself into an enemy. When everyone could go everywhere, when no boundaries remained intact, total collapse might not be far off.

For Seneca to express such dour views, even from exile on Corsica, would no doubt have been risky. Tragic dramas, which tended to center around arrogant or deluded monarchs, were always risky under the principate; Tiberius had once ordered a playwright executed for a single line about the blind folly of kings. It is not clear that Seneca ever had his plays performed or even allowed them out of his house. There is no evidence they were known in his day, and Seneca himself says nothing about them elsewhere in his writings. Perhaps they were private documents, shared with a trusted few—a way to vent worries that a ruling princeps would not have welcomed.

After 49, *Medea* would have been risky for another reason. It portrayed a powerful wife wreaking havoc on an imperial house. Agrippina, Seneca's friend and patroness, could not have relished such a plot, in the wake of her marriage to Claudius. And she would have been even less pleased by *Phaedra,* Seneca's other great portrayal of a destructive queen.

Adapted (as was *Medea*) from a more famous play by Euripides, *Phaedra* tells of the second wife of Theseus, a mythic Athenian king. Phaedra conceives an irresistible passion for Theseus' grown son, Hippolytus, and tries to seduce him, but he recoils. Rejected, Phaedra becomes a monster of vengeance. She kills herself but leaves behind a note accusing her stepson of rape, knowing it will prompt Theseus to destroy him. The play evokes that familiar folktale type, the wicked stepmother, made more monstrous here by incestuous lust.

To Roman readers in A.D. 49, *Phaedra* would have raised uncomfortable associations. They saw Agrippina as a tempestuous, controlling, and highly sexual woman, not unlike Seneca's heroine. She had already been accused of incest with both Caligula and her brother-in-law Lepidus; she was now incestuously married to her uncle Claudius. And she had become a stepmother. The chances that she would be a wicked one, given that she had a son of her own to protect, seemed high. Seneca's *Phaedra* would have been perilous for its author indeed, if released against this backdrop.

Was palace life imitating Seneca's art, or were things the other way around? Could we determine the date that *Medea* or *Phaedra* were written, we would know the answer. For lack of any chronology, we can only muse on this tantalizing circumstance: Rome's greatest tragic playwright had landed at the court of a queen plucked straight from tragedy. The curtain was going up on the drama of Agrippina's reign.

Concern over how Agrippina would treat Claudius' children, Britannicus and Octavia, had already been raised before the wedding. Vitellius, chief flack and spin doctor of the Claudian regime, had addressed this concern in the Senate: "To *her*"—Agrippina—"Claudius can entrust his innermost counsels, *and* his young children," he declared with studied confidence. But nothing in Agrippina's background gave grounds for this assertion. She had been a bitter enemy of Messalina, Claudius' prior wife, and could be expected to hate the children on their mother's account, or they her. More troubling was her obvious devotion to Domitius, whose odds in a succession struggle were certainly, by this time, better than even.

Claudius could not have been blind to the risks of his new marriage, but he did little to protect his children. He stood aside as Agrippina began to promote her son's interests over those of Britannicus. Our sources depict Claudius as passive and manipulable, Agrippina as ruthless and clever, but it seems more likely that, in the matter of succession, the two were in cahoots: both recognized the need to merge the bloodlines of the imperial house. Their own marriage had been one step in this direction; the betrothal of Domitius to Octavia had been another. The logical third step was not long in coming: Claudius prepared to adopt Domitius, the great-great-grandson of Augustus, as his son.

It was contrary to Roman law for a man with a living son to adopt another. Such an arrangement would clearly threaten the rights of his natural offspring. But Nature had already been superseded by Law when the Senate voted that Claudius could marry his niece. On February 25, A.D. 50, the senators passed a special act of adoption requested by the princeps himself. Claudius gained a new son and gave him a new name: Nero Claudius Caesar Drusus Germanicus, or as he soon became known, Nero.

A rivalry for succession had begun, and it soon held all Rome in suspense. Not since the legendary days of Romulus and Remus had two boys who were brothers, in legal terms at least, been so much at odds. Every public appearance by the imperial family was scrutinized for clues as to which boy was the presumed heir. Coins struck at state mints, usually vehicles for glorifying the reigning emperor, became for the first time an indicator of who would replace him. Those struck at Rome increasingly featured Nero, while those in the provinces continued to favor Britannicus, or else they put the profiles of both boys together in an overlapping arrangement called jugate. One issue minted in the Greek city of Pergamon hedged its bets: it featured Nero's portrait on one side and that of Britannicus on the other, as though the outcome of the rivalry rested on the toss of a coin.

Nero had not only purity of blood but seniority in his corner. He would reach all the stages of political maturity more than three years before Britannicus: at fourteen, the donning of the *toga virilis,* the wool tunic signifying adulthood and responsibility; at twenty, the minimum age for officeholding; at twenty-five, the right to sit in the Senate. It was not clear how many of these milestones a youth had to pass to qualify for the principate. But Nero was almost sure to pass more of them, during Claudius' lifetime, than his stepbrother.

Nero's partisans were evidently eager to increase his lead, for they rushed him to the first milestone a year ahead of schedule. At age thirteen, in early 51, Nero received his adult's toga and was escorted into the Forum, the arena of public affairs. He was as yet too young to hold office, but the Senate reserved a consulship—the annual magistracy carrying the state's highest authority—for him in the year he would turn twenty. Similar measures had been taken under Augustus in order to hurry young heirs toward the throne. Nero was quite clearly being groomed for rule.

Pergamon coin issue showing Britannicus and Nero on flip sides.

As a consul-to-be, Nero was entitled to exercise proconsular power—like a modern teenager driving with a learner's permit—and to wear special clothing and insignia. His new stature was therefore highly visible in the streets of Rome. At a special round of games put on to mark his elevation, he was presented to the crowds wearing his new markers of high office, while Britannicus appeared beside him in the simple cloak of a boy. The contrast was a humiliation for Britannicus and a clear indication of the new order of things.

He had the heart to lift the seed of alien blood above his own son, says a character in *Octavia* with disgust, looking back at Claudius' elevation of Nero in 50 and 51. The sidelining of Britannicus shocked and puzzled many observers. Could a father be so unfeeling toward his own flesh and blood? Some thought the preferment of Nero was an accident of timing. Claudius, they guessed, would advance Britannicus in the same way three years later and would make the two youths joint heirs—a strategy that previous emperors had used. Others thought Agrippina, with her rumored sexual wiles, had addled Claudius' brain.

In back rooms of the palace, factions jockeyed for influence, one supporting Britannicus' right of succession, the other championing Nero. Claudius' two most powerful Greek freedmen—ex-slaves on whom he increasingly relied as chiefs of staff—were divided. Narcissus had feared

Agrippina from the start and had tried to persuade Claudius to remarry
Aelia Paetina, his own ex-wife, instead. His rival Pallas, with a better eye
for picking winners, had all along backed Agrippina as Claudius' spouse
and now backed Nero as his heir.

Seneca had no choice but to take Nero's side, despite the fact that in
Consolation to Polybius, sent from Corsica, he had effused over the young
Britannicus. "Let Claudius confirm his son, with lasting faith, as steersman of the Roman empire," he had written. But that was before a second
son had appeared on the scene, and before that boy's mother had become
his patroness. Now Rome needed clarity and decisiveness about the way
forward.

Seneca never commented, in any extant work, on the palace rivalry,
but a line he quoted from Vergil seems to address it indirectly. In A.D. 54,
when Nero was already on the throne but Britannicus' claim was still supported by many, Seneca imagined one of the Fates saying:

Death to the worse; let the better one rule in the empty throne room.

The verse comes from Vergil's *Georgics,* and gives instructions for
managing a hive that has two "king" bees (Romans thought hive leaders
were male, not female). Seneca quoted it in another context, but he must
have been aware, given the tension surrounding the succession question,
of its grim relevance.

While the fortunes of Britannicus declined, those of his sister Octavia, perhaps a year or two older, were on the rise. By betrothing her to
Nero, Claudius had raised her chances of becoming empress and, eventually, queen mother, but he first had to cease being her father. Since Nero
was now, in law, Claudius' son, Octavia had to become some other man's
daughter; even a regime founded on a union of uncle and niece could
not sanction that of brother and sister. Octavia was adopted by a patri-
cian family so that she might marry *insitivus Nero,* "grafted-on Nero," the
sneering title she gives her husband in the play *Octavia.*

By the start of 53, the reengineering of the imperial family was complete. Claudius had a new wife and a new son; Nero had a new name

A statue from Claudius' era, thought
to depict his daughter Octavia.

and a new father; Octavia had a new father and a new fiancé. Britannicus
alone remained unreconstructed. He had been the great loser in all these
transactions, and he simmered with impotent anger. One day he let that
resentment show, perhaps involuntarily, as he passed his "brother" in the
palace halls. Though Nero had been adopted many months earlier, Britannicus saluted him as Domitius, the name he had held before joining
the imperial family.

Agrippina seized on this greeting as evidence of ill will, even of a
conspiracy to overthrow the regime. She denounced Britannicus, now
perhaps nine years old, to Claudius and demanded that he take action.

Whatever his feelings may have been for his sidelined son, Claudius acceded to his wife's wishes. Britannicus was stripped of the tutors who had helped raise him, his closest confidants and supporters; one of them, Sosibius, was put to death as an insurgent. A new staff of minders was called in, whose loyalty to the new order was firm and who could be counted on to isolate the boy.

Britannicus had been fenced off from all he held dear, perhaps even from his father. He had landed exactly where his partisans feared he would land: in the grasp of a stepmother.

Agrippina had gotten all that she sought. She had elevated Nero to presumptive heir and greatly diminished Britannicus. Her own stature had risen along with her son's. Shortly after his transformation from Domitius to Nero, she had received a new name of her own, the honorific title *Augusta*. Only the most revered imperial women had borne this title before her, and only as widows or mothers of emperors. Agrippina was the first to claim it as *wife,* and the shift betokened a new definition of the role. An Augusta was now—or so Agrippina hoped—the female counterpart of a Caesar, entitled to sit beside him in the halls of state, to take part in his privy councils, to appear on the backs of his coins, or even to share the front face with him in jugate profile.

But Agrippina's self-assertions did not stop there. In her second year as empress, she boldly intruded into the most sacred preserve of male power: the military.

A British resistance leader, Caratacus, son of Cynobelinus (Shakespeare's Cymbeline), had been brought to Rome in chains that year. Claudius arranged to receive his submission in a grand ceremony: Caratacus and his family were marched up to an imperial dais behind a procession of spoils, with the whole Praetorian Guard, clad in full armor, lining their route. Beside Claudius on that dais, surrounded by the standards that symbolized command of the legions, sat Agrippina, claiming her right as Germanicus' daughter to occupy such a place. When Caratacus delivered his plea for clemency, he addressed *both* members of the royal

Agrippina, wife of Claudius after A.D. 49.

couple, and when clemency was granted, it was granted by both. "This was a new thing, unknown to the ways of our ancestors—a woman sitting before the Roman standards," comments Tacitus, no friend of powerful women.

Agrippina's paternity gave her enormous credit with the army. So did her name—a feminine refashioning of that of her grandfather, Marcus Vipsanius Agrippa, the general responsible for Augustus' greatest victories. Alert to the value of these assets, Agrippina found an ingenious way to advertise them to the world.

Agrippa had founded a town in Germany as a haven for the Ubii, a tribe he had brought under Roman dominion. His son, Germanicus, later made it his base of operations. Agrippina herself had been born there, during her father's glorious campaigns. This place, as yet only a regional outpost called Ara Ubiorum, was the focal point of her family's heroic legacy, and Agrippina knew it. She persuaded Claudius to upgrade it to a *colonia,* a high-ranking Roman town with full legal status, and to name it after *her.* Never before had a Roman foundation commemorated a woman. Its full name, Colonia Agrippinensis, "Agrippina's *colonia*," proved too cumbersome for many Roman tongues, and so over time a shortened version, *Colonia*, gave rise to the modern name, Cologne (or Köln).

Agrippina had gained power unprecedented for her gender, greater even than Messalina's, and she was even better than her predecessor at putting it to use. A familiar pattern emerged, in which enemies of the empress—in particular, attractive, marriageable women—suddenly found themselves labeled enemies of the state. Lollia Paulina was one of these—a fabulously rich widow whom Claudius had looked at as a possible bride, before deciding to marry Agrippina. Agrippina accused her of treason, on the grounds she had consulted astrologers in an attempt to win the marital contest. Lollia was stripped of her wealth and sent into exile, presumably to the Pontine Islands. When she was safely out of the public eye, a Praetorian was dispatched to kill her and, according to Dio, bring back her severed head.

Not only female rivals but rivals for palace influence troubled Agrippina. Among them was the man who had long enjoyed Claudius' confidence, the Greek freedman and palace staffer Narcissus. This sharp operator had himself brought down many enemies in the days of Messalina. He might have been a helpful henchman to Agrippina, but the two instead were at odds. Narcissus was leaning increasingly toward Britannicus in the rivalry over succession.

Agrippina wanted Narcissus humbled. When a huge public works project that Narcissus headed came a cropper, her opportunity arrived.

Under Narcissus' oversight, a crew of 30,000 had worked for eleven years to dig a drain for the Fucine Lake, about fifty miles east of Rome. Claudius meant to shrink the lake and reclaim arable land from its shores. It was an enormous undertaking: a tunnel had been chiseled through the rock, much of it hard limestone, for a distance of three miles, so that the lake's waters would flow into the nearby river Liris. The rubble had to be hauled out laboriously by winches through shafts in what is today Monte Salviano. Vast amounts of cash had been spent on the project, and Narcissus had a huge stake in its success—a point that did not go unnoticed by Agrippina.

Claudius staged an elaborate celebration for the tunnel's opening. Crowds came from Rome and all the surrounding towns to watch the festivities, with the emperor presiding in full battle garb, and Agrippina beside him in a *chlamys,* a military cloak, adorned with threads of gold. As a prelude, Claudius assembled thousands of condemned prisoners and put them on warships for a battle to the death. The start of the ceremony was signaled by a trumpet blast from a mechanical statue that arose automatically from the center of the lake.

But at the tunnel's moment of truth, the flow issuing from its mouth was only a trickle. Narcissus' engineers had erred. The crowds went back to Rome, and the crews went back to work. In due course, a second opening ceremony was arranged, again with elaborate entertainment, including a dignitaries' banquet held at the tunnel's mouth; this time the tunnel worked *too* well. A jet of water erupted from it with a roar, tearing away chunks of the dining platform and sending the banqueters fleeing in panic.

Agrippina saw a chance to take Narcissus down, and she pounced. The freedman's great wealth—he was reputed to be the richest man of his time—made charges of fiscal malfeasance all too credible. Of course, graft could explain only the first tunnel debacle, not the second; but an ingenious rumor was spread that Narcissus had contrived the banquet cataclysm as a way to divert attention from his juggled books.

Narcissus survived the Fucine Lake disasters, but they weakened him. Meanwhile Agrippina advanced Pallas, her own freedman partisan, to the lead position in the palace hierarchy. With the support of Agrippina, his patroness and—so the public believed—his lover, Pallas rose to heights never before reached at Rome by a foreigner or a former slave.

In 52, the Senate, at Agrippina's behest, awarded Pallas the insignia and powers of a praetor—one-upping Narcissus, who had received only those of a quaestor. Pallas was also offered a vast sum of 15 million sesterces from public funds. When he graciously refused the money—he was already wealthy beyond measure—the Senate ordered that fulsome praises be inscribed on a brass plaque and displayed in the loftiest of places, affixed to a statue of Julius Caesar in the Forum.

To heap such honors on an ex-slave was an embarrassing show of the Senate's servility. But one clever senator, Cornelius Scipio, devised a way to save face. An Etruscan prince, also named Pallas, had lived near Rome in mythic times, according to Vergil's *Aeneid,* and had died in battle while fighting on the side of Aeneas. Speaking before the Senate, Cornelius addressed the freedman Pallas as "one sprung from the kings of Arcadia," implying that the shared name indicated lineal descent. The man whom the Senate had just anointed was no mere freedman, but the progeny of an ancient hero.

Elevating the lowborn or fallen, thereby making them dependent and loyal, was a time-honored strategy for Roman rulers, as it has been for autocrats everywhere. Agrippina had already used it to great effect with her recruitment of Seneca, whom, like Pallas, she had gotten appointed praetor. Their shared reliance on Agrippina gave Seneca and Pallas, the Roman moral philosopher and the Greek palace lackey, something in common. Both men, moreover, had seen their brothers promoted to coveted positions—another tactic by which Agrippina bound supporters to herself. For a man who had a brother in high office had *two* lives at stake, should the empress become displeased.

By a curious coincidence, the careers of these two brothers—Seneca's older brother Novatus, and Pallas' brother Antonius Felix—are bound together by an unlikely thread: the travels of the apostle Paul.

Paul was among the followers of a man whom the Romans knew as Christus or Chrestus, if any at Rome had yet even heard his name. In the 50s the movement begun by this man was still a minor and foreign disturbance, a doctrinal dispute among Jews in the East, especially in the territories that the Romans called Judaea (Israel, Palestine, and neighboring regions) and Achaea (Greece). As things turned out, Seneca's brother Novatus—by this time he had taken the name of a wealthy aristocrat who had adopted him, and was called Gallio—was serving as proconsul, or governor, of Achaea in the early 50s, just when Paul arrived there.

Felix, brother of Pallas, had taken up a parallel post in Judaea at the same time. Judaea was then a nominally independent kingdom, governed by its own monarchy, but Roman agents like Felix, called procurators, nonetheless helped keep the peace there.

Paul's travels through Greece resulted in his famous epistles to the Corinthians, in which he explained his new doctrines to skeptical Jews. The head rabbi of Corinth, Sosthenes, was in fact sympathetic to Paul and allowed him to teach in the city's synagogue. But the congregants were angered by what they regarded as heresy. They brought Paul before Gallio, Seneca's brother, and demanded punishment.

Gallio had no desire to meddle in the doctrinal disputes of zealous monotheists. Since no crime had been committed, Gallio declared, a Roman proconsul had no role to play in Paul's fate. Like Pontius Pilate, who had faced a similar situation decades earlier in Jerusalem, Gallio washed his hands of the matter. He even refused to intervene when the Jewish plaintiffs vented their frustration on Sosthenes and beat him to death outside Gallio's chambers.

The episode has earned Gallio a small, undistinguished place in the Bible, in chapter 18 of Acts of the Apostles. Meanwhile in Judaea, Felix, brother of Pallas, was having his own difficulties with the Jews. These too would be recorded in Acts of the Apostles, at greater length than Gallio's because they had far greater repercussions.

Felix was a violent and selfish man. He provoked Jewish ire from the moment he landed in Caesarea, Judaea's administrative capital. When the Jews' head rabbi, Jonathan, began carping at him, Felix hired thugs to stab the man to death with the short daggers they carried under their cloaks. These coldhearted assassins had a ruthlessly effective technique: they struck stealthily, then hid their daggers and, rather than run away, melded into the crowd surrounding their victim. The Sicarii, "dagger men," became Felix's personal hit squad and began terrorizing the province.

Tensions in Judaea rose to alarming levels. An insurrectionist known as "the Egyptian" gathered thousands of followers for an attack on the Roman garrison in Jerusalem. Felix countered by unleashing his troops on the crowd. The walls of the holy city were drenched in gore. A man who did not belong in a sensitive post, put there because his brother had friends in high places, was trying to hold on to power by the brutal use of force.

In the midst of this violent upheaval, the apostle Paul sailed from Greece to Judaea, continuing his mission to the Jews of the East. Despite numerous prophecies that he would meet disaster in Jerusalem, he made his way to the holy city, just as the Roman search for the insurgent "Egyptian" was in full force.

One day a Roman officer in Jerusalem learned that someone was causing an uproar inside the Jews' holiest shrine, the Temple. He thought it must be the Egyptian and had the man arrested and hauled away for torture. But then he heard his prisoner speaking in civilized Greek. It was Paul he had captured. The uproar had been caused by Jews outraged at Paul's teachings, just as the Jews of Corinth had been outraged. Paul was thrown into prison by authorities who had no idea what to do with him, a pattern that was to prevail for the rest of his life.

Eventually Paul was taken to Caesarea and brought before Felix and his wife Drusilla, daughter of the Jewish royal family. Felix was impressed by what he heard about universal love and salvation through faith. Over the next two years, Felix had Paul fetched from his cell on several occasions, and he and Drusilla listened raptly to his preachings. It was a strange confluence that brought a Jewish princess, a Christian apostle, and the brother of Claudius' most powerful freedman together in the same room, but such were the complexities of the Roman world in the first century A.D. Stranger still was the fact that Paul, the only person in that room with no freedom, wealth, or power, was also the only Roman citizen.

Felix was finally recalled from his procuratorial post in A.D. 60. His abuses of power would surely have incurred punishment, except that his connection to Pallas placed him beyond the law. He left Paul to rot in jail in Caesarea, but Paul invoked his legal right to an appeal before the emperor himself. Paul was shipped off to Rome, still a prisoner, but on arrival he was allowed enough freedom of movement that he was able to proselytize, crossing paths perhaps with his fellow apostle Peter.

Almost nothing is known of Paul's life in Rome. But a curious legend holds that while there, he struck up a warm friendship with Seneca.

A collection of letters survives that purports to be a correspondence between Seneca and Paul, each expressing admiration of the other's teachings and even arranging meetings to learn more. Almost certainly these letters are spurious, but the idea that the two great moralists of their age were in some kind of dialogue is hard to resist. Their two ethical systems, Stoicism and Christianity, had much in common, and early Church fathers would one day consider Seneca a kind of proto-Christian, based partly on the "evidence" of his correspondence with Paul.

Felix's departure from Judaea did not bring the troubles there to an end. Subsequent Roman procurators continued to use the Sicarii as hit men and squeezed the province badly with tax levies. Late in Nero's reign, a second revolt would break out there, far more serious than that of the Egyptian. Rome would finally crush Jerusalem in A.D. 70 and destroy its Temple, leaving only one wall—today's Western Wall—standing in place.

But by that time, Paul would be dead—as would Seneca, Pallas, Gallio, and the entire imperial family. Felix alone, of all those who came to prominence in this treacherous era, would ride out its turbulent currents and survive into the next.

While Felix was being taught by Paul in Judaea, Seneca was conducting lessons in a different classroom, in Rome. His student, heir apparent to rule the Roman Empire, was in dire need (as time would prove) of his teachings. But Seneca did not have a free hand in setting the curriculum, or in anything he did for that matter.

Agrippina did not think much of philosophy and did not want her son exposed to it. Intellectual musings, she felt, were not what a future emperor needed. She wanted her son taught the more practical arts he would need as princeps, above all rhetoric and declamation. The emphasis that these subjects got is attested by Tacitus, who imagined Nero giving credit to Seneca, later in life, for his eloquence. "You taught me not only how to express myself with prepared remarks, but how to improvise," the princeps tells his tutor, a remark no doubt invented by Tacitus but based on primary research.

Eloquence was still an essential concomitant of power in Rome, even under the autocracy. A princeps was expected to deliver speeches, in both Latin and Greek, before the Senate, the army, and the populace. His security might depend on how well he handled these situations and whether he could show confidence and control. The style of the speech mattered, too, for verbal elegance helped carry conviction and project power.

At some point, possibly as early as Nero's first public declamation at age thirteen, Seneca began serving not only as a speaking coach but as speech*writer*. This was a new thing in the history of the principate. Earlier emperors had written their own public addresses, each in his own distinctive style. But Nero's literary interests ran to poetry, especially plangent odes set to the music of the Greek lyre. He had little inclination toward the more sober medium of Latin prose. Beyond that, he was a passionate fan of the chariot races, a far more exciting diversion than could be found in forensic rhetoric.

Early in his career, Seneca himself had had ambitions as an orator and had spoken well enough to draw the envy of Caligula. But chronic respiratory illness made public speaking hard for him. Looking back on this early period, he wrote that he had stopped wanting to speak in public *and* that he had stopped being able—presumably because of his weak chest. Now he had the chance to get his words heard across much of the globe. His partnership with Nero, in this arena at least, was highly complementary.

There was another way in which Nero and Seneca complemented each other: the teenage boy lacked a father, and the fifty-year-old man lacked a son. Indeed, the infant son that Seneca had lost to illness, on the eve of his exile to Corsica, would have been just a few years younger than Nero, had he lived. Seneca had never had another child and never would. Nero, for his part, had lost his father at age three and had spent his life in the care of powerful women: his paternal aunt Domitia Lepida and the formidable Agrippina. For a boy just entering adolescence, the presence of a mature male teacher—even one whose temperament differed radically from his own—must have been a source of comfort.

Tacitus, who knew far more about this relationship than we do, attests that it included bonds of affection. Imagining how Nero might have looked back on these years, the historian has the princeps say to Seneca: "You nurtured my boyhood, then my youth, with your wisdom, advice, and teachings. As long as my life lasts, the gifts you have given me will be eternal." He goes on to call Seneca *praecipuus caritate,* foremost in the ranks of those he holds dear. The phrase is ironic, given that the two men had by this time come to hate each other. But Tacitus regarded them as words Nero might plausibly have used.

Seneca never described what went on in these palace tutorials or discussed his *in loco parentis* role. He once wrote disdainfully, in general terms, about students who sought out teachers "for the sake of improving their talents but not their souls." Perhaps he had the young Nero in mind.

Seneca's own education had been very different. At Nero's age, he had "laid siege" to Attalus' classroom, arriving early and staying late by the side of his great Stoic model. Now he was limited to practical instruction. But he had a chance, if only by way of his presence, to change the future princeps for the better. And by changing a princeps, he might change the world.

In A.D. 53, under a bloodred sky that seemed to onlookers to be on fire, Nero was married to Octavia, daughter of Claudius. He was then sixteen years old, she a few years younger. The celebrations at Rome must have been intense, though no descriptions have survived. By the union of this pair, the two sides of the imperial family would be fused, and a half-century-old problem resolved. The principate's future would be on a much sounder footing—provided the couple could have children.

But Nero was not eager to impregnate his wife. Marriage to Octavia was an unwelcome prospect. He had known her for years as his adoptive sister, long enough to know she was not at all his type. Reserved and decorous, high-minded and proper, she was the last partner he would have chosen for himself, to judge by his later selections.

According to Suetonius, some members of the court suggested to Nero, no doubt delicately, that he ought to show his wife more affection. Nero's reply was imperious. "She should be content with *uxoria ornamenta*—the trappings of a wife," he said, punning on the *ornamenta consularia,* the consular regalia sometimes awarded as a hollow show to men who were not in fact consuls.

Octavia could not have cared much for Nero either. The author of *Octavia* thought the union broke down thanks to *her* dislike of *him,* not the other way around. "The soul of my wife was never joined to mine," he imagines Nero complaining to Seneca, almost petulantly, some eight years down the road.

It did not matter much how the young couple felt about each other, for imperial unions were hardly love matches. Their function was to produce an heir and to win Roman hearts by showing them a model of virtuous womanhood. From this second perspective, Octavia made an ideal empress. The Romans liked what they had seen thus far of her sobriety and self-possession. As time went on, Octavia's popularity would rise ever higher, and Nero's mistreatment of her, as will be seen, would provoke riots in the city's streets.

Seneca's marriage was very different—a true partnership, if we judge by his rare mentions of it in his extant works. In one of them, he describes his wife's tender fretting when he insists making a journey while ill. "Her life's breath depends on mine," Seneca wrote to his friend, a man named Lucilius. "I can't ask her to be any braver in her love for me, so she asks me to love myself more carefully" (that is, to take better care of himself). It's one of few candid glimpses we have of Seneca's family life—if even this one can be taken as authentic.

The woman who was so anxious over Seneca's safety was Pompeia Paulina, the daughter of an *eques* from Gaul. Seneca had been married to her since at least 49 but possibly a good deal earlier. We don't know whether it was Paulina, or an anonymous first wife, who bore him a short-lived son in 41 or who sat beside him later in the 40s, as pictured in *De Ira,* while he reckoned up his moral failings each night. He does not name the spouse with whom he shared those moments. If it was indeed Paulina, she must have been less than twenty years old when he married her, for he makes clear in the letter to Lucilius that Paulina was a good deal younger than he.

For Paulina and her family, marital connection to a palace insider brought swift political advancement. Pompeius Paulinus, Seneca's father-in-law, attained the high office of *praefectus annonae,* superintendent of Rome's grain supply, at around the time Seneca became Nero's tutor. Seneca's rising fortunes were lifting those of his entire family—but the effect could be reversed if those fortunes fell. In fact, Paulinus seems to have suffered just such a reversal in 55, in an episode reflected in one of Seneca's moral treatises.

In 55, Seneca suffered a setback at court at the hands of Agrippina, who by then had become his determined rival. Agrippina flaunted her victory by installing one of her partisans, Faenius Rufus, as *praefectus annonae*—which meant that Paulinus, Seneca's father-in-law, had to step down. Demotion would embarrass both Seneca and Paulinus, unless it could be portrayed as something voluntary and noble: a philosophic retreat. Such, it seems, was in part the purpose of Seneca's *De Brevitate Vitae,* "On the Shortness of Life," a treatise addressed to Paulinus and urging him toward just such a retreat.

"Withdraw yourself into calmer, safer, and greater things," Seneca told his wife's father. "Do you think these tasks are comparable: to see that grain is transferred to storehouses without being pilfered or neglected in transit, that it's not damaged by moisture or exposed to heat, that it tallies up by weight and measure; or to approach these holy and lofty matters: to learn what substance God is made of, what experience awaits your soul, what it is that holds the heavy matter of this earth in the middle of the cosmos, raises lighter things above it, and drives the fiery stars to its highest point?"

De Brevitate Vitae is much more than a call to one man to retire. It roams over a wide turf and addresses a wide audience. Seneca here expounds some of his central ideas about time, mortality, and the quest for a good life. Only philosophic contemplation, he argues, can fulfill that quest. Only those who study philosophy are truly alive, in that they move outside the prison of time into the realm of eternals. All others, those who follow worldly pursuits, are squandering their time, merely running out the ever-ticking clock of mortality.

The final address to Paulinus stands out from the treatise, and from Seneca's other works, by its pointedness and detail. Nowhere else did Seneca deal with the unique circumstances of his addressee. The anomaly has struck many readers, including Miriam Griffin, a leading Seneca scholar. It was Griffin who first proposed that *De Brevitate Vitae*—which cannot on other grounds be dated—was written soon after Paulinus' dismissal from office. On this theory, the work's final segment is an ingenious face-saving device, a loftier version of the modern cliché about wanting to spend more time with family.

The interpretation detracts somewhat from *De Brevitate Vitae*, a beautifully written and stirring exhortation toward the examined life. But it fits all too well with the pattern of Seneca's earlier works, in particular the *Consolations* addressed to Marcia and to Polybius. There his deft control of language and argument allowed him to do two things at once: expound his Stoic ideals and improve his political image. It seems he continued that double game into his early years in the palace—and perhaps, as will be seen, to the last moments of his life.

The marriage of Nero and Octavia spelled triumph for Agrippina. By 53, she had succeeded in making Nero's succession likely, though not inevitable. And she had taken other steps to shore up her ability to control events. She was proving herself to be, by any account, one of the all-time master strategists of the game of dynastic politics.

By the fourth year of her marriage to Claudius, Agrippina had reshuffled the imperial hierarchy in her own favor. She had overhauled the palace staff, raising up Pallas, the Greek freedman who had loyally supported her cause, while thrusting aside Narcissus, who had not. Narcissus was a dangerous adversary whom Agrippina watched carefully. His great wealth, obtained by years of grafting, made him able to do her harm, as did his control of the emperor Claudius' private papers and correspondence.

Agrippina had also done much work on the Praetorian Guard, the army unit that would, when the time came, acclaim the new emperor. She spent years winnowing out those she mistrusted and promoting her own partisans. And she made a crucial change in the guard's leadership. She removed its two coprefects, holdovers from the days of Messalina, and replaced them with her own selection. The guard henceforth would have a single commander, a man named Afranius Burrus.

Burrus was an undistinguished officer from the middle ranks of society, like Seneca an import from the provinces (Gaul in this case). His family belonged to the equestrian, not senatorial, ranks. Burrus had a maimed hand, perhaps from a war injury, which made his future as a career soldier uncertain. His appointment as head of the Praetorians greatly increased his fortunes and his social status. Burrus, like Seneca, would feel enough gratitude to do whatever his patroness wished, or so Agrippina might hope.

Month by month the foundations of Agrippina's power, and of Nero's succession, were becoming firmer. But Britannicus was also growing up.

Early in 53 Britannicus turned twelve, one year younger than Nero had been when he received his adult toga and an array of titles and honors. His supporters, Narcissus among them, watched anxiously for signs that Britannicus, too, would "graduate early." Perhaps, this faction believed, Claudius had advanced Nero only to cover the three-and-a-half-year gap until his own son came of age. He might still intend to give the empire joint heirs, or a sequential succession in which the older boy would rule first but pass on power to the younger. Such arrangements had been made by emperors before, though not carried out after their deaths.

Claudius was growing older as well, which added to the urgency of the question. Now in his early sixties, suffering from tremors and digestive ailments, the emperor did not seem likely to reach his seventies.

Astrologers had predicted his death nearly every month since he came to power—or so said a wisecracking character in a farce written by Seneca. Whoever was to be heir might be called upon very soon.

At around this time, Claudius did fall seriously ill, and Rome went into a deathwatch. Agrippina seized the opportunity to further spotlight her son, arranging for Nero to sponsor public games in honor of Claudius' recovery. Nero provided horse and chariot races out of his own pocket, a public show of filial piety. His real feelings, though, must have run in the opposite direction. Plainly there was no better moment, from Nero's perspective, for Claudius to die, than during the interval between his own attainment of manhood and that of his brother.

Claudius wrote to the Senate from his sickbed, proclaiming Nero qualified to take the reins in the event of his death. But then, to everyone's surprise, he recovered. And as his health revived—what little he had ever had—so did the hopes of Britannicus' supporters.

Narcissus now went on the offensive against Agrippina, denouncing her openly and claiming that "the palace is being torn apart by the schemes of a *stepmother*." His own fate was sealed no matter who succeeded, he said—evidently feeling that his betrayal of Messalina had made him an enemy to one heir, his enmity with Agrippina, to the other—but he could at least hope to safeguard his master, Claudius. His clear implication was that Claudius, if Nero was designated successor, would soon fall victim to Agrippina—and to Pallas as well, who had now, as Narcissus claimed, become the empress's lover.

Charges of low-life, adulterous, or incestuous sex were a highly effective tactic in Roman politics. Such charges had been brought against every imperial wife and daughter; they had already been flung at Agrippina for most of her life and would continue up to her death. Judging their truth content is almost impossible today. (Imagine assessing tabloid accounts of modern celebrity sex lives from a distance of two millennia.) All we know for certain is that such charges were guaranteed to stick and to leave a nasty smear.

Also hard to assess are behind-the-scenes tales about what now took place in the palace. Our sources report that the emperor's favor began

A weary-looking Claudius, in a bronze
portrait probably made from life.

to shift, away from Nero and toward his natural son. Suetonius says
Claudius would hug Britannicus and urge him to grow up quickly, sug-
gestively quoting an old Greek proverb: "The one who wounded you"—
meaning himself—"will heal you." Tacitus attributes such gestures only
to Narcissus, not to Claudius. But he does give some support to the idea,
prominent in other sources, that Claudius was growing mistrustful of
Agrippina's conduct, especially her sexual comportment. (When he was
congratulated for having presided over the conviction of an adulteress,
Claudius allegedly punned that his own wives were likewise *impudica sed
non impunita,* "sleazy, but they won't get off easy.")

Claudius drew up his will at this time and had it put under official
seal. He could not simply pass on control of the empire as if it were a family heirloom, but bequeathing his personal wealth, an essential resource
for anyone running the government, would amount to the same thing.

What was in that document, or in Claudius' mind, concerning his sons? The will was later suppressed, leaving historians both ancient and modern to argue about its contents. Perhaps, as Tacitus, and some modern scholars, believe, it confirmed the selection of Nero; but why then would Nero suppress it? The motive Tacitus gives—that the will would have upset the populace by preferring a stepson over a son—sounds specious, given that entirely scuttling the will risked inflaming them even more.

Barbara Levick, the leading modern biographer of Claudius, reasons that no logical man would derail the standing order, which for years had favored Nero, at this late stage. But moves made by aging emperors do not always accord with logic. Tiberius, who had faced a similar dilemma to that of Claudius—whether to prefer a grandnephew, Gaius, over his own grandson, based on age and purity of blood—avoided making a decision as long as he could, then designated *both* boys joint heirs. Even at the doorway of death, Tiberius seemed unable or unwilling to make the fateful choice. According to a report by Seneca, in his final moments Tiberius removed the signet ring from his hand as though to pass it to a successor. But instead he held on to it, and then, just before collapsing, put it back on his own finger.

Was Claudius in a similar quandary in October 54? Or was he still convinced, as he had been for four years, that Nero was the best way forward? Did Agrippina perceive a growing change of heart in him? Did she then take steps, as most sources agree she did, to stop that heart, before it could change further?

Poisoning stories bedevil the modern historian even more than scandalous sex tales. No autopsies were held after the death of an emperor. The Romans, like all peoples everywhere, enjoyed skullduggery and conspiracy theories. These were vastly more entertaining than reports of sick old men slowly declining toward death. The truth of whether Claudius was murdered can never be known for certain, and some scholars do not believe he was.

That said, the timing of Claudius' death is highly suspicious. It fell some three months before Britannicus' majority, during the last stretch of Nero's three-year edge. If Claudius had indeed expressed to anyone, or written in his will, any doubts about Nero's succession, this would have been the perfect time to strike.

According to Tacitus, Agrippina plotted Claudius' murder carefully. She first sent away Narcissus, the emperor's most watchful partisan, to Sinuessa, a spa town where he could take the cure for his gout. Then she commissioned Locusta—"the Crayfish"—a Gallic woman convicted of poisoning but sprung out of jail on condition she work for the palace. Agrippina wanted a carefully calibrated drug, one that would not kill Claudius quickly—a sudden, violent death would be too obvious—but rather would destroy his mind, so that he could neither protect himself nor elevate Britannicus.

This custom-made toxin was passed to a eunuch named Halotus, the emperor's server and food taster, who introduced it into a plate of mushrooms, one of Claudius' favorite foods. Dio concurs with Tacitus' account and adds a memorable detail: Agrippina had only one mushroom poisoned, the biggest and most succulent on the plate. She shared the dish with her husband to put him off guard, but then insisted, as loving spouses do, that he help himself to the best one.

Claudius quickly fell into a stupor and was carried from the banquet hall; but then—again following Tacitus' account—the plan went awry. After emptying his bowels of the toxic meal, Claudius began to recover. Agrippina panicked, recognizing that her husband must now suspect her intentions and would act swiftly against her.

Luckily she had other palace lackeys ready to do her will. Xenophon, a Greek physician who attended on the imperial family, was called in and prescribed a therapeutic purge. He produced a feather to induce vomiting; it had been coated with a fast-acting poison. This second drug finished Claudius off, during the night of October 12.

Such is the tale of Claudius' demise as told by Tacitus. It is contradicted on details by other ancient historians and mistrusted by some modern ones. But many of those who today deny that Claudius was murdered nonetheless agree that a dish of mushrooms was the cause of death.

If such was the case, the lethal fungus seems far more likely to have been poisoned than merely poisonous, given the timing of its appearance on the emperor's table.

The moment for Nero's accession was at hand, a moment Agrippina had long anticipated and that she now choreographed with consummate skill. Before news of Claudius' death could leak out, she made use of the Praetorian Guard, the corps of soldiers she had carefully groomed over preceding years, to seal off the palace. No one was to learn of Claudius' death until the time was right. Meanwhile she detained Britannicus in his chambers and kept his sister Octavia close by her side.

When morning came, and a troupe of comedians arrived to entertain the emperor, the soldiers admitted them. It was important to convey a sense of routine to those passing by. Finally, at around noon—an hour of good omen, according to superstitions of the day—Agrippina launched into action.

The palace doors were thrown open, and Nero came grandly forth, accompanied by Burrus, prefect of the Praetorian Guard. A brief announcement was made of Claudius' death to the soldiers on duty outside, who took their cue from Burrus and saluted Nero as leader. Or at least, most did. Tacitus reports that a few looked around anxiously and asked one another why Britannicus had not appeared. But as critical seconds ticked away, Britannicus stayed off the scene.

Rome had as yet no rituals for the acclamation of a princeps. Only twice before had there been an orderly transfer of power. For lack of a longer tradition, the soldiers adopted the procedure used for Claudius the last time around. Nero was taken in a covered litter to the Praetorian camp outside the city walls. There he delivered a speech—Dio specifies that Seneca had written it for him—to the assembled soldiery. He accompanied his grand words with a grand gift: as much as 20,000 sesterces, or two decades' worth of pay at the centurion salary level, per man. The soldiers hailed him as *imperator,* as they had done for Claudius.

Nero proceeded to the Senate house and spent several hours there.

The senators, too, greeted Nero adoringly. They immediately voted him the rights and powers accruing to his new status. This outdid Claudius, and Caligula as well, both of whom had waited weeks to receive these honors.

By the end of the day on October 13, as her son made his way back to the palace, Agrippina could look with immense satisfaction on what she had wrought. Nero was princeps, and Britannicus was disinherited. The Praetorians had dutifully played their part. The machinery she had set in place had worked.

Narcissus, in Campania, got word of Claudius' death and hurried back to Rome. Perhaps he still hoped to rouse support for Britannicus, but he was too late. As soon as he entered the city, he was arrested and thrown into prison. The new regime, only a day or two old, had committed its first abuse of judicial procedure.

Meanwhile, in the skies above Rome, Claudius' spirit made its limping way toward heaven, to join the company of the gods. As the Senate would shortly decree, Claudius had become a god, Divus Claudius, at the moment of his death.

The upward progress of Claudius' ghost would soon be described by a most unlikely "witness"—the former senator who was now the close adviser, speechwriter, and moral conscience of the new regime, the philosopher Seneca.

CHAPTER 3

Fratricide

(A.D. 54–55)

"That which transpired in heaven, on the third day before the ides of October, Year One—the beginning of a most blessed age—I wish to commit to record," begins a text with the curious title *Apocolocyntosis Divi Claudii*—"Pumpkinification of the Deified Claudius." The narrator, an unidentified political insider with a snarky tone and a habit of suddenly breaking into verse, promises to relate the events of October 13, the day after Claudius' death. The author, improbably enough, was Seneca.

Nearly everything about this work is a mystery, including the meaning of its title, for the text as we have it nowhere refers to pumpkins. The invented Greek word *apocolocyntosis,* coined by analogy with *apotheosis,* may simply be intended to convey the spirit of the ludicrous. For Rome had witnessed a truly ludicrous event by late 54: the official deification, sponsored by Nero and Agrippina, of Claudius.

It was the first time in almost two decades that such an honor had been granted, and only the second time a princeps had received it. Augustus, of course, had been the first. The notion that Claudius ranked with his most sanctified predecessor was patently absurd. Seneca's older brother Gallio, formerly called Novatus, quipped to his cronies that Claudius had been hauled up to heaven with a hook—meaning the hook the Romans used to haul the corpses of criminals through the Forum, before they were dumped into the Tiber.

Laughable or not, the move held advantages for Nero. He could now be called *divi filius,* son of a god, as he soon was on coins and in inscriptions. By a twist of irony, the same rise in stature accrued to Britannicus, Claudius' natural son, the new emperor's chief rival and foremost threat.

Agrippina too had much at stake in Claudius' divinization. She could now hope to follow the example of Livia, the wife of Augustus, and exploit the power that belonged to a god's widow. Livia had become priestess of Augustus' cult and was thereafter accompanied by a lictor—a bearer of bundled rods, symbolizing the right to use force as an instrument of control. Agrippina, in fact, saw to it that she would outstrip her predecessor. The senatorial acts that deified Claudius awarded her *two* lictors to Livia's one. They also set aside funds for a colossal new temple in central Rome, to be superintended by Agrippina as *flamen* or head priestess.

It was this solemn act of deification, this prop to the authority of both Nero and Agrippina, that Seneca mocked in *Apocolocyntosis.* Abandoning the reserved, high-minded tone of the moral treatises, he here writes in such an uncharacteristically funny, irreverent voice that, were it not for a chance comment by Cassius Dio, no one would ever think the work was his.

The day described in *Apocolocyntosis* begins with the death of Claudius. After the Fates snip the thread of the emperor's life, Claudius farts loudly and pronounces his last words: "Oh Lord, I think I've shit myself" (to which the narrator adds, "Whether he did or not, I can't say, but he certainly shit all over everything else"). The palsied, limping emperor appears at heaven's gates and is greeted as a deformed monster. An assembly of gods is convoked—a parodic version of the Roman Senate—to debate Claudius' request for admission, and stern voices are raised in opposition. The deified Augustus rises to condemn Claudius' abuses, recounting with outrage the murders that have thinned out the imperial family.

Rebuffed from heaven, Claudius is sent down to the underworld.

There he is greeted by throngs of his victims—thirty-five senators and 321 knights, together with countless commoners, according to the exacting records of Aeacus, judger of souls. Sentence is passed in the work's last lines. Claudius will have an eternal low-rank post on the staff of Caligula, shuffling legal papers for one of the mad emperor's freedmen.

Seneca's motives in writing this work are extremely hard to discern. Editors of a recent translation suggest he wanted revenge, since Claudius, at the behest of Messalina, had sent him to exile on Corsica thirteen years earlier. Other readers have suggested it was written during the Saturnalia, a winter solstice holiday that granted license to servants to make fun of their masters. But if so, Seneca took that license to a risky extreme, ridiculing one of the first, and most sober, undertakings of Nero's administration.

In fact, there is more than satire and holiday fun in *Apocolocyntosis*. Even in its first sentence, the work employs a complex mixture of serious and comic tones. The dateline includes the phrase *anno novo,* "in the first year," as though Nero's accession has begun the world anew, ushering in "a most blessed age." In these phrases Seneca appears to be playing it straight; even while lampooning the recently deceased princeps, he lavishes praise on the current one. It's a tricky balancing act—and it gets even trickier as the praise becomes more elaborate.

Seneca describes the snipping of Claudius' thread in lines of tragic verse, parodically grandiose in style. But the tone turns suddenly rapturous when the author's attention turns to Nero. The Fates are seen spinning a new life, using an endless, and golden, thread. The god Apollo appears to proclaim that this golden life will bring a new golden age. He compares the man it represents to the sun rising up after long night. "That's the kind of Caesar who's come," Apollo effuses; "that's the Nero Rome will soon gaze upon."

The lines ring out like a martial anthem in the midst of an opera buffa. Seneca wrapped this flattery inside a comic, satiric package, just as he had wrapped praise of Claudius inside his philosophic *Consolation to Polybius.* That work of ten years earlier was patently out of date, now that

Claudius was down and Nero was up, and Seneca, according to Cassius Dio, tried to have it suppressed. In another decade, he would have cause to regret these verses of *Apocolocyntosis* as well.

With this weird combination of back-slapping levity and solemn fanfare, Seneca enacted for the public his close bond with the princeps. Together they could have a laugh kicking dirt on Claudius' corpse. The work has the feel of an inside joke, shared in the clubby atmosphere of a palace back room. One theory holds that it was composed for a single Saturnalian banquet, with Nero himself enjoying the fun—and flattery—between goblets of Falernian wine.

Rome now had the youngest ruler the Western world had ever seen. Even Alexander the Great, the paragon of precocity, had entered his third decade before assuming rule over Macedon and starting his conquest of the East. Nero was still sixteen, yet reigned over an empire larger than Alexander's had ever been. And his talent for leadership, his inclinations toward command and rule, were nothing like Alexander's. Lacking in self-assurance, easily seduced by fantasies and whims, Nero was going to be vulnerable to intimidation and control. So at least his mother might hope, for it was she who planned to control him.

Nero's youth, idealized for public consumption in the vigorous portrait statues of the day, posed a welcome contrast to the decrepitude of Claudius. Rome's hopes for a bold new beginning were high. Poems and pamphlets—among them Seneca's *Apocolocyntosis*—proclaimed the dawn of a new golden age. Such sentiments were by now de rigueur at the accession of an emperor, but they seemed more convincing when addressed to a trim, athletic, moderately handsome teenager.

Beneath the celebratory mood lurked painful memories of the last youthful princeps, Caligula, installed at age twenty-five amid equally bright expectations. Within two years the energies of that youth had turned to sadistic caprice. No outward signs had forewarned of Caligula's madness; just so, there was no way to know, at Nero's accession, what weaknesses were lurking in the boy's nature. The principate, that great magnifier of mental flaws, would bring them out in time—but few could have guessed how soon.

Other than Agrippina, Seneca was closest to Nero and best able to gauge his fitness to rule. If the sage harbored fears for the future, he never expressed them—or at least, never more pointedly than his fervid depictions of a coming apocalypse. He must have harbored doubts, having seen in Caligula's case that youthful arrogance and absolute power made an explosive combination. If we can trust a report by Suetonius, Seneca had had a dream, on the night after his appointment as Nero's tutor, that he was in fact teaching Caligula. The story, perhaps spurious, supplies our only clue that Seneca, after one brief look into Nero's soul, might have dreaded the path before him.

Caligula was not the only nightmare that the Roman elite were trying to escape. Claudius, too, had murdered large numbers of them (or in a more generous mood, had forced them to commit suicide). He had used the vague charge of *maiestas,* treason, to arrest his enemies, then tried them in secret proceedings within closed chambers of the palace. Messalina and palace freedmen often joined him on these tribunals, sitting in judgment over men indicted on their say-so. Acting in concert with high courtiers, playing on Claudius' fears and superstitions, his wife and her allies had often goaded the emperor into a guilty verdict.

Claudius' regime was widely disliked by the Senate for these abuses. But Claudius was also the source of Nero's legitimacy, since it was he who had adopted and promoted the boy. The first challenge facing the new princeps was what posture to take toward his predecessor. A balance had to be struck between the reverence befitting a son and protégé, and the reckoning up of past abuses.

The task of navigating between these poles fell to Seneca, who now took up his official duties as speechwriter. In his first big assignment, however, Seneca stumbled.

Claudius' funeral was an elaborate ceremony held six days after the emperor's death. Nero delivered the eulogy, before the assembled Roman elite. Seneca framed the speech in heroic language, seeking to reaffirm the

Nero in his late teens.

power of the principate and the close bonds between Claudius and Nero. But he miscalculated and overshot his target. As Nero read out fulsome praises of Claudius, snickers could be heard in the crowd. Seneca had crossed the line—unintentionally this time—into satire.

The historian Tacitus, writing many years later, notes the sophistication of the funeral speech and remarks on Seneca's "pleasing talent, well suited to the ears of that time." Given the patent fictions the speech contained, this praise is ambiguous, one of Tacitus' many multilayered comments on Seneca's career. "The ears of that time," after all, were accustomed to hearing doublespeak and empty flattery. Tacitus was himself both a writer and a courtier, who had survived the reign of the despotic Domitian only by carefully adapting his words. He had sympathy for Seneca's plight—but a certain contempt as well.

Whatever ground the new regime lost in this first address was quickly made up in the second. Nero's inaugural speech to the Senate, again composed by Seneca, struck all the notes that the beleaguered senators longed to hear. The practice of holding closed-door trials would stop. The new princeps would not act as sole judge, nor delegate power to freedmen lackeys, as his predecessor had done. The Senate would have its ancient dignity, and many of its lost jurisdictions, back again. "My youth was not troubled by civil wars and family feuds," Nero proclaimed, distinguishing himself from previous palace-raised emperors. "I bring with me no hatreds, no scars, no lust for vengeance."

The promise of a clean slate, a return to amity between ruler and aristocracy, coming from one so young and so seemingly sincere, stirred the senators deeply. They voted to have this speech inscribed on a column covered with silver plate and read aloud every year in the Senate house when incoming consuls took office. It was an unprecedented honor for a public address. A compact of mutual respect had been struck between Senate and princeps, as in the days of Augustus. The nightmare of Caligula seemed to be gone, the policies summed up in a slogan that Seneca quoted on three occasions, always with revulsion: *Oderint dum metuant*— "Let them hate, as long as they fear."

In framing this compact for Nero, Seneca was addressing his own former colleagues. A senator himself, though now working for the palace, he had a unique role to play, well suited to his diplomatic mien. He had been a victim of Claudian injustice, at first sentenced to death, then exiled to Corsica after the sentence was commuted. He knew abuse of power at first hand. No one had better credibility as an advocate of restraint.

The ideas Seneca put into the inaugural speech share a common outlook with *De Ira*, which by now was certainly in circulation. That work taught the powerful and proud that it was better to ignore a wrong than stoop to anger. "To fight against an equal is risky; against a higher-up, insane; against someone beneath you, degrading," Seneca wrote in *De Ira*. He gave the example of Cato, that Stoic nonpareil who, when spat upon in public by an adversary, merely wiped his face and returned a good-natured quip. If one could not turn a blind eye, one could at least forgive, knowing that all human beings are prone to do wrong.

In both the inaugural speech and *De Ira*, Seneca was eager to banish discord and vengefulness, but he knew this took constant effort. He himself practiced a Zen-like exercise to restrain his own anger, if we can trust the self-portrait he paints in *De Ira*. Every night before bed, Seneca confides to his readers, he sat quietly beside his wife and took stock of his day, reviewing moments when he gave in to his passions. Perhaps he grew too hot during a dispute, or spoke more sharply to an underling than the man could handle. In each case, he tells himself: "See that you don't do that again, but now I forgive you."

Seneca then broadens the scenario and writes as though all Romans are performing the same exercise. Perhaps one is offended by drunken jesting at a dinner party. Perhaps another is jostled at a rich man's door by a self-important doorkeeper. A third is seated at a banquet table in a spot lower than he feels he deserves. Seneca urges his readers to forgive such slights and take themselves less seriously: "Pull further back, and laugh!"

With an unerring eye for detail, *De Ira* caricatures the self-regard and self-importance of the Roman nobility. The work even explains these traits in a way that might look familiar to a modern psychologist. The wealthy and powerful indulge their children and give them no training in overcoming indignities. "The one to whom nothing was refused," Seneca writes, "whose tears were always wiped away by an anxious mother, will not abide being offended." The ability to laugh, he suggests, is an antidote to the petulance that comes with privilege.

But not everyone was able to take the laughter cure. Seneca was about to confront a woman who, as far as evidence reveals, had not the slightest trace of a sense of humor. He had poked fun at her, indirectly, in *Apocolocyntosis,* for she considered herself the widow, and priestess, of a god. To her, apotheosis was no laughing matter.

That woman was, of course, the imperious Agrippina, once Seneca's greatest patron, but now looming as his greatest problem.

While Claudius lived, the task of getting Nero onto the throne had kept Agrippina, her son, and her son's tutor in close alignment. Now that this goal had been achieved, their relations had become far less stable. Much would depend for Seneca on how he negotiated the change in the troika.

Stoicism had taught him much about managing emotion and keeping the rational mind in control. But how rational could he remain amid the wrath of a possessive, domineering woman, still vigorous in her late thirties, and the rebellious, impetuous urges of a seventeen-year-old boy?

Nero started off by paying public tributes to Agrippina. When the captain of the guard asked the princeps, on the very first night of his reign, for the watchword that would give security clearance, Nero made it *optima mater*, "best of mothers." It was a phrase from epic poetry, found once in Vergil's *Aeneid*, and thus a gift of heroic stature for Agrippina. It

Relief from Aphrodisias in modern Turkey showing
Agrippina crowning her son.

was more than mere whimsy, for Nero knew that she had carefully cultivated the allegiance of the Praetorians for years. They were loyal more to her than to him. He had much to gain from seeming, in their eyes, a devoted son.

The reliance of the son on his mother was underscored in statuary, especially in a bas-relief sculpture found in Aphrodisias (a Romanized town in what is now Turkey). Uncovered only in 1979, this relief, part of a gallery of imperial portraits, depicts Agrippina gazing at Nero with maternal adoration as she places a laurel wreath on his head. Nero, dressed as a soldier, does not return her gaze but looks outward, coolly, impassively, at the tasks before him. The scene clearly configures Agrippina as the source of her son's power. The image seems to have derived from an original displayed at Rome.

In his first coin issues—always an emperor's most far-reaching medium of communication—Nero gave his mother a prominent, virtually coregnant, role. Under Claudius, Agrippina had appeared in jugate arrangements, her husband's profile stamped over hers, or else she was relegated to the reverse—"tails"—side. Now a new format appeared, never before seen at Rome: Nero and Agrippina were shown in symmetrical profiles, gazing at one another on the "heads" side. Neither profile was larger than the other. The image suggests an intimate conversation, a moment of perfect concord, with each partner unafraid to hold the other's gaze.

The message sent through these media was clear: Nero meant the public to see Agrippina as a sharer in rule. It was an obvious move for a youth who had been promoted to the principate in his teens, but it posed considerable risks. Romans who had witnessed the depredations of Messalina, or the machinations of Livia, Augustus' wife, before her, were not eager to see another woman grasping the levers of power. The specter of *impotentia,* the will to power that Roman men demonized in Roman women, was again rearing its head. It did not help that Agrippina had already raised that specter in the reigns of Caligula and Claudius, seducing (so it was thought) the men from whom she could gain, and destroying those who opposed her.

Coin issue of 54 showing Nero and
Agrippina. Significantly, her name and
titles are seen on the "heads" side of the
coin, his on the reverse.

It was not long before Agrippina began playing her folktale role all
too close to type. She used her new power to order two assassinations,
eliminating one potential threat and one long-standing enemy. According to Tacitus, Nero was not involved in either move.

Marcus Junius Silanus, brother of the suicide who had spoiled Agrippina's wedding day, now forty years old, was serving as governor of western
Turkey and doing no one any harm. But his blood made him dangerous.
His descent from Augustus marked him as a likely alternative, should the
Romans decide someday to oust Nero. Agrippina dispatched two envoys
who gave him the same poison used on Claudius—"too openly to be
missed," according to Tacitus. Apparently she wanted other Julian males
to know whom they were dealing with.

Next Agrippina did away with Narcissus, Claudius' devoted freedman, who had remained in custody since the death of his master. Not
only did Agrippina bear him an old grudge, but the man knew too much.
She ordered Narcissus to commit suicide, a more benign fate than execution since he could still pass on property to his heirs. Before his death,

perhaps in exchange for this privilege, he burned the private papers he had amassed—documents that could have done Agrippina much harm.

Agrippina's purge might have gone further, but Seneca moved to curb it. He could not stand by and watch as these Claudian tactics resumed, tactics that Nero, speaking Seneca's words, had promised the Senate were over. Tacitus, who otherwise loved to dramatize scenes involving either Seneca or Agrippina, does not show us how this confrontation played out. But he does say that Seneca's policy of restraint was seconded by a crucial ally at court: the new prefect of the Praetorian Guard, Afranius Burrus.

Burrus and Seneca made an odd pair, one a career soldier, the other a moralist and writer who had never borne arms. But they had by now built a bond of mutual trust. Together they worked to guide the young Nero and counter the sway of his mother. "They exercised different but equal influence [on Nero]," Tacitus comments admiringly, "Burrus by his soldierly sense of duty and his gravity of character, Seneca by his instruction in eloquence and his upright civility." It was a rare instance when men who might have been rivals became collaborators, aided by shared goals and, increasingly, a common enemy.

Seneca explained his philosophy of executive restraint in *De Ira*. There he compared a leader's handling of the state to a physician's care of the body, an analogy he would often return to. Just as a good doctor seeks the least aggressive cure, a leader should use the gentlest methods of correction. He should chastise with only words if possible, then proceed to the mildest of blows. Execution should be only a last, desperate resort, for those who are so morally "ill" that death is, in effect, euthanasia.

Had Agrippina been permitted her own turn on this medical metaphor, she might have argued the benefits of prophylaxis. Sometimes tumors had to be excised *before* they turned malignant. Or she might have fired back at Seneca the line he had recently quoted himself, from Vergil's guide to beekeeping: "Death to the weaker; leave the stronger to reign in the empty throne room."

. . .

For the moment Agrippina did not proceed with her purge. But she soon created a new problem when she claimed a role in privy councils of state.

As Claudius' wife, Agrippina had once appeared on the emperor's dais, dressed in military garb, to receive the surrender of British insurgents. Now she wanted to be present at even more important occasions. The Senate's chambers were barred to all outsiders, but Agrippina contrived to move its meetings to a room in the palace and to listen in on deliberations from behind a curtain. Everyone knew she was there, taking note of every word that was said.

Another defining moment in the palace power struggle came early in 55, when Nero's reign was a few months old. A foreign policy crisis had presented itself. On the empire's eastern frontier, Rome's ancient enemy, the Parthians, had decided to test the new emperor's mettle. An uprising in Armenia had pushed a Roman puppet off the throne there, and the Parthian king seized the opportunity. He installed his brother, Tiridates, as ruler of Armenia, in effect claiming this crucial buffer state as his own.

The provocation demanded a riposte—but who would deliver it? Some Romans fretted that a youth just turning seventeen, governed by his mother and his teachers, was not up to the task of waging war in the East. Others reasoned that Seneca and Burrus were experienced men who would help the young emperor get through. Everyone waited to see who would be put in command, a real soldier or a mediocrity who could be counted on not to outshine Nero.

Agrippina, daughter of the greatest soldier of the century, expected to help manage the crisis. This was a red line for the male leaders of the regime. An Amazon could not lead Rome into war, even if she was the last living child of Germanicus. A court audience for the Armenian ambassadors was chosen as the place to make a stand.

Seneca and Burrus sat beside Nero on the high platform that denoted imperial power. Agrippina entered the room and made clear she intended to join them on that platform. The idea struck horror into the minds of the onlookers, but the three men had devised a countermeasure. At Seneca's cue, Nero stepped down off the dais and met his mother at ground level, pretending to greet her but blocking her progress. The episode appeared to outsiders to be merely a tender exchange between mother and son, not a determined test of wills. The proceedings were then adjourned or moved to a new location. An open clash might have ensued had Nero reascended the dais, and foreign eyes might have glimpsed the rift in the regime.

Nero, prompted by Seneca, had stood up to his mother with a small but strong gesture. He soon followed it with equally confident moves to counter the eastern threat. Troop strength was boosted, and plans were laid to bridge the Euphrates and invade Parthia. Nero gave Domitius Corbulo, an iron-hard disciplinarian who had beaten the Germans under Claudius, command of the invasion forces. That move was hailed as a sign that Nero, advised by Seneca and Burrus, did indeed have the strength to face a barbarian foe.

The Parthians quickly backed down. Their surrogate in Armenia relinquished power and turned over hostages to Corbulo as guarantees of nonaggression. A grateful Rome showered honors on Nero, erecting a statue in the temple of Mars as large as that of the war god himself.

Agrippina accepted her second check but nursed her wounded pride. She was far from ready to cede the role of chief regent to Seneca, still less to Burrus. She was determined to show who had more influence over her son, she or they. As it happened, her next opportunity was not long in coming, and her efforts to exploit it would forever destroy what concord remained in the palace.

Like most Romans, Seneca mistrusted ambitious women, especially mothers who sought power through their sons. In a letter to his own mother, Helvia, from his exile on Corsica, Seneca had praised her for keeping out of politics even with two sons in the Senate: "You did not make use of our influence as though it were family property. . . . The only things that touched you from our elections to office were the pleasure they gave you and the costs they imposed." Helvia's passivity posed a stark contrast, Seneca wrote, to "those mothers who wield the *potentia* of their sons, with the *impotentia* of women." His wordplay contrasts political governance—normally the province of men—with female inability to "govern" desire and emotion.

Seneca never mentions Agrippina in any of his surviving writings. Indeed his moral treatises deal only infrequently with women in general. *De Ira* characterizes anger as a "womanly and childish vice," but its cases in point come from the realm of adult males. Even in *Apocolocyntosis,* his scathing satire on the abuses of Claudius, Seneca mentions Messalina— the moving force behind numerous executions, and his own exile—only as a victim, not as a perpetrator, of crimes.

By contrast, Seneca's tragedies are dominated by women. Two of his best plays, *Phaedra* and *Medea,* revolve around powerful women and their passions, love in the first case, anger in the second. Phaedra conceives a desperate passion for her stepson, Hippolytus, then destroys him after he spurns her. Medea, barbarian wife of the Greek hero Jason, murders her children to get revenge on her adulterous husband. It is tempting to think that Seneca wrote the first in the era of Messalina, the second in that of Agrippina, women whose prevailing passions sort well with the heroines he portrayed. But there are no clues, either within the plays themselves or in other sources, that allow us to establish their dates.

Few today would think to read *De Ira* together with *Medea,* though the two works might well have been composed concurrently. Indeed, among dozens of modern editions of Seneca, a huge array of anthologies that organize his works for modern readers, only a single volume dares to package tragedies and prose works together. For why would any reader— still less, any *writer*—choose to inhabit two nearly opposite moral universes at the same time? *Medea* shows anger run amok, mushrooming into gigantic and hideous forms. "*Ira,* I follow wherever you lead," Medea says as she stabs her sons to death, one after the other. But in *De Ira,* Seneca argues that anger can and must be subdued so that the rational mind can prevail. Our exemplar is Seneca himself, sitting with his wife as evening falls, calmly chastising himself for raising his voice that day.

Interpreters have struggled, and will struggle forever, to understand how one mind could have produced both bodies of work. It is as though Emerson had taken time off from writing his essays to compose the opera

Faust. Some have described Seneca's tragedies as inversions of his prose works—instruction by negative example—but that is too pat an explanation. The author of the plays expresses thoughts that the author of the treatises seems unable even to entertain. The last couplet of *Medea*, spoken by Jason as he watches his murderous wife escaping in a dragon-drawn flying chariot, resounds with nihilistic horror:

> *Make your way up, through the high expanses of heaven;*
> *Proclaim, wherever you go, that there are no gods.*

The tragedies feature many such moments. One would guess that their author was well acquainted with despair, even madness. But the prose treatises are optimistic and pious. They proclaim everywhere that there *are* gods, or God—as proved by the divine power of Reason within every soul.

In which body of work do we hear the real Seneca? Or are they two equally authentic expressions of what has been called his "compartmentalized mind"? Did he write his tragedies as a covert cri de coeur, a release of moral revulsion he could not otherwise express? That certainly seems the case, as will be seen, with his most ambitious, most harrowing drama, *Thyestes*—perhaps the last play he completed and the only one that can be securely dated to his years under Nero.

In *Medea* and *Phaedra*, Seneca plumbed the depths of what he saw as a typically female affliction, *impotentia*—an inability to master lust, restrain envy, or tamp down the need for control and power. It was a condition he, and other Roman males, feared in all contexts but particularly when it entered the political realm. The passions of unbridled women could destroy that realm and rush the world headlong toward apocalypse.

It was these fears of female *impotentia* that Rome, and Seneca, confronted as they watched Agrippina suddenly come unglued in early 55. What prompted the tempest was not an issue of statecraft but an affair of the heart.

. . .

Nero had married Octavia a year or two before his accession, but the union was a cold one. The young emperor did not much care for the high-minded princess his mother had chosen for him. Octavia was central to Agrippina's plan to knit together the Julian and Claudian lines and secure the future of the dynasty. The birth of a son would have sealed that future and cemented Nero's position, but Octavia had not yet conceived. Perhaps she was not able, but it is likely that her disdainful husband did not give her many chances.

Nero's interest in sex was as strong as any adolescent boy's, but like many smothered sons of the elite, he craved the exotic and outré. He had not been in the palace long when an Asian freedwoman named Acte, a member of the foreign-born staff assembled by Claudius, caught his eye and came into his bed. She was everything Octavia was not—above all, she was not his mother's choice.

Emperors felt entitled to any woman they desired, regardless of either party's marital status. Nero's passion for Acte was not in itself worrisome. Indeed, it brought relief to many, who had seen Caligula debauch himself with the wives of senators and consuls, humiliating the elite with rape and degradation. The affair with Acte harmed no one—but it sent Agrippina into a rage. She regarded it as a betrayal by her son and a challenge to her authority. "A *handmaid* for a daughter-in-law!" she exclaimed to her partisans, and demanded of Nero that he end the liaison. "*I* made you emperor," she reminded him, implying that she might undo what she had done.

Nero had had enough. His mother's carping and bullying had annoyed him before, so much that he had threatened to abdicate and run off to Rhodes, far from her influence. Now he was ready to risk a true breach, and he turned to his best natural ally, Seneca.

Seneca had aided Nero early on in the affair with Acte, directing his close friend Annaeus Serenus, newly appointed as head of Rome's *vigiles* (a combined police and fire-fighting corps), to help conceal it. Serenus pretended to be Acte's lover, passing along Nero's gifts to the girl as though they came from him. It was a sneaky and passive form of support—given no doubt in hope the affair would soon run its course—but it showed plainly where Seneca's sympathies lay. If mother and son were going to war, he would side with the son.

The choice could not have been an easy one. Agrippina was his patroness, the woman who had brought him back from exile and given him the power he now enjoyed. He would lose that power, and perhaps his life, if he fell on the wrong side of the rift. Agrippina might even go over the edge if she was pushed too far, a dangerous outcome that Seneca could not have hoped for. Even if Nero *must* triumph in the end, Seneca had nothing to gain—and indeed had much to lose—from the total estrangement of his two masters.

The contretemps took a seemingly benign turn. Unable to bully her son, Agrippina suddenly turned cloying. Outpandering Seneca and Serenus, she offered Nero her own palace rooms for his trysts with Acte, and the use of her wealth to subsidize his pleasures. It was a transparent attempt at manipulation, and Nero's friends urged him not to take the bait. The emperor nonetheless had pangs of regret. Knowing well his mother's taste for feminine finery, he picked out some clothes and gems from the palace treasury and sent them to her as a peace offering. Agrippina only bridled when she got them, claiming that the crown jewels she had given her son were being returned to her in niggardly dribs and drabs. The attempt at reconciliation ended up widening the breach.

Nero decided to neutralize one of Agrippina's chief supporters, the freedman Pallas. Officially minister of the exchequer, but party to all backroom schemes, Pallas had amassed enormous influence and more wealth than anyone in Rome—except his deceased former rival, Narcissus. For seven years, he had used his sway on behalf of Agrippina, but now Nero wanted his mother disarmed. He cut a deal with Pallas, allowing the freedman to take his loot with him, no questions asked, if he would leave without making trouble. Pallas exited grandly, accompanied by crowds of attendants and bearers—a rare political gambler who had beaten the house and, for the moment at least, got out with his winnings intact.

The loss of her principal ally turned Agrippina apoplectic. A few weeks earlier, she had touted her role in securing the throne for Nero; now she spoke openly of her power to take it away. Britannicus was about to reach manhood, she pointed out to her son, and could easily reclaim his patrimony. In an inversion of her former line, she portrayed Nero as an interloper and a usurper of Britannicus' rights. It was by the grace of the gods, she said, that Britannicus still lived. She would take him to the Praetorians' camp and present him for acclamation; the soldiers would take *her* part against her rivals at court.

"It'll be a daughter of Germanicus on one side, and on the other Burrus the cripple and Seneca the exile—one with his maimed hand, the other with his schoolmaster's tongue, yet they seek rule over the whole human race!" she cried, gesturing wildly and invoking the shades of her victims, the two Silanus brothers and the now-deified Claudius.

A young man's dalliance with a servant was spiraling into a crisis. Agrippina was lashing out viciously at her son, with her uncanny instinct for what would threaten him politically and terrorize him psychologically. There was no doubt of her standing with the Praetorian Guard, the keystone to control of the throne. The guard had always been fiercely loyal to the house of Germanicus, whose memory they deeply revered. With the guard behind her, Agrippina could, if it came to that, destroy Seneca, Burrus, and Nero together, as easily as she had created all three ex nihilo.

The triumvirate forged at the end of Claudius' regime—the strange triangle of Agrippina, Nero, and Seneca—had collapsed. It was now a game of two against one, with Agrippina desperate not to end up on the losing side. She had shown her willingness to use any weapon, to escalate to the highest pitch of emotion, in order to hold Nero's allegiance. For Seneca, adherent of Reason, advocate of moderation and the suppression of anger, it was not clear whether, or how, to fight back.

Britannicus was approaching his fourteenth birthday. With it would come an adult toga, a ceremonial entry into the Forum, and implicitly, eligibility for rule. The seniority advantage that Nero had enjoyed would soon be at an end, forever.

Though sidelined from power, Britannicus had made plain that his hopes were not extinguished. In December 54, when Nero had been two months on the throne, the imperial family had one night relaxed with a role-playing game, and Nero had been made king-for-a-night. The new princeps imperiously commanded his adoptive brother to stand and sing before all. Britannicus, unbowed by the bullying, sang a tragic lament about the loss of patrimony and rule. It was the same sort of pluck the boy had shown years earlier, if he indeed had ignored Nero's adoption and deliberately called him Domitius.

Had Claudius wanted his natural son to inherit the throne on coming of age? Some believed his will had made such provisions, but Agrippina and Nero had suppressed it. In any case, what mattered to Nero now was not his adoptive father's intentions but those of his mother. Even if the will had not named Britannicus heir, Agrippina could claim that it had—and who would gainsay a grieving widow, daughter of Germanicus, and priestess of her deified husband's cult?

Agrippina had shown, in the Acte crisis, that she would use Britannicus at any opportunity to gain leverage. She had the supreme weapon that could be held over a princeps, a viable replacement. Only when this weapon was defused could Nero hope to control his mother—though she would still have in her arsenal the support of the Praetorians, the heroic legacy of Germanicus, and a remarkable ability to lavish or deny maternal love.

The date of Britannicus' upcoming birthday grew more threatening as it drew closer. Nero decided he must make that date a deadline in the literal sense—the date by which Britannicus would be dead.

It was as much his mother as his adoptive brother that Nero was striking at. He was not strong enough to order violence against Agrippina, though soon the wish to do so would consume him. For now, he could murder her by proxy.

Nero used his mother's own hired poisoner to accomplish the deed, the Gaul Locusta, "the Crayfish." Unlike his mother when she killed Claudius, though, Nero did not care about acting in stealth. Locusta at first concocted a slow-acting poison that only made Britannicus vomit; Nero became so agitated that he struck her. The woman explained that she had only been trying to help keep the crime concealed. "So I'm afraid of the Julian law, am I?" Nero asked, mocking the idea he could be tried under standing statutes.

Locusta obliged by providing a stronger dose, testing it on a goat and a pig to make certain. Speed and openness were desirable now. Nero wanted Agrippina to see that he had the courage to act.

Did Seneca help Nero carry out his first assassination? Was he at least informed of the plot? None of our sources imply either proposition, but the logic of the court demands that they be considered. Seneca had been Nero's ally against Agrippina from the start, as well as his chief adviser and guide. It is hard to know whether Nero could, or would, have pulled off the crime without him.

By custom, the imperial family dined together, but with younger members sitting upright (as only children did in Rome) at their own table. Britannicus took his meals here, alongside his close friend Titus, son of the general Vespasian—both of whom would one day become emperors themselves. Nero and his wife Octavia sat apart, reclining on dining couches in adult fashion. Hierarchies of place, posture, and diet thus separated Octavia from her younger brother. The paths of the two orphans had diverged widely since *insitivus Nero,* "grafted-on Nero," had arrived in their midst.

Tasters routinely sampled all drinks and dishes to guard the family against poisons. But every system has its loopholes, and Nero exploited one of them. Since it was winter, wine was drunk warm, mixed before-hand with hot water. Britannicus' cup was duly tasted and passed to him. But the drink had been made too hot for the young man's liking. He pushed it away, and an obliging servant added melted snow to temper it. The drink, now containing the poison, was not tested a second time. Britannicus sipped it and fell stone dead.

There followed a stunned silence in the dining hall, during which all present felt, as one historian has put it, "the need of seeing into the minds of others while concealing one's own." Some made a hasty exit from the room. Agrippina and Octavia, who were among those taken by surprise, stood transfixed, striving (according to Tacitus) to keep their faces expressionless. All eyes turned toward Nero. The emperor reminded those present that Britannicus had suffered epileptic attacks since childhood; the boy would no doubt soon recover his health. No one contradicted him, and the meal grimly resumed.

Rome had seen dynastic murders before, but never such a brazen one at a large gathering. The openness of the deed sent a clear message, intended for Agrippina above all. She would not be allowed to bully or blackmail her son. Nero would stand on his own, or rather with Seneca and Burrus, not his mother, to aid him.

Nero (left) and Britannicus, in a relief dating
from before Nero's accession.

Locusta had done her job well. She received an imperial pardon for her prior crimes and an award of rich lands outside Rome. On these estates, according to Suetonius, she founded a kind of poisoning academy in the service of the princeps. Her drugs had so far carried off two of three surviving Claudians, slowly in the first instance, in the second with terrifying speed. Nero would have cause to call on her one more time, in the years to come.

Somehow the poison given to Britannicus also got into the system of Titus, his best friend and dining companion, and made the young man ill for weeks (or so Suetonius reports). Titus would, after becoming emperor a quarter-century later, portray himself as Britannicus' posthumous champion. In the short time he occupied the principate, from A.D. 79 to 81, he issued coins bearing Britannicus' image and commissioned two costly statues: a gilded one that stood in the palace, and an equestrian portrait, plated with ivory, that was carried, alongside images of gods and heroes, into the Circus Maximus at the start of a yearly sports festival.

By that time, a link to the Claudians had become an asset for reigning emperors, since Nero had trashed the reputation of the Julians. Britannicus came to stand as a shining symbol of what might have been.

Postmortem rites for Britannicus had to be carefully stage-managed, just as they had been for Claudius. The young man's death had to seem like a natural event, even if the palace knew otherwise. When it was discovered that Locusta's toxin had darkened Britannicus' skin, Nero reportedly had the body painted over with chalk to whiten it again. A cremation ceremony was held either that very night or the next, despite heavy rain. Later it was rumored that the rain washed away the makeup from Britannicus' face, as though the gods themselves sought to reveal the truth.

Britannicus' ashes were interred, quickly and quietly, in the mausoleum of Augustus, formerly reserved for emperors and members of the Julian line. But despite the honorary resting place, haste and lack of ceremony aroused public resentment. Nero was forced to publish an edict the day after the interment. It was good Roman custom, Nero asserted, to forgo rites for those who had died in youth, lest the lingering presence of a young corpse bring bad luck to the family. This thin pretext was the best the regime could manage, even with Seneca's ingenuity.

Agrippina, according to two sources, went into open mourning for the young man whose cause she had espoused so recently and with such fatal consequences. Perhaps her tears were political theater, designed to arouse opposition to Nero, but she also had grounds for remorse. Her best means of restoring her waning power at court was gone. She had used Britannicus as a pawn in a high-stakes showdown, and her son had bested her with a lightning blow.

Agrippina's fortunes went into a steep decline, clearly signaled by imperial coinage. Her image was no longer shown facing that of Nero. For a brief time, she appeared in jugate, the profile of the princeps overlaying hers, as she had been portrayed under Claudius. Then she disappeared from state coinage entirely within the year. The "best of mothers" had been thrust from her son's favor. Spurned, she gravitated toward another outcast at court, her stepdaughter Octavia, orphaned daughter of Claudius and Messalina, now Nero's unloved teenage wife.

Octavia's plight, in the aftermath of Britannicus' death, was truly piteous. In seven years, she had watched as her father killed her mother, her stepmother killed her father, and her husband killed her brother. She had somehow survived, along with her half-sister Antonia, in a regime run by strangers and enemies. Her husband rejected her and sought the embraces of an ex-slave instead. The loss of her brother Britannicus left her utterly alone, perhaps afraid even to grieve, as the author of *Octavia* imagined:

> *My fear forbids me to weep for a brother,*
> *He in whom my last hope was lodged,*
> *He who gave a short respite from pains.*
> *Living only to mourn my kin*
> *I linger on, the shade of a once-great name.*

The historian Tacitus confirms the tragedian's portrait: "Despite her youth, Octavia had already learned to conceal her sorrow, her love—all her emotions."

Britannicus had other partisans at court, and in the Senate and the street, but Rome stayed quiet. Though an earlier princeps, Tiberius, had once endured widespread outrage at the suspicious death of Germanicus, in this case no protests arose to trouble the new regime. The public was not even provoked by a disturbing report, of uncertain credibility, that Nero had raped Britannicus some days before the fatal dinner, to demoralize his enemy before striking him down.

Many suspected foul play, but they bowed to the logic of history, according to Tacitus: in royal families, brother had ever been at war with brother; the principate could not be shared. "Death to the weaker; leave the stronger to reign in the empty throne room," Seneca had written, probably only a few weeks earlier, in *Apocolocyntosis,* quoting Vergil's advice on ending strife in a beehive with two "kings."

But in *Apocolocyntosis,* Seneca had also depicted Augustus, among the company of the gods, thundering disdain at Claudius for killing members of his family. And in *De Ira,* he had compared a princeps to a gentle physician, administering death only as a form of mercy when a patient was beyond cure. For the author of those two works, the murder of Britannicus raised disquieting questions.

Was a moral principate, an administration compatible with Stoic precepts, going to be possible? Seneca had based his vision of good governance on the regime of Augustus; but the regime to which he belonged, dominated by an insecure, spoiled teenager and his unstable mother, seemed a long way off from that shining ideal. He stood closer to the moral universe of his tragedies, works like *Medea* and *Phaedra,* than to *De Ira* and his other prose works.

Seneca had to consider not only his own principles but his reputation among the elite. He had crafted Nero's inaugural speech to the Senate, an address that promised an end to abuses of power. That historic speech had been inscribed on silver tablets and hung on a column for all to see. But those tablets were now badly tarnished. The fresh start that the regime had enjoyed months earlier, its repudiation of Claudian paranoia and subterfuge, had been given the lie.

Even if Seneca had played only a passive role in the murder—and some surely suspected it was more than that—he was nonetheless tainted by it. "Not stopping a wrong is the same as spurring it on," Seneca had written in one of his plays, a line that, if any among the elite had heard it, might now have been spat back in his face. It did not help that in all likelihood, Seneca was among those to whom Nero gave shares of Britannicus' property. This distribution caused revulsion in official Rome, according to Tacitus: "There was no lack of those who took issue with this: that men who affected moral seriousness were splitting up houses and estates like booty."

Not least of Seneca's concerns, in the days after Britannicus' death, was his own safety. Any illusion that partnership with Burrus, who controlled the Praetorians, would protect him had now been dispelled. In the balance-of-fear calculations that governed palace relationships, poison was a great trump card. Nero now had an expert poisoner in his service and, more important, the courage to deploy her weapons. The threat that Nero's power posed must have been present to Seneca's mind at every state dinner thereafter.

In the tragedy Seneca wrote near the end of his life, *Thyestes,* the climactic scene shows a king destroying his brother by feeding him a toxic meal. On one level, the scene evokes the murder of Britannicus, for the victimized brother had been just on the verge of assuming joint rule. On another, the victim is Seneca himself, for the play portrays this man as a mild-mannered sage returning from exile. By the time he wrote *Thyestes* or soon afterward, Seneca's life had also been threatened by poison, as we will see. In the play, he seems to recall Britannicus' deadly last dinner but also to put a version of himself in the boy's place at table.

The dilemmas Seneca now faced—ethical, political, and deeply personal—would grow more complex and pressing through the decade he was to spend at Nero's side. To judge by his few oblique references to them, he was never to find resolution. He would describe himself, near the end of that decade, as suffering from an incurable moral illness, able to gain partial relief but no cure. Perhaps that was the necessary outcome of his decision, long before, to enter politics even while pursuing his Stoic moral pilgrimage. He had attained both the wisdom of a sage and the power of a palace insider—but could the two selves coexist?

Seneca was not ready to give up on the ideal of a moral principate. His greatest assets, virtuosic eloquence and literary ingenuity, were still as potent as ever. Twice before, he had used these gifts to accomplish feats of dexterity: preaching acceptance of death while also begging for recall from exile, in *Consolation to Polybius;* viciously lampooning a dead princeps while exalting a living one, in *Apocolocyntosis.* His command of words was such as to make any goal seem possible. Perhaps it could even hold together his swiftly diverging paths.

In the wake of Britannicus' death, Seneca set out to write his most eloquent, most audacious, most ingenious prose work yet. This time he would not only ventriloquize Nero, he would preach to him, asserting the privilege of a teacher to lecture his pupil. He would erase the recent assassination and start the regime over again, on a firmer ethical footing this time. He would show that if Nero went down the road of Claudius or, worse, of Caligula—banishments, executions, rigged trials held in the emperor's bedroom—he, Seneca, would not stand by idly, or at least could not be held to blame.

Such thinking, at any rate, is one way to explain the genesis of *De Clementia* ("On Mercy"), the most inspiring political treatise produced under the Roman principate—or, perhaps, the cleverest piece of propaganda.

CHAPTER 4

Matricide

(A.D. 55–59)

"Have I, out of all mortals, found favor, and have I been chosen to take the role of gods here on earth? Am I the judge who marks out nations for life or for death?" Such are the awestruck words of eighteen-year-old Nero looking out upon his realm, as Seneca imagines them. Seneca opens *De Clementia,* "On Mercy," by giving voice to Nero's thoughts, a new device for allowing Rome once again to hear *his* words issuing from the emperor's mouth.

Seneca depicts Nero as an omnipotent but morally serious adolescent. Like a modern teenage superhero, the princeps knows that great powers confer great responsibilities. Principles of justice, mercy, and restraint guide his every move. Whether dealing with foreign foes or the troublesome mob of his fellow citizens, he keeps "harshness sheathed, but mercy battle-ready," an instance of Seneca's favorite metaphor, moral effort as hand-to-hand combat. "If the gods today ask me for an accounting, I stand ready to tally up the whole human race," Seneca/Nero concludes—meaning that, as shepherd, he has not allowed his flock to diminish by even a single head.

Of course, the flock *had* been diminished, and recently, by one very important head, and those reading Seneca's treatise knew it. The death of Britannicus casts a long shadow over *De Clementia,* especially since Seneca goes on to proclaim, in his own voice this time, the spotlessness of Nero's record. He affirms Nero's boast of "never having shed a drop of human blood anywhere on earth"—a claim that rings all the more hollow for being literally true; Britannicus had been poisoned rather than put to the sword. Seneca willfully wipes the slate clean, as though allowing the year-old regime a do-over. If Nero could be given a pass for that one life, Seneca must have reasoned, many more might be spared.

By his own account, Seneca was moved to write *De Clementia* after witnessing a behind-the-scenes moment of palace life. Burrus, the Praetorian prefect and Seneca's own staunch ally, needed the emperor to make out warrants for the execution of two robbers. Nero kept postponing the unpleasant task, until Burrus finally drew up the papers and presented them for signing. "If only I were illiterate!" Nero reportedly sighed, as he validated the warrants. Seneca effuses that this should be the quip heard around the world, that it bespeaks the guiltlessness of a golden age when all men are brothers. It shows Nero already in possession of perfect *clementia,* Seneca claims, ingeniously concealing instruction behind a screen of flattery.

The essay claims not to teach Nero anything but to show him his own moral brilliance, as if in a mirror. Its real goals, of course, are more complex.

Seneca's target audience in *De Clementia* was not so much the emperor but the senatorial class, the Roman political elite. The treatise sought to reassure these aristocrats that Nero's character, on which much of their own safety depended, was in good hands. Despite the red flag that Britannicus' murder had raised, Seneca showed that he was still restraining the young emperor, keeping him off Caligula's path. It would be Seneca's humane principles, here superimposed onto Nero by rhetorical sleight of hand, that would guide the regime.

Seneca expounded those principles more fully in *De Clementia* than he had in *De Ira.* (The two treatises are in a sense complementary, since *ira* seeks to impose punishment while *clementia* remits it.) Both essays take the position that all humankind is prone to err and therefore all deserve mercy. But *De Clementia* is more emphatic on this point. "We have all of us done wrong," Seneca intones here, in words that would not be out of place in a modern Christian sermon, "some seriously, some lightly, some intentionally, some pushed into it by accident or carried away by the wrongdoing of others; some have stood by our good designs not firmly enough and have lost our guiltlessness, unwillingly, while trying to keep our grasp on it." That last case sounds strikingly like Seneca's own.

Everyone should be merciful, given the universal guilt of humankind; but, Seneca claims, emperors—*and kings*—have even greater reason to do so. Remarkably, he does not blush to dust off the old, vilified word *rex* as a virtual synonym for *princeps*. For more than five centuries, Rome had held *reges* in contempt, which meant that emperors had to conceal their true status. The Roman state was, in theory, still a republic, with the Senate gently guided by a "first citizen."

In *De Clementia*, Seneca drops the veil of pretense. Rome has become an autocracy, he grants—and a good thing, too, for the alternative is chaos. Should the mob ever throw off its "yoke," he asserts in the essay's opening words, it would harm itself and everyone else—an assessment that had propped up the Caesars for a century but that no one had yet dared admit.

Seneca begins *De Clementia*, then, by ceding Nero absolute power; but then he shows why his power should be restrained. Kindness from rulers wins adoration from subjects and results in a long, secure reign; severity breeds fear, and from fear springs conspiracy. The divine Augustus is brought forward, as in other Senecan works, to exemplify the former approach. Augustus, Nero's great-great-grandfather, found out that a trusted subordinate, Lucius Cinna, was plotting against his life. After a long, tense parley with Cinna, Augustus, far from imposing punishment, awarded him an appointment as consul—the highest political honor. "He was never again the target of anyone's conspiracies," Seneca concludes.

Nero's role, as defined by *De Clementia*, is absolute monarch in law but pious servant of moral principle. He can choose—or already has chosen, under the conceit that Seneca is only showing Nero his own perfection—to rein in power voluntarily. If his fellowship with the all-fallible human race does not compel him, self-interest will.

To highlight that fellowship, Seneca uses a novel analogy to illustrate the role of the princeps. Roman writers had often portrayed their leader as a father raising his children or, in more effusive moods, as the sun shining down on the earth. Seneca introduces a new model. He compares Nero to a *mind,* controlling the limbs of the citizen body. The analogy virtually embodies Reason, the Stoic school's greatest good, in the person of the emperor.

The second section of *De Clementia* has not survived intact, but here Seneca went in for theory: defining what *clementia* is, how it arises and functions. Notionally he was still addressing Nero, but readers knew that the princeps had not the slightest interest in such things. *De Clementia,* like most of Seneca's writings, targets multiple audiences and strives for multiple goals. It shows that pure ethical philosophy, the source of Seneca's high repute, was an ongoing project, though not part of his official brief.

De Clementia is a hugely ambitious effort to hold together a fragmenting life. Perhaps Seneca could accomplish what Aristotle, four centuries earlier, had attempted (in popular legend at least) with Alexander the Great: to bring enlightenment to a global ruler. Perhaps Stoic virtue could after all march hand in hand with power; perhaps the principate could in fact be built on a moral foundation. At least he, Seneca, could be seen making the attempt—a point that would be crucial, should the experiment fail.

What Nero thought of getting such instruction in public is not known. It's unlikely he cared much for philosophy during his late teenage years, or ever afterward for that matter. Had he tried, Seneca would have had trouble finding a student who was less apt for his lessons. Nero was busy exploring the possibilities that his new powers had brought him—to commit murder, for one, but also lesser crimes, illicit pleasures, and carefree assaults on Roman society. If any philosophic text caught his attention, it was not one of Seneca's high-minded treatises but Plato's *Republic*, with its famous story of Gyges' ring.

In the *Republic,* Plato portrayed Glaucon, a youth about Nero's age, in conversation with Socrates, a man about Seneca's. At one point, Glaucon relates to Socrates how a Lydian named Gyges found a magic ring. If twisted a certain way on the finger, the ring would make its wearer invisible. Glaucon then asks Socrates, What would prevent Gyges from donning the ring to steal from the marketplace, to rape women, and to beat or kill whomever he chooses? Surely, Glaucon says, any man would do these things if invisible, no matter how seemingly upright his nature.

Socrates' rebuttal plays out over the remaining nine books of the *Republic*. Under the guidance of a master teacher, Glaucon comes to realize that justice brings far greater happiness than injustice. It was precisely the outcome Seneca might have hoped for in his tutelage of Nero. But Nero was no Glaucon, and Seneca, as time would reveal, was no Socrates.

Nero had in fact set out on exactly Gyges' path. He regarded the principate as his ring of invisibility, a license to do what he pleased.

Nero began sallying out of his palace incognito on rapacious nighttime jaunts, helping himself to merchant goods, drinking and carousing, assaulting passersby. Caught up in the exuberance of power, he wilded in the streets of the city, sexually molesting women and boys alike. It was an early sign of the troubles that awaited Rome. The new princeps was turning out to be a lawless teen with no moral compass.

Nero feared no legal consequences, but the drubbings he might take while in disguise posed a problem. One incident did indeed end badly. A young man of senatorial rank, Julius Montanus, enraged by the rape of his wife, viciously beat a man whom he failed to recognize as the emperor. Nero went home and hid from sight until his bruises healed. He was disinclined to punish a man for an honest mistake—but Montanus somehow learned who his victim was and sent a letter of apology, which changed everything. Nero could not abide a subject who knew he had beaten up the princeps. Montanus, informed of the emperor's displeasure, forestalled the inevitable by taking his own life. Thereafter Nero was careful to bring soldiers along on his forays, ordering them to stand at a distance but come to his aid when called.

Seneca did not interfere with Nero's Hyde-like escapades; nor did Burrus, Seneca's close ally. These two men might have reined in the wild energies of Nero's youth, but, according to Cassius Dio at least, they had been cowed by the murder of Britannicus. The princeps had struck a blow for independence, not only from his mother but from his two senior advisers as well.

Nero's young friends, companions of his wilding sprees like Marcus Otho and Claudius Senecio, egged on the princeps to defy these two father figures. "Are you afraid of them?" they asked, knowing they would score points by irreverence. "Don't you realize that *you* are *Caesar*—that you have power over *them*, not they over you?" The slow unraveling of Nero's trust in Seneca had begun—a process that would take ten years to play out and would result in disaster for both men.

Nero extended his newfound license to the commoners: he removed the armed details that kept order in Rome's open-air theaters. Fans of various pantomime dancers—balletlike performers whose sensuality made them the sex symbols of their day—used this freedom to start factional fights in the stands. Nero went to the theaters in disguise and watched these frays with delight, or even took part, throwing stones or broken bits of bench along with the most rabid brawlers. Finally the disorder became so grave that even Nero felt it had to be stopped. He ordered all pantomimes out of Italy, to give the fevered audiences a chance to cool off, and reinstated military patrols of the theaters.

It was not a dancer but a musician who most fascinated young Nero: a Greek singer and lyre player named Terpnus ("Delight"). The emperor installed this man in the palace and had him perform after dinner, often staying up late to listen, enraptured, to his languorous, passion-filled songs. Terpnus' art form was imported from Greece, like the pantomime dance, and Romans found it seductive and sensuous—an effect mistrusted by the elite, though the mob adored it. Nero, too, was captivated and soon undertook to learn the art himself. His voice was not naturally musical, but he took every measure taught by Terpnus to beautify it, including purgatives, enemas, special diets, and an exercise for the diaphragm done while lying under lead plates. He had taken his first steps on the path that would lead him, over the next decade, from princeps to performing artiste.

Amid Nero's experiments in anomie and cultivations of his voice, Rome somehow had to be governed. It was becoming clear that the princeps had little interest in statecraft, and no talent for it. His one big initiative in these early years, a proposal to abolish all indirect taxes—customs duties, tolls, and the like—had to be scuttled by embarrassed advisers, on the grounds that it would cause financial ruin.

Seneca and Burrus seem to have kept Rome in order to a large degree, though just how large is a matter of debate. Our sources have little to say about governance during these years, preferring personal dramas and court intrigues—the events that, for them, defined Nero's reign. Tacitus merely implies that the state was being run, without Nero doing much to run it. Seneca and Burrus, aided by a staff of Greek freedmen inherited from the days of Claudius, most likely had their hands full.

Then there was Agrippina, eager to do whatever she could—which was considerably more than what most Romans wanted.

Though the poisoning of Britannicus had deprived her of her ultimate weapon, Agrippina was attempting to regroup. She had begun amassing money to buy influence and cultivate support among the disaffected. Nero preemptively bribed many of his courtiers with lavish gifts—rewards for their complicity in Britannicus' death—but Agrippina had a large estate and could hope someday to outbribe him.

More disturbing to Nero were the bonds Agrippina was forging with Octavia, his unloved bride. Concord between these two outcast women portended no good to him. Agrippina could use Octavia to play the succession card, as she had once done with Britannicus, rallying support to the Claudian banner. She could promise Octavia as a marital prize, a guarantee of legitimacy, to a usurper.

The warning shot that Nero had fired had clearly not humbled his

Agrippina.

mother, and sterner measures were needed. Nero ordered Agrippina stripped of her bodyguard, the band of German toughs who had been a visible marker of her status (only the princeps was similarly attended), and of the Praetorians who patrolled her quarters. Finally he turned her out of the palace altogether, claiming—an obvious pretext—that daily gatherings of her dependents were crowding the halls of state.

Agrippina at once became marked as persona non grata in the eyes of Nero's regime. Her friends made haste to abandon her, fearing that any association might be held against them. When Nero went to visit her new abode, he took a conspicuous armed guard with him. He wanted to convey to all observers that she was a dangerous woman.

Then one night, as Nero was relaxing over drink and song, news arrived that seemed to confirm his worst fears about his mother.

By A.D. 55, there were four men alive whose lineage made them potential rivals to Nero. Two belonged to the ill-fated Silanus family, direct descendants of Augustus as Nero was (a distinction that had already brought death to two of their kin). A third was Rubellius Plautus, the only child of Tiberius' granddaughter and therefore connected to the line of Augustus by adoption. The last was Faustus Sulla, not descended from any emperor but a Julian nonetheless, great-grandson of Augustus' sister Octavia.

These men could not simply challenge Nero to some Arthurian trial by combat. But they could be backed by rebellious foreign legions, as Germanicus once had been, or by a mutinous Praetorian Guard, like Claudius. Or their cause could be embraced by the third of Rome's king-makers, Agrippina.

In Nero's eyes, Plautus gave the most cause for concern. He had a high reputation for strength of character; he lived a simple, unambitious life, in accord with his Stoic beliefs. His wife, Antistia Pollitta, was also well respected and had good political pedigree, being the daughter of a consul serving that very year. Sulla was almost as worrisome as Plautus, having married Antonia, Claudius' daughter by his second wife (the predecessor of Messalina). And Sulla's name linked him to a formidable ancestor of an earlier century, Lucius Cornelius Sulla—a military strong-man whose memory could still stir restive troops.

The messenger who knocked on Nero's door that drunken evening was a freedman named Paris, an actor, one of Nero's favorite performers and perhaps (so Tacitus implies) a visitor to his bed. Paris carried information he had received from Julia Silana, a woman who had continued talking to Agrippina even after her fall from grace. According to Julia's report, Agrippina was planning a coup that would put Rubellius Plautus in power. She would get him divorced from Antistia, then marry him herself and become coruler of the empire, as she had been in the days of Claudius.

There were reasons to doubt this tale, since Julia, its source, bore an old grudge against Agrippina. Nonetheless Nero went into crisis mode. The specter of his mother's power to undo him, so recently suppressed, sprang back out with terrifying force. He wanted his mother put to death immediately, and he also, according to one of Tacitus' sources, demanded a new Praetorian prefect—he now mistrusted Burrus as Agrippina's appointee. Only Seneca's intervention, according to this source, prevented the second move, but Nero seemed intent on carrying out the first.

Burrus was summoned to Nero's chambers and ordered to kill Agrippina. Only with difficulty could the prefect persuade the princeps to wait until morning, when the wine would have worn off and the matter could be weighed in full. At dawn the next day, Burrus was sent to interrogate Agrippina, accompanied by a worried Seneca.

Neither man wanted this showdown between mother and son. Not many months had elapsed since the murder of Britannicus. The public had accepted one apparent assassination, but a second one, of a far more powerful figure—the daughter of Germanicus—would not sit well. Then too Seneca and Burrus had their own futures to consider. They had risen in Nero's graces by opposing Agrippina, but if that great counterweight were removed, the emperor's trust might disappear as well. Already it seemed to be slipping away: Nero had sent his own freedmen along to witness the questioning of Agrippina, as though he were suspicious of collusion.

Agrippina's self-defense speech, as preserved by Tacitus, relied on chopped logic and feigned maternal affection. All her accusers had ulterior motives, she pointed out, and the principal one, Julia Silana, was childless; *she* could not know the warmth of a mother's love. "Parents don't switch children the way a cheap adulterer changes lovers," Agrippina argued, ignoring the fact that, a few months earlier, she had done exactly that—threatening to advance Britannicus over her own son. Then, changing tack, Agrippina called to mind all she had done to put Nero into power. She claimed she had no hope of survival were Plautus, or anyone else, to take the throne. Only her own flesh and blood could keep her safe, she said, again ignoring patent facts: it was because of her flesh and blood that she was now fighting for her life.

The speciousness of these arguments did not matter. Seneca and Burrus knew that they must bring about a reconciliation between mother and son or face a very uncertain future. They persuaded Nero to meet his mother face-to-face, and somehow—Tacitus does not say what took place in their closed-door meeting—the crisis was defused.

The price of reconciliation was steep. Knowing he must find a modus vivendi if he was not going to kill Agrippina, Nero had to make highly visible concessions. The court hierarchy had to be rebalanced so that Agrippina's accusers were banished and her partisans promoted. Recent appointees had to be deappointed, and not even Seneca's family was spared: his wife's father, Pompeius Paulinus, now lost his post as prefect of Rome's grain supply, to make room for Faenius Rufus, a protégé of Agrippina. This may have been the occasion, as seen earlier, for Seneca's plea to Paulinus to retire into philosophy—the essay *De Brevitate Vitae,* "On the Shortness of Life."

Whatever ground Seneca had lost in *l'affaire Plautus,* Burrus had lost more. On the panicky night when the rumor first broke, Burrus had perhaps narrowly escaped dismissal; then he had been forced to decline a direct order from Nero. In the wake of the crisis, an opportunist named Paetus, a man who made a disreputable living buying and selling bad debt, tried to curry favor by tying Burrus to a new conspiracy, this one centered on Faustus Sulla. To make the charge more convincing, and a conviction more appealing, Paetus accused Agrippina's former lackey, the freedman Pallas, of being Burrus' accomplice.

It was a probe of the new rifts in the palace, but Nero, perhaps at Seneca's urging, stood by Burrus. As though to belittle Paetus' charges, Nero empaneled Burrus as one of the judges deciding the case, thereby ensuring acquittals all around. The tempests passed, and court hierarchy was restored.

Nero went on with his nighttime diversions: mayhem in the city streets, singing lessons with Terpnus, the warm embraces of Acte. But his mind was more troubled than before by Rubellius Plautus and Faustus Sulla. No evidence had been found against either, but loose talk alone gave grounds on which to mistrust them. By the twisted logic of autocracy, a man cast as usurper in a fictional conspiracy became an enemy in reality. Whomever rumor settled on, this logic ran, was the man the public would turn to if they ever demanded a change of princeps.

Rumor had also cast Agrippina as a foe of the regime, ascribing to her a plan to marry Plautus. Though there may have been no substance to the accusation, its plausibility gnawed at Nero's mind. Nero had already watched his mother remake the imperial family from top to bottom, after marrying Claudius. She might pull off the same trick a second time. She might even—she was just now reaching forty—bear a second son to some new Julian husband, an heir to displace Nero from his throne and from her affections.

A mother who could seduce and control powerful men, who hated her son for not bending to her will, who had threatened in a heated moment to advance Britannicus—such a woman seemed capable of anything. There would be a reckoning between Nero and Agrippina someday, though none could tell as yet what form it might take.

In 55 or (more likely) 56, Seneca attained the highest constitutional office in the Roman state, that of consul. The post carried less power than his unofficial role as *amicus principis,* friend of the princeps, but it was a towering achievement nonetheless. Seneca's elder brother Gallio, returned to Rome from his proconsular post in Greece, attained the same honor at about the same time. The two boys from Corduba, provincials born into the equestrian class, sons of a crusty rhetorician who had never made it to the Senate, had come far indeed—a mark of what the emperor's favor might bring, in Rome's winner-take-all political system.

High office was not the only way Seneca's fortunes had changed. During the six or seven years since his return from Corsica, he had gotten rich.

Exile to Corsica had stripped Seneca of half his estate, but Agrippina's recall had restored it, and thereafter his closeness to Nero had made good the loss many times over. Some gifts came from the emperor himself; others were from those who sought favors or access. By the late 50s Seneca owned estates in Egypt, Spain, and Campania, the fertile and fashionable region centered around Neapolis (Naples), as well as others in unspecified locales, along with plenty of cash. His gardens were famed for their size and magnificence. In the early 60s he would add another property, a choice vineyard, to his holdings, at Nomentum, north of Rome.

Both Tacitus and the satirist Juvenal called him *praedives,* a milder term than our *filthy rich* but certainly not an epithet Seneca would have been proud of.

These estates brought in a modest income from the sale of produce, especially wine. Seneca counted himself an expert vintner and was said to have gotten more than 180 gallons of wine to the acre. But better profits could be gained from lending money at interest, and Seneca pursued this revenue stream as well.

Provinces newly added to the empire were hungry for capital—the wherewithal to develop trade and begin tapping Roman markets—and willing to pay high rates. Seneca invested in Britain, the newest and hungriest province. This was good foreign policy, for Roman funds helped to make British warlords tractable, but it was also good business. Cassius Dio's estimate of Seneca's British stake, 40 million sesterces, is perhaps an exaggeration. But whatever the amount involved, it is clear that Seneca's portfolio was targeting aggressive growth.

The paradox of a moral philosopher who was rich and getting richer raised concern in Seneca's time, as it has in ours. Other sages had enjoyed royal subsidies—Aristotle, for one, had profited handsomely from his friendship with Philip of Macedon, Alexander the Great's father—but none had been quite so intent on building a fortune. Indeed, the two Greek thinkers most admired for their lifestyles, Socrates and Diogenes, were famous for their disregard of wealth. Socrates had been poor by birth and remained so through inattention to his trade; Diogenes the Cynic was an ascetic by choice. He rejected his family's bourgeois status, got himself exiled from his native city, and went about in a threadbare cloak with only the barest possessions, a bag for his crust of bread and a cup for scooping water from fountains. When one day he saw a boy drinking from his hands, he smashed the cup, disgusted by his own love of luxury.

Seneca was a Stoic, not a Cynic like Diogenes, and for the Stoics wealth did not present so grave a problem. They counted it as one of several "indifferents" that contributed neither to happiness nor to unhappiness. Moderate Stoics even conceded that wealth could add to happiness, not least because it made possible virtuous deeds. But Seneca had been attracted, from his earliest writings, by a harder, tougher regimen, bordering on Cynicism in its disdain for wealth.

In his letters from exile, Seneca had celebrated life as an unaccommodated man, his view of the open sky unblocked by mansions and banquet halls. He had praised a member of Claudius' court who "pushed riches away, and sought no better profit from his ease in acquiring them than contempt of having them." He had sworn, in *De Ira,* that all the world's gold mines, heaped up into a single pile, "would not be worth the frown on the face of a good man"—the frown that owning them would surely cause. "No one excelled this millionaire in singing the praises of poverty," writes his biographer Miriam Griffin.

Seeming contradictions between word and deed emboldened Seneca's enemies. By now he had plenty of them, and not only in Agrippina's circle. A principal foe was Suillius Rufus, who had himself gotten rich as a *delator* under Claudius and Messalina—a lackey who prosecuted those whom the princeps disliked, in exchange for reward. Suillius was not faring well under Nero; a move by the Senate threatened to fine or even punish those who took pay for legal services. His back against the wall, Suillius tried to deflect blame onto a new target. If the senators wanted to punish ill-gotten gains, he said, they need look no further than Seneca.

"By what kind of wisdom, by what teachings of the philosophers has Seneca heaped up 300 million sesterces in four years as a palace insider?" Suillius ranted in the Senate. "The childless and their estates are being scooped up in his net; Italy and the provinces are being drained away by his outrageous moneylending. I will endure anything—any accusation or trial—rather than rank my long-standing honor, won by my own efforts, below his windfall profits!"

The brazenness of this attack was breathtaking. The idea that Suillius had *earned* his money, albeit by slandering the innocent, whereas Seneca had merely got his handed to him, or that Claudian fortunes were more honorable than Neronian ones, relied on tortured moral logic. So too did a comparison that Suillius drew between his own courtroom rhetoric—which he described as "vigorous and blameless"—and the "indolent" discourse Seneca practiced on innocent youth. Suillius compounded the outrage by resurrecting the old charge of adultery with Livilla, Caligula's sister, for which Seneca had once been exiled. After eight years in Corsica paying for a crime he may well have been innocent of, Seneca now had to suffer this from Suillius: "Should we deem mine a weightier offense— getting a reward for decent labor, paid by a willing defendant—than sullying the bedrooms of royal women?"

Suillius' charges went nowhere; Nero's regime was not about to see its senior minister defamed. Instead, Suillius' dirty deeds under Claudius were dredged up and used to discredit him. When he claimed he had merely followed orders, Nero dutifully checked his father's papers and reported he could find no such orders. Suillius ended up exiled to the Balearic Islands with the loss of half his estate. But the caricature he had drawn of Seneca—a portrait of a venal upstart, an outsider conniving his way into power, money, and the beds of princesses—could not be so easily banished.

Others besides Suillius attacked Seneca during these years. Some said he seduced the young men he pretended to teach, others that *he* had been seduced—by Agrippina. Some claimed he kept five hundred citrus-wood dining tables in his home for lavish dinner parties. The most damning charge of all, because it could not be refuted, stemmed from his close collaboration with Nero. "Even after denouncing tyranny, he had become a *tyrannodidaskalos*—a tyrant-teacher," Dio quotes Seneca's critics as saying, using a rare and potent Greek word. *That* charge has shadowed Seneca for two millennia.

Seneca prided himself on his self-restraint, especially restraint of anger. In *De Ira,* he held up the model of Cato, who kept his cool even when a man publicly spat in his face. But the carping of those who took issue with his wealth got to him. In a portion of his treatise *De Vita Beata,* "On the Happy Life," he hit back.

In the main, *De Vita Beata* gives an exposition of Stoic values, enshrining Reason and Virtue as the sources of happiness. A *sapiens* or wise man—the perfect master of the Stoic creed—will require nothing more than these. But, Seneca concedes, those less perfect, those still making their way toward wisdom, can use some help from Fortune. That leads him to consider a philosopher's relationship to money, and his essay takes a surprising turn.

Seneca suddenly replies directly to his attackers, first restating their charges in scathing detail: "Why do you speak better than you live? . . . Why are your country estates farmed beyond what natural use requires? Why do you not dine as your own writings dictate? Why does your furniture gleam? Why is the wine drunk at your house older than you are? Why is gold on display there? Why are trees planted that will supply nothing but shade? . . . Why do you have land overseas? Why more land than you can even keep track of?" The questions go on and on, with Seneca mocking his accusers by exaggerating their taunts.

Seneca's line of defense relies on his earlier distinction between the *sapiens,* complete in Stoic wisdom, and others still striving. "I am not a *sapiens,* nor—let me give you food for your malice!—will I ever be," he replies to his accusers. "Demand from me not that I be equal to the best, but better than the bad. . . . I have not attained good health, nor will I; I mix only pain-killers, not cures, for my gout." Riches do not befit a wise man, Seneca concedes, but since he is not one, the rule doesn't apply. He argues, in effect, that he need not practice virtue until he has attained it—even if, as his critics would no doubt counter, such practice might advance him toward his goal.

Seneca asks his critics to see the glass of his character as half full, not half empty, and to pardon his moral failings. More arguments follow. Seneca says he has less interest in money than his accusers. He does not depend on riches for happiness; why should he not then possess them, since he is immune to their toxins? Finally he channels Socrates, imagining, in a long speech, what his great forerunner would say in a similar position. It is not the first time, nor the last, that he fuses himself with this most exalted of models, though it is strange that he does so in a discussion of wealth—an area in which he and Socrates had little in common.

The last sentences of the treatise as we have it—spoken by either Seneca or the ventriloquized Socrates, or both at once—contain a disturbingly dark message to Seneca's accusers: "Looking down from on high, I see the storms that are looming, ready to break on you with their black clouds, or even drawing near, right next to you, about to whisk away you and all you possess." Seneca seems, inescapably, to be issuing threats—referring obliquely to his ability to pull imperial strings.

After one more fist-shaking sentence, *De Vita Beata* breaks off. An accident of transmission—a leak or infestation of worms that destroyed part of an early manuscript—created the break. But the resulting text gives the impression of an author suddenly realizing he has gone too far.

Seneca had allowed his critics to get under his skin. His outrage at being attacked by lesser men made him zealous in his rebuttal. Though he invoked Socrates as his spokesman, he seems not to have learned from his great forerunner about staying above the fray. The rough and tumble of politics, and the intoxicant of proximity to power, were taking their toll on his Stoic serenity.

While Seneca was battling his critics and adding to his huge estate, Nero was occupied with a different distraction. He had fallen in love.

The princeps had continued sleeping with Acte during his four years in power, while also maintaining his sham marriage to Octavia. But recently a woman eight years his senior, the wife of his best friend, had roiled his emotions. She was among the most beautiful, desirable, and sexual women of her day, and above all, she was fertile—an important point for Nero who, though only twenty, had much to gain by siring an heir. Her advent would provoke the third and greatest mother-son crisis to rock the imperial household, destroying the uneasy concord of the past three years. Her name was Poppaea Sabina.

A haughty whore, bedecked with what she despoiled from my house—so Octavia, portrayed as the virtuous wife par excellence, characterizes Poppaea in the play *Octavia*. Ancient historians concurred, painting Poppaea as a ruthless, scheming seductress—the perfect match, it would seem, for a boy raised by Agrippina. No doubt the Roman dread of female *impotentia,* the same dread that colored male views of Agrippina, was at work

Poppaea Sabina.

again here, distorting Poppaea into a caricature. But Poppaea and Agrippina *did* have much in common. As might be expected, each quickly formed a deep-seated hatred of the other.

Poppaea was already married, divorced, and remarried when Nero fell for her, and she had a young son from her first marriage. It seems that Otho, her second husband and Nero's close friend, first brought Poppaea and the emperor together, though just how is unclear. Tacitus gives two different reports, one making Otho the instigator of the affair—he boasted of Poppaea's beauty so ardently that Nero had to see for himself— the other suggesting that Nero wanted Poppaea all along and got Otho to marry her as a cover. Whatever the circumstances, Otho ended up far from Rome, dispatched to a provincial post in Lusitania, while Poppaea, now his ex-wife, stayed behind.

Nero seems to have intended from the start to marry Poppaea and make her empress—an outcome Poppaea must have demanded, if ancient reports of her ambitiousness have any bearing on truth. To accomplish this, however, Nero would need to divorce Octavia, against the express and urgent wishes of his mother. Fidelity to Octavia had already been a flashpoint in Nero's incendiary relations with Agrippina, years earlier when Acte first came on the scene. The prospects of a fresh blowup, now that Nero was contemplating not just a new lover but a new wife, were very real.

Poppaea dared Nero to stand up to his mother and reject Octavia, playing on his male pride. She sneeringly called him a *pupillum,* a helpless dependent, lacking both power and freedom. Or perhaps, she taunted, he was afraid to marry a woman who would show him what Agrippina *really* was: a greedy, arrogant shrew despised by the public. Poppaea threatened to abandon Nero and return to Otho, her previous husband. Above all she worked on him with her erotic charms, which by all accounts were considerable.

Agrippina recognized the threat from Poppaea and took countermeasures. In the days of the Acte crisis, when faced with a similar challenge, she had at first cozied up to her son, offering him money, gifts, and affection. It seems she tried this ploy again now in more extreme form, offering him *herself.* According to most ancient accounts, Agrippina, fighting Poppaea's sexual fire with fire, tempted Nero toward incest, visiting him in alluring outfits after he had gotten drunk at his midday banquets. Tacitus, quoting his sources, does not say that consummation occurred—if it did, could anyone have witnessed?—but he does speak in lurid tones of "erotic kisses and endearments that are forerunners of sin."

Incest rumors were a powerful smear tactic in Rome, but this one came, according to Tacitus, from Cluvius Rufus, a court insider with no ax to grind. Tacitus claimed that it was well supported and contradicted by just one dissenter—who took issue only by claiming that Nero, not Agrippina, initiated the affair. Suetonius endorsed this alternate version, while Cassius Dio preserved a bizarre third variant in which Nero made love to a prostitute dressed to look like Agrippina, then boasted in jest that he had slept with his mother. The truth lies beyond our grasp, as with many turning points in this strange mother-son saga. But Cluvius' story cannot be dismissed.

Cluvius also made an interesting claim about Seneca's part in the drama. He reported that Seneca used Acte, Nero's ever-adoring bedmate, as a counterweight to Agrippina, who was herself trying to counter Poppaea. Sending Acte in to visit the princeps at opportune moments, Seneca tried to divert the young man's lust to a more appropriate object. Seneca reportedly asked Acte to bear a message on her seductive missions: the Praetorian Guard, Nero's guarantors of rule, would never stand for an incestuous affair within the royal household.

Cluvius gives us a painful picture of Seneca's role at court, five years into the reign of Nero. The high-minded Stoic, who had begun by setting Augustan goals and guidelines for the regime, had been sucked ever deeper into the mire of family intrigue. He was struggling to hold on to his influence over Nero, believing he could still do some good. But the methods he now had to use were expedient in the extreme. To act as imperial panderer, dispatching an ex-slave to the princeps to stop him from sleeping with his mother, brandishing Burrus and the guard as an implicit threat—these were hardly roles he had envisioned when he returned to Rome from Corsica, his trunk full of ethical treatises.

Seneca and Nero had been together for ten years now. Nero had grown up, and Seneca had grown old. The princeps had found new allies, among them another former tutor, a Greek freedman named Anicetus ("Invincible"). Nero had elevated this man to admiral of the Misenum fleet, a naval force he was grooming to be his own *corps d'élite*—the Praetorians being more devoted to his mother. Other freedmen, slaves, and foreigners had begun to rise at court, men whose complete dependence and subservience gratified Nero. The voices that whispered against Seneca and Burrus had grown in number and stridency, and Nero had shown more willingness to listen.

It was to Anicetus, not to Seneca or Burrus, that Nero turned as he approached the great crisis of his reign, in the summer of 59. By that time, the young man's love for Poppaea had brought him to a pitch of dire resolve. He had decided on a crime *that the future will believe with difficulty, and ages to come, with reluctance,* as the play *Octavia* forecast—correctly. He had decided to kill his mother.

. . .

It was what he had wanted to do years before but was prevented by Seneca and Burrus. Now, abetted by Anicetus, Nero found the courage to act. Perhaps Poppaea goaded him on, as Tacitus claims, by insisting she could never be his wife as long as Agrippina lived. But Nero needed no Lady Macbeth to harangue him into crime. He had already killed his adoptive brother on his own initiative; his mother posed a greater threat and caused him greater psychic torment.

Did Seneca take part in Nero's matricidal plan? Tacitus wondered but didn't know. Dio made Seneca chief instigator, though like much of his testimony on Seneca, this seems little more than slander. The question of collaboration is indeed hard to resolve. A princeps could not have easily hid such a plot from a high-ranked counselor, but perhaps Seneca no longer ranked very high. If Nero kept him in the dark, declining to consult his old ally against Agrippina, then relations between teacher and pupil had truly gone downhill. If Seneca *was* consulted, he may have seen he could not prevent Nero from acting but could at least help him succeed. Under that scenario, he may have consented to murder if it could be done cunningly, so as to look like an accident.

Cunning was indeed what was needed, for a daughter of Germanicus could not be attacked either with blades or legal writs. Poison too was out of the question; Agrippina, having long suspected Nero's intentions, had taken precautions, perhaps even fortifying herself with antidotes. A technologically savvy method was called for, and Nero was a great lover of technology. One day he saw in the theater, according to Dio, a collapsible boat that fell apart when a lever was worked, simulating a shipwreck. The idea took root in his obsessed mind. With a move as clean and remote as the proverbial push of a button, Nero could crush his mother, or drown her, or both, far out in the water and away from the public's eyes. He delegated the mission to Anicetus.

Constructing the trick ship in secret was no simple task. Anicetus no doubt recruited his best shipwrights at Misenum and also trained loyal sailors who would crew on the fateful voyage. Meanwhile Nero set about making up with his mother. The two had become estranged of late— some breakup had followed their overly intimate union—but Nero hastened to repair the breach. He had to regain Agrippina's trust enough to get her on that boat.

Writing in jocular tones, admitting to having lost his temper, Nero cajoled his mother into joining him at Baiae, the sumptuous resort surrounded by lakes and a quiet bay, for the celebration of that year's Quinquatria, a rite of Minerva held at the spring equinox.

Both Nero and his mother had villas at Baiae, as did many of the Roman elite. The place was famous for high living, loose morals, and easy pleasures, a den of vice that good men should shun, in the eyes of Seneca—though he did sometimes go there. In his disdain, Seneca painted a vivid picture: "Why do we need to see drunken men wandering the beach and boaters on riotous pleasure cruises, and the lakes resounding with songs of musicians? . . . Do you think Cato would ever have lived there, to count the adulteresses as they sail past, the many kinds of boats painted with vivid colors, the roses bobbing everywhere on the lake's surface?" *No* was of course his answer, though he perhaps made the high season at Baiae sound more appealing than he meant to.

Boating was the great thing at Baiae. Because most of the villas stood along a curving shore, or across a small bay at Puteoli, partiers could get from house to house by boat, putting in at small private docks. In her grander days, Agrippina had plied these waters in a state warship rowed by picked sailors. Just down the coast from her villa, an estate called Bauli, was the naval station at Misenum, where such ships and crews stood ready. Now, though, it was a different boat that arrived from Misenum for her use, a luxury yacht fitted out with regal ornaments, manned by a special crew—many of them Anicetus' trained assassins.

Nero had this boat moored at a Baiae villa, where he had arranged a grand dinner party in Agrippina's honor. He presented the boat to his mother after dinner as a gift. It was only one of the many filial gestures he made that night, in an effort to overcome her distrust. Agrippina had her guard up, for she had long suspected her son might seek her life. But the splendidly arrayed ship appealed to her vanity, and Nero's kisses, as he put her on board, seemed sincere.

It was a cloudless, windless night, "with a calm that seemed sent by the gods to reveal the crime," as Tacitus says in one of his most memorable sentences. The ship slipped along through shallow water, on its coasting voyage from Baiae to Bauli. Agrippina reclined with a friend, Acerronia, on a special couch on the vessel's rear deck. The two women talked warmly of the evening's entertainment and of the fond attentions of Nero. Nearby stood another of Agrippina's entourage, her *procurator*—manager of her estates—Crepereius Gallus.

Without warning, a section of roofing above these three collapsed, slamming onto Gallus with the full force of its lead-reinforced weight. The man was immediately crushed to death.

Had Agrippina not been reclining on her couch, or had Acerronia not been sitting lower still as she bent over her friend's feet, both would have died with Gallus. But the couch saved them. Its back and arms extended high enough to block the force of the falling lead. The two women got out from under the lethal weight and emerged into a frantic scene.

Anicetus' agents among the crew were trying to complete their mission. They had expected the ship to break apart and pitch Agrippina into the sea, but this had failed to happen. Confused and seemingly lacking a backup plan, they rushed about on the boat's splintered deck. Some had the idea of capsizing the craft by putting all their weight on one side. But other crewmen who were not part of the plot, perhaps surmising what their comrades were up to, countered them by running to the opposite side. Shouts echoed across the bay's still surface, barely heard, if at all, by those on shore.

As the boat gradually tipped, Agrippina and Acerronia slid into the water. Acerronia, perhaps failing to see the design behind the calamity, called out that *she* was Agrippina and asked for rescue. Her cries drew a hail of blows from oars and other naval gear, as nearby assassins saw a chance to finish their job. Acerronia was clubbed to death in the water, while Agrippina, who had kept a prudent silence, took only a hit on the shoulder. Glimpsing the lanterns of some fishing smacks nearby, she swam off unnoticed. Indefatigable to the last, she had escaped Nero's deathtrap.

Safely returned to Bauli, Agrippina reflected on her position. Nero clearly meant to kill her but had gone to extreme lengths to keep the crime secret. Her high stature as daughter of Germanicus, and her son's timidity, had prevented an open attack, and these might now be enough to save her. She sent a messenger to Nero to inform him of the night's events, pretending it had all been a freak accident. If she could feign trust in her son, prevent him from striking a second blow, she could somehow rally support and strengthen her position. Already crowds of well-wishers, festival-goers who had heard about the collapse of the ship, were gathered outside her villa. She had a fighting chance, if she could only survive this night.

Meanwhile at Baiae, Nero, accompanied by Anicetus, had fretted for hours awaiting word of the plot's outcome. The news that it had failed sent him into a tailspin. He knew that his mother would now spot his intentions. Wounded but not killed, Agrippina would become more dangerous than ever. She might march on his villa that very night with a band of armed slaves, or make her way back to Rome to denounce him before the Senate. Nero was determined that his mother must die before the next day dawned, but he had no idea how to proceed. In despair, he sent for his two senior counselors to be roused from their chambers—Seneca and Burrus.

None of Seneca's meditations on morality, Virtue, Reason, and the good life could have prepared him for this. Before him, as he entered Nero's room, stood a frightened and enraged youth of twenty-three, his student and protégé for the past ten years. For the past five, he had allied with the princeps against his dangerous mother. Now the path he had first opened for Nero, by supporting his dalliance with Acte, had led to a botched murder and a political debacle of the first magnitude. It was too late for Seneca to detach himself. The path had to be followed to its end.

Every word Seneca wrote, every treatise he published, must be read against his presence in this room at this moment. He stood in silence for a long time, as though contemplating the choices before him. There were no good ones. When he finally spoke, it was to pass the buck to Burrus. Seneca asked whether Burrus could dispatch his Praetorians to take Agrippina's life.

Now it was Burrus' turn to face the awful choices that came with collaboration. He too declined to do what the situation, and what full loyalty to Nero, demanded. The Praetorians, he said, had too strong an allegiance to Agrippina, and to the memory of her father. He suggested that Anicetus and the sailors at Misenum finish what they had started.

Nero's old guard had temporized at a critical pass and thus ceded power to the new. Anicetus eagerly took on the task that Seneca and Burrus had cast off, and Nero instantly affirmed how highly he rated this boon. "Only today did I get control of the empire," he declared, "and it was a mere freedman who conferred such a great gift." This barb was aimed at Seneca who, despite having worked for a decade to firm up Nero's power, had now been found wanting. The sage's influence over the princeps, long in decline, had taken another lurch downward.

With opportune timing, the messenger sent earlier by Agrippina, Agerinus, now arrived with news of his mistress's "accident." Nero was grateful for a pretext, however slim, to move openly against his mother. As Agerinus delivered his message, Nero dropped a sword by the man's feet and ordered him seized as an assassin. Then he dispatched Anicetus to Bauli.

It was well past midnight when Anicetus' hit squad arrived at Agrippina's villa. In spite of the hour, the grounds and beach were thronged with Agrippina's well-wishers. Anicetus ordered them to disperse, then broke down the door and began removing household slaves.

Agrippina was in her bedroom with a lone servant, but even this last companion disappeared when armed men were heard in the house. The queen mother was alone when Anicetus and two other officers burst into her room. She had been hoping it was her messenger Agerinus arriving; his long delay meant she was still in grave danger.

Agrippina's only chance was to shame her attackers out of completing their mission, to remind them of the glory of her line. But she was exhausted, shaken from the night's ordeal, and wounded. The best she could manage, according to Tacitus, was to protest that Anicetus must have made some terrible mistake. Surely Nero would never order her death.

The captain accompanying Anicetus, a man named Herculeius, answered by hitting her on the head with a club. The other officer standing by, Obaritus, drew his sword. Agrippina was all out of stratagems. There was little left for her but to die.

Agrippina had been betrayed by those she had put in power, by Nero above all, but also by Burrus, Anicetus, and not least, Seneca. The sage she had rescued from Corsica, who owed all he had to her, had declined to raise his voice against her murder. Politics had first made bedfellows of her and Seneca—in the literal sense, some claimed. But politics, and her son's disordered mind, had arranged things such that only one of them could survive.

The foremost woman of her age—sister of one emperor, wife of a second, mother of a third, the last of Germanicus' children—was about to die, friendless, abandoned, alone. One last, bold gesture remained to her, a gesture reported by three ancient sources. The author of *Octavia* describes it best:

> *Dying and wretched, she makes one last request of her assassin:*
> *to sink his lethal sword in her womb.*
> *"Here's where to bury your sword, right here—*
> *The place from which such a monster came. . . ."*
> *After those words, she lets her sad soul*
> *seep out through savage wounds*
> *together with a final groan.*

CHAPTER 5

Maritocide

(A.D. 59–62)

The deed that Nero had yearned to achieve brought him no relief. Back at his Baiae villa, informed of his mother's death, he could only peer vacantly into the darkness, starting up suddenly from time to time as though in fear. The enormity of the vacuum he had created was now becoming apparent. The central force in recent politics, the woman who had held sway in the palace for more than ten years, the last of the nine children of her great father, was gone. Nero, an insecure, self-indulgent twenty-three-year-old, had made himself an orphan.

Burrus tried to bolster the young man's nerves by sending in Praetorians to greet him. The guard had been Agrippina's most loyal partisans, and Nero had cause to fear them. Cued by Burrus, though, they made clear they would change sides, congratulating the young man on having escaped his mother's "plot." The pale pretext created by dropping a sword at a messenger's feet was to be the official version of the night's events. Nero, it was to be proclaimed, had been the intended victim, not the perpetrator, of violence.

At Bauli, meanwhile, Anicetus oversaw Agrippina's cremation, done by the simple expedient of burning her body on a dining couch. No state funeral or pyre was held, and it is unclear whether Nero even came from Baiae to view the corpse. No burial was performed or monument constructed; Agrippina's followers heaped only a low dirt mound over her ashes. (The grand Campanian ruins known today as Agrippina's Tomb are in fact the remains of a theater built much later.)

The most important cleanup task in the wake of the messy matricide fell to Seneca. There were concerns that the senators back in Rome, to whom he remained principal liaison, might decry Nero's deed in the Senate house or conspire with the Praetorians to remove the princeps from power. Seneca was charged with winning their acquiescence. Despite his decline at court, his verbal dexterity was still a vital asset to the regime, as was his high standing among the elite. Here, at least, was a job that toughs and parvenus like Anicetus could not do.

Seneca now undertook the most difficult writing assignment of his life. In the letter Nero would send to the Senate, under his own name but without pretense of authorship, Seneca had to justify as an act of policy a crime that was neither justifiable nor primarily political. He had to brazen out a family murder before the same body of men who had been promised, some five years earlier, an end to family murders. He had to win pardon for the princeps whose great virtue, as he had proclaimed in *De Clementia*—even then at risk of his own reputation—was not to have shed a single drop of human blood.

What clever turns of phrase, what sinuous rhetoric, could accomplish such a task? Only one sentence of the letter survives, in a chance quotation, but Tacitus preserves a record of its content and structure.

The letter began with the main cover story, the discovery of a weapon on Agerinus' person. Agrippina had plotted a coup and, it was asserted, had taken her own life when the plot was uncovered. The letter went on to discuss the larger threat that Rome had been under while Agrippina lived: a usurper, and worse, a woman, had sought supreme power. Agrippina had pressured the Praetorians and the Senate to swear allegiance to *her,* the letter alleged; then she had withheld gifts and handouts from the guard if they refused—a subtle reminder that Nero was at this moment arranging gifts and handouts for that very body. Agrippina had tried to enter the Senate house, the letter went on, and to represent the Roman state in dealings with foreign ambassadors. Ever since marrying Claudius ten years before, she had grasped at the throne.

But even while claiming to have escaped a monster, Nero, as represented by Seneca, affected filial grief. To celebrate the death of a mother, even the nightmarish figure conjured up in the letter, would be unseemly. "I neither believe nor rejoice that I am still alive," Seneca had Nero say, employing a parallel-with-contrast structure typical of his style.

The letter's sternest challenge was how to present the bizarre events leading up to Agrippina's death. The collapse of the rigged boat—witnessed by many and, in light of the later killing, clearly intentional—was a subject perhaps better passed over in silence. But Seneca must have felt that even a transparent lie was better than no explanation at all. His letter portrayed the collapse as a shipwreck, an accident that showed the gods themselves intervening to save the state. Nero's troops had only completed the design of Providence.

This was going too far. For the second time in his political career, Seneca had overstepped the bounds of propriety with his ready support of the princeps. "It was not Nero—whose monstrosity precluded any complaint—but Seneca who was in a bad odor, because he had written a defense speech using this kind of rhetoric," says Tacitus.

One senator in particular, a stiff-necked Stoic named Thrasea Paetus, silently walked out of the chamber after the letter had been read. Thrasea, like Seneca an admirer of Cato and other heroes of conscience, disliked the servility of his colleagues. The fictions of Seneca's letter, and the Senate's willingness to countenance them, finally pushed him past his breaking point. By modern standards, his was a mild protest, a simple declaration of nonsupport. But in the Roman autocracy, even such small gestures carried huge significance and incurred huge risks.

No senators followed Thrasea's lead, though many no doubt wished to. Instead they declared their total acceptance of the account contained in the letter. They voted that annual games be held at the time of the Quinquatria to celebrate the salvation of the princeps. A gold statue of Minerva—the goddess to whom the spring festival was devoted—would be set up beside that of Nero in the Forum. There was to be no public reckoning for matricide.

But as they fawned, the senators silently pondered the new course on which Nero's regime was set. They were getting a clearer view of the emperor's emerging character. His matricide presented a strange admixture of cravenness and cruelty. Nero had lacked the courage to proceed openly against his mother or even to acknowledge that he had killed her. Instead he had shown himself nervous and needy, trying to win hearts and minds in the Senate before daring to enter Rome. Indeed, long after the senators had voted to honor him, Nero lingered in Campania, fretting over what reception he would get in the capital.

Such a man might be just as dangerous as Caligula, though for different reasons. He would want reassurance and flattery and even—though few in Rome had yet glimpsed his ambitions as a performer—the cheers of sycophantic crowds. His subjects would be required to show not just loyalty but something more, a sort of affection. He would hate anyone in a position to judge him, which meant the entire political class. The aristocracy might again be haunted by old specters—treason trials, banishments, executions, and forced suicides—arising this time not from the whims of a sadist but the demands of a petulant child.

A waggish actor named Datus, star of the clownish performances called Atellan farces, highlighted the new dangers in a performance he gave shortly after Agrippina's death. During a comic song that contained the line "Farewell father, farewell mother," he mimed the motions first of drinking, then of swimming. Claudius had in fact died from a poisoned meal, not a drink, and Agrippina had escaped the waters to be killed in her bed, but the references were clear enough. Then when Datus came to another line, "Orcus guides your steps," he pointed to the senators seated before him in the front rows of the audience. The god who had charge of souls of the dead, he implied, was awaiting them in the underworld.

After spending nearly three months in Campania, Nero and his court returned to Rome in June. The long delay, and the work done by handlers in the interim, had primed the populace well. Romans turned out in droves to welcome Nero home, even setting up bleachers along his route; the senators put on festal attire. The people strove to show their princeps that they would turn a blind eye to murder.

Beneath these displays, however, revulsion simmered. In anonymous pranks and graffiti, Nero was made to recall his crime. One wag hung a leather sack from a public statue of Nero, implying that the princeps belonged inside one—for Romans sometimes punished parent slayers by sewing them up in a sack, together with various wild animals, and casting the whole lot into the Tiber to drown. Meanwhile a different message appeared on a statue of Agrippina that had been draped in cloth, a temporary measure to conceal it until it could be pulled down. On the pretense that the cloth was a veil of modesty, someone affixed a sign that represented Agrippina speaking to Nero: "*I* have some shame; *you* haven't."

Nero bore all this with a degree of patience that bewildered the ancient chroniclers. Perhaps relieved to have incurred some penalty, or (as Dio speculates) not wishing to give substance to rumors by prosecuting them, he ignored all jibes. Even when informers, eager for advancement, reported the names of the graffitists, Nero refused to take action. He preferred to distract and cajole his public, and set about to mark the death of Agrippina with magnificent spectacles and games.

First came the Ludi Maximi, spread over many days and occupying multiple theaters. Bizarre new spectacles were staged for the crowds, including an elephant that walked down a sloping tightrope carrying a rider on its back. Ancient nobility, coerced into taking the stage, were seen dancing, acting, and even fighting as gladiators against wild beasts, roles that had long been considered out of bounds for aristocracy. Meanwhile commoners in the stands were showered with handouts and prizes. Live birds, valued as pets, rained down on them by the thousand. Vouchers in the form of inscribed balls were tossed out by the emperor's troops, redeemable later for horses, slaves, precious metals, even whole apartment buildings. Nero was going all out, and digging deep into his own purse, to win his people's love.

Another lavish event, the Juvenalia—a "youth festival," marking the first time Nero shaved off his whiskers—followed soon after. Officially a private party held on imperial land, it was attended by large crowds of *equites* and plebeians, the classes whose favor Nero had chosen to court. As in the Ludi Maximi, aristocrats were made to perform in roles that defied social conventions. A noblewoman in her eighties, Aelia Catella, was shown dancing in a pantomime, the most risqué genre of popular theater. Other members of great houses were recruited for choral dances. When some came onstage in masks to hide their identities, Nero insisted the masks be removed. He meant to show all Rome that even the high and mighty were sharing his carnival fun.

At the culmination of the Juvenalia came an event that Nero's advisers had long dreaded, though they had no choice but to take part. For the princeps no longer wished merely to practice his singing in private. He had determined to go on the stage.

Of many shocking firsts in the history of theater, perhaps none rivals the moment when a Roman emperor, the apex of the social pyramid, appeared in the long cloak and high boots of a Greek citharodist, saying "Please hear me graciously, masters." It was no spontaneous whim but an entrance Nero had planned and prepared and for which he had written a musical ode, "Attis or the Bacchantes," an ardent story of lovestruck madness. He had also ensured that his reception would be favorable. Gallio, Seneca's brother, an ex-consul, brought the emperor onstage and introduced him, while Seneca himself (according to Dio), together with Burrus, was stationed where he could be seen signaling approbation, waving his toga-clad arms high in the air.

Nero had brought with him his newly organized corps of thuggish cheerleaders, the Augustiani ("Augustus' men"). Tall, strong, and fierce in their devotion to the princeps, they sent a clear message by their very presence—an implied threat against dissenters. Their number would eventually grow to 5,000, and Nero would take them on tour with him as his performance career expanded. He had them trained to use special clapping rhythms, though at the Juvenalia, in their first appearance, they merely shouted rapturous phrases like "Oh Apollo!"

One man in the crowd that day distinguished himself by his unwillingness to applaud. For the second time that year, Thrasea Paetus, the senator least inclined to kowtow to the princeps, chose silence and dissent over noisy collusion. And for the second time, his recalcitrance did not go unnoticed.

For Seneca, dissent was not an option. His position required him to show support for Nero's singing debut, however much it disturbed him. Perhaps he even had to assist it, for Dio reports that the sage was enlisted to prompt Nero should he forget his lines. He was being used by the regime, exploited for his tarnished but still lustrous public image, and he knew it. If Seneca observed Thrasea Paetus in the crowd that day, he no doubt envied a man—a Stoic thinker and writer like himself—who could exercise the simple freedom of doing nothing.

Nero had grown up. His moves at Baiae, undertaken without the help of his teacher and guide, served as his rite of passage, a perverse coming of age. He had committed the most audacious murder of the century and had gotten clean away with it. After his self-liberation, he could no longer be told what he could and could not do, least of all by a grave-faced man four decades his senior.

Encouraged by the success of his singing debut, Nero sought to break yet another propriety barrier and race in a four-horse chariot. In earlier days, Seneca and Burrus had forbidden it as an insult to the office of princeps. Now they had too little control to prevent it, but the senior advisers did win a shift of venue. Across the Tiber and outside the city, on the Vatican hill, stood a little-used racecourse begun by Caligula. The track—today St. Peter's Square, with its original Egyptian obelisk, erected as turning post, still standing—had by this time been completed. Nero was persuaded to do his racing in this more discreet location, with slaves and paupers for an audience.

It was a humble victory for Seneca but perhaps a comforting one. He could still do some good for the principate, the institution that had required him to do much evil. If he ever argued to himself his reasons for clinging to power, as he argued in *De Vita Beata* his reasons for amassing wealth, it must have been on this basis: Nero would be a worse princeps, and Rome would be subject to worse abuses, were he to leave the scene.

Seneca had made the bargain that many good men have made when agreeing to aid bad regimes. On the one hand, their presence strengthens the regime and helps it endure. But their moral influence may also improve the regime's behavior or save the lives of its enemies. For many, this has been a bargain worth making, even if it has cost them—as it may have cost Seneca—their immortal soul.

There was of course another reason Seneca stayed by Nero's side. He had described in *De Ira* how autocrats exerted control by their power to harm family members. He told the story there of Pastor, a victim of Caligula, who had to smile at the murder of his son because he had *another* son. By A.D. 60, Seneca had helped Nero acquire several hostages of this kind—including a remarkably gifted nephew, the closest thing Seneca had to a son of his own.

Marcus Lucanus, son of Seneca's youngest brother, Mela, had come to Rome to join Nero's court. Though still in his late teens, the boy had already shown huge literary talent, outpacing in poetry his uncle's immense prolixity in prose. In him, the fantastic wordiness of the Annaeus clan, passed down from its rhetorician patriarch Seneca the Elder, had reached its acme. He is known to the modern world as Lucan.

Lucan was two years younger than Nero. He first came to the attention of the princeps when, at age fourteen, he gave an impressive recitation in both Latin and Greek. Nero was then newly installed on the throne, with Seneca at his side, and Lucan had an easy entrée to power. But the young man left Rome and landed in Athens, a serene place of study and contemplation. He seemed at that point to share his uncle's literary gifts and passion for Stoic philosophy, but not his attraction to politics.

Several years later, probably about the time of Agrippina's death, Lucan received a summons to return to Rome and enter Nero's service. Why the princeps called him back is unclear. Perhaps Seneca, troubled at his own prospects, had suggested the move as a way to bring the boy near him; for he had described, many years earlier, the release from sorrow he felt the moment his eyes lighted on his charming nephew. "There is no torment of the heart so great, or so fresh, that he will not soothe it with his embrace," he had declared to his mother, Helvia, in a rare outpouring of familial affection. Lacking a child of his own, and increasingly estranged from Nero, Seneca must have greeted Lucan's return with joy and relief—though no doubt also with some anxiety.

Nero, for his part, was so enthralled by his new recruit as to immediately make him a quaestor, several years before he was eligible for the post. In the past, only members of the imperial family had been given such exemptions; Nero had launched Lucan on a very fast political track. Perhaps he felt a kinship with a precociously talented poet, since he increasingly fancied he was one himself. He had begun collecting at court those who seemed to embody his own idealized self-image—rulership perfectly harmonized with the gentle arts of music and verse. "Apollo's lyre is plucked by the same hands that draw his bow," wrote one contemporary poet, flattering Nero by extolling this ideal.

By this time, Lucan had begun work on a radically daring and ambitious epic poem, the *De Bello Civili* or *Civil War*. The plan for this work was unique in many ways, above all its focus on recent Roman history—the civil wars that had brought Augustus to power—where all previous epics had dealt with the mythic past. Lucan made many innovations in style and method to suit his subject matter. *Civil War*, which survives today in incomplete form, reveals the audacity of its author—a youth who had set out in his teens to reinvent the most revered of ancient genres, the medium of Homer and Vergil.

Though the Roman civil wars had taken place a century before Lucan's time, they were hardly politically neutral, as Lucan himself understood. The characters who loomed large in his story—the assassins Brutus and Cassius; Cato, the Stoic suicide; and Julius Caesar himself—had by Nero's day become potent ideological symbols. The birthdays of Brutus and Cassius were observed every year by stiff-necked Thrasea Paetus, in ceremonies that celebrated senatorial autonomy. Cato, too, was widely revered in contemporary writings, as has been seen. Lucan was going to

The only known portrait of
Seneca's nephew Marcus Lucanus,
known today as Lucan.

have to walk a thin line in writing about such men while serving under Nero, a descendant of the man slain by them.

Perhaps out of self-protection, Lucan chose to open *Civil War* with effusive praise of Nero, a passage so overwrought that some have read it as satire. All the bloodshed of the civil wars, Lucan claims, should be glorified, not regretted, since they made possible Nero's reign. Then, turning from the past to the future, Lucan imagines the day when Nero will take his place in the heavens, among the gods. Take care not to seat yourself at either pole, Lucan cautions the princeps, lest your weighty presence tilt the cosmos out of balance. Stick to the middle, the zodiacal belt. The air is clearer there and clouds less frequent, so our view of your starry form will not be impeded.

The imperial favor Lucan enjoyed, and his willingness to court it, were vividly displayed in August 60. That month Nero introduced his Greek-style sport-and-arts festival, the Neronia. He had set prizes—gold wreaths, a lavish Roman adaptation of Greek laurel garlands—for recitations of poetry and oratory, as well as for music, song, and athletic events.

Lucan took the stage in the poetry contest with a composition called *Laudes Neronis,* "Praises of Nero," and won first prize. Nero looked on approvingly from his imperial dais, not yet willing to enter the contest himself. But Lucan, with touching deference, removed his crown and awarded it to the princeps. The winner of the rhetorical competition followed suit.

Lucan's gesture underscored the tension inherent in his relationship to the princeps, a tension felt by other writers too, including Seneca. Nero was not just a patron of the literary arts but an artist himself. He liked to join his court bards as a fellow member of their guild. Lucan's brilliance gratified Nero's vanity; but the threat that such brilliance posed, the danger of a rivalry that the princeps would inevitably lose, was lurking below the surface. It would not be long before it emerged.

For Seneca, the close and rapid bonding between his nephew and the princeps was a mixed blessing. It augmented the dilemmas begun by his own entry into imperial service, followed by that of his brother Gallio. Three prominent Annaei now had their fates tied to the emperor's favor. They had risen together, thanks to the reliance of Roman politics on family-based loyalties, but they might easily fall together as well.

The role Seneca had carved out for himself had become vastly harder to maintain, in the wake of Agrippina's murder. But the cost of deviating from that role had also greatly increased.

Nero kept other authors at his court in these days, men who shared his table while indulging his artistic ambitions. He liked to bandy verses with this crowd, beginning a line of poetry in a meter of his own choosing, then challenging a dinner guest to finish it in the same meter. The game allowed him to enjoy the fellowship of poets but also make clear who was calling the tune.

But maintaining a literary coterie was an expensive undertaking, and this was only one of many cash drains Nero had taken on. Prodigality was becoming a hallmark of his reign and was soon to give rise to its deepest troubles.

Games and festivals were among Nero's largest expenses. Even before Agrippina's death forced him to fatten his entertainment budget, he had put on bizarre and inventive displays. The oval interior of his new wooden amphitheater could be filled with salt water to make an artificial sea, and he staged mock naval battles on it, with pelagic fish swimming among the ships for extra effect. Other beasts emerged after the water was drained off, sometimes appearing out of the floor by means of pulleys and trapdoors (stagecraft later expanded in the famous Colosseum). The opening ceremonies of this grand structure featured exotic creatures from far-off lands, including elks, hippopotami, and seals, the last chased by what appear to have been polar bears.

But Nero's priciest innovation was the Neronia, instituted in 60 with the idea that it would repeat every five years. Fearing that conservative Romans might scorn this Greek-style event, Nero laid out liberal prizes to attract their participation. He built a new gymnasium and bath complex adjoining the grounds, with olive oil—the Greeks' favorite skin-cleansing ointment—supplied at his own expense.

Games, shows, theaters to hold them in, handouts for the crowds— all this drained the state coffers, and since it was Nero who had to refill them, the expense was essentially his. In theory, the imperial treasuries were separate from the emperor's property, but in practice, boundary lines were hard to draw. As the ultimate home-office worker—all Rome being his place of business—Nero could use public monies for private purposes and vice versa. Officials in charge of keeping accounts, by a reform enacted under his reign, were his own appointees.

Then, too, Nero spent wildly on private festivities, including lavish palace banquets and late-night parties. These fetes took on new energy in the 60s thanks to a man who dazzled Nero with his refined tastes and easy hedonism. Gaius Petronius, famous for sleeping all day and spending his nights in pleasure seeking, received an appointment as *arbiter elegantiae,* officer in charge of protocol and entertainment. A free-living, free-speaking aristocrat who took nothing seriously, Petronius made a huge impression on the young princeps. Nothing seemed à la mode to Nero unless it came from Petronius, Tacitus noted.

The swift ascent of Petronius pointed the way for other courtiers. Those seeking advancement found it politic to encourage Nero in his excesses or to furnish him with new pleasures and spectacles. Ofonius Tigellinus, the head of Rome's safety and fire brigade, rivaled Petronius at this game, except that where Petronius was effete and devil-may-care, Tigellinus was tough, street smart, and determined. He too rose in Nero's esteem and became a trusted insider—as Romans would soon learn, to their woe.

Most profligate of Nero's expenditures were gifts to court favorites and pets, already outlandish enough in Nero's teenage years to alarm his mother. When Agrippina heard that Nero planned to give 10 million sesterces to a freedman, she had the coins piled in a heap so that her son could behold his extravagance. Ever eager to defy his mother, he took one look at the pile and ordered it to be doubled, saying, "I did not realize I had given so little." Ultimately more than 2 billion sesterces would be spent on such bequests, so much that Nero's successors tried (with little success) to get most of it back. Acte the ex-slave, Menecrates the lyre player, Spiculus the gladiator, Paneros the moneylender, and many others walked away with fortunes.

Of a different order were the gifts Nero bestowed on his inner circle, including on Seneca. They allowed Nero to create bonds of obligation and collusion. Tacitus remarks on this kind of giving when discussing the distribution of Britannicus' estate after the boy's assassination. Many observers, says the historian, thought that Nero, conscious of his guilt in the eyes of the public, was trying to buy a kind of redemption. If good men were seen accepting the proceeds of crime, the crime became less heinous.

Seneca had been the recipient of many such gifts over the years. Gardens, villas, and estates, including some that had perhaps belonged to Britannicus, made him vastly wealthy. But accepting them had made him an accomplice in the rough methods by which they were obtained. That Seneca was struggling with this problem is clear from a treatise he published in the late 50s or early 60s, *De Beneficiis,* a long meditation on the topic of giving and receiving.

The Latin word *beneficium* includes notions of "gift," "good turn," and "favor." Seneca used the concept as a prism through which to examine social relations of all kinds, including those of business, friendship, and politics. It was essential to him that giving be done well—meaning, in a spirit of generosity, even love. Again and again, he invokes the models of nature and of divinity, which provide nurture for humankind without reckoning up what is owed. Our goal in performing *beneficia* for our fellow men, Seneca insists, should be to emulate the gods.

De Beneficiis is a long work, Seneca's longest treatment of a single topic. It weaves in and out of many themes, some of them touching closely on the author's own circumstances—though the relevance, as always, remains implicit.

One problem Seneca deals with is that of gifts given by kings and tyrants, which cannot be refused, yet cannot be recompensed. He recalls that Socrates was invited to join the court of a Macedonian king but declined on the grounds that had he accepted, he would not have been able to return the royal largesse. Seneca admires Socrates for avoiding what he calls a life of "voluntary servitude." One senses that in talking about Socrates, he is, as in *De Vita Beata,* talking about himself.

Here Seneca imagines an objection: "Socrates *could* have declined [the king's gifts], if he had wanted to." But, he responds as though on his own behalf, a king cannot abide such treatment, regarding it as a mark of scorn. "It makes no difference whether you refuse to give to a king, or refuse to accept gifts from him; he takes both, equally, as a rejection," Seneca says. This was an important point for him, since his own wealth, much of it gained in service to Nero, had come under harsh attack. Refusing such rewards, he makes clear, would have been hazardous.

According to Seneca's definition in the treatise, Nero's giving had been not a *beneficium,* an act of generosity, but a means of asserting power and imposing obligation. In the early 60s, Seneca was feeling the weight of that obligation as never before, and he began searching for a way to unburden himself. In 62, he would make an attempt, as will be seen, to divest himself of all he had received and reclaim his autonomy. If Nero's giving had made him a captive, perhaps he could free himself by giving back.

Before reaching that point, however, Seneca, and the rest of the palace staff, had a foreign policy crisis to deal with, the worst Rome had faced in decades. It was an acute crisis for Seneca, because many at Rome felt, rightly or wrongly, that he had caused it.

In the fog-bound glens of eastern England, Boudicca, warrior-queen of the Iceni, was gathering a mighty host determined to end Roman rule. At her hands, more than 80,000 Romans and their allies would soon be killed, and the Roman army would come within a hairsbreadth of an epic disaster. If not for the iron resolve of her opponent, Suetonius Paulinus, Rome would have likely disgorged Britain from its empire and never set foot there again, abandoning what Claudius had achieved, with such proud self-celebration, a generation earlier.

Boudicca's rebels had chosen an opportune moment to strike. Paulinus had gone off on an invasion of Mona, the island off Wales now called Anglesy, with two of the four legions then serving in Britain. The town of Camulodunum (modern Colchester), settled by aged-out veterans and their dependents, had some warning that trouble was afoot but could do nothing; it had no walls or fortifications, having never needed them before. Some townsmen took refuge in the Temple of Divine Claudius, Camulodunum's most secure structure, and held out there for two days. But Claudius was no better a warrior as a god than he had been as an emperor. Camulodunum was wiped out and its people put to the sword. A legion sent to relieve them from Lindum (Lincoln), 150 miles to the north, was smashed to pieces en route.

Word of the disaster reached Paulinus in Wales, and had he begun building ships for an evacuation, many of his troops would have thanked him. The situation was dire and about to get far worse, for Paulinus' best hope of reinforcement—the ninth legion, stationed in the west of Roman Britain—refused orders to join him as he returned south. It seemed suicidal to enter the killing zone, where rebel forces, outnumbering Romans many times over, had already shown they were not interested in taking prisoners.

Undaunted, Paulinus brought his men through hostile territory to Londinium (London). He arrived safe, without encountering Boudicca's forces, but decided he could not defend the sprawling, unwalled trade mart on the Thames. Roman businessmen who could ride or fight were evacuated with the army column, but tens of thousands were left behind, begging Paulinus for aid even as he gave the order to march. The Britons soon visited the same horrors on these tradespeople as they had on the veterans of Camulodunum. They saw no point in holding hostages; should their revolt succeed, they would have gained all they wanted, and should it fail, Rome would not bother to negotiate.

Failure did not seem possible to Boudicca as she closed in on Paulinus' army. She had a string of massacres and one battlefield victory to her credit, and her forces had a numerical advantage of perhaps twenty to one. If there is any truth in the long speeches Dio assigns her, she regarded Romans as a decadent people, unable to stand up to Britons in war. Perhaps she had heard of Nero's recent singing performance, as Dio represents, and saw it as proof of her adversaries' mettle. "They are slaves to a lyre player—and a bad one at that," she reportedly told her troops, improbably mixing diatribe and music criticism.

But overconfidence had made Boudicca overbold. She accepted battle at a site that Paulinus had chosen, where the Romans had woods and high ground protecting their flanks and rear. She let her troops bring their wives along to watch the anticipated rout, parking them in a row of wagons encircling her own back lines. The Britons advanced; the Romans hurled javelins and charged.

Boudicca launched her war chariots, the tanks of their day, but the drivers, unprotected by metal breastplates, were easily dispatched by well-aimed arrows. The discipline of Roman troops, always Rome's greatest military asset, held up under the blows of British axes. The battle may have lasted all day, as Dio records, or only a short time, as Tacitus implies, but its outcome was decisive. Boudicca's troops were turned, and as they tried to flee, they found themselves trapped by their own wagon train and by the corpses of those felled in the javelin volley.

Before the end of the bloodletting, Boudicca's army had lost a stag-

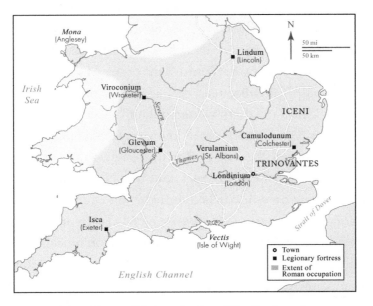

Map of Roman Britain at the time of Boudicca's revolt.

gering 80,000, paying back life for life the fatalities inflicted on Rome. At one stroke, the rebellion was smashed and Roman control of Britain restored. Boudicca fled back to her home province, where she either poisoned herself, according to Tacitus' account, or, in Dio's, died of disease.

Fresh Roman troops streamed across the channel to ravage rebel lands. The Britons were already depleted by famine, since warriors on the march had had no chance to sow next season's crop. The Iceni had beaten their plowshares into swords, thinking they would soon dine on captured Roman provisions. All told, hundreds of thousands died in England within a year's time, the worst cataclysm yet suffered under Roman imperial rule.

In the aftermath, official Rome sought the causes of the disaster, and some held Seneca to blame.

According to Dio's account, before the rebellion began, Seneca had called in his loans to British tribal leaders, abruptly and on harsh terms. That put many Britons into bankruptcy, while others were broken by the corrupt finance officer in charge of the region, Decianus Catus. Together,

Dio suggests, Catus and Seneca forced Britons into a corner where they had nothing to lose by revolt. Tacitus, by contrast, says nothing of Seneca's moneylending in Britain, though he confirms that Catus had made enemies there by rapacity. For Tacitus, the principal spark of the conflict was the flogging of Boudicca and the rape of her daughters, committed by arrogant Roman troops grown scornful of British tribesmen.

Dio's hostility to Seneca is well known, yet some modern historians credit his account of the start of Boudicca's revolt. One has even ingeniously linked it to a report by Suetonius that Nero at one time considered withdrawing from Britain and shrinking the empire. Suetonius gives no time frame, but Nero could have entertained such an idea only prior to the rebellion; during or afterward, Rome had too much at stake to let the island go. If Nero, in the late 50s, had indeed voiced doubts about keeping Britain Roman, those in the know would have hastened to call in their chips. On this theory, the rebellion was ignited by a shrewd piece of insider trading.

Did Seneca indeed touch off Rome's worst provincial uprising by carrying his profiteering too far? The answer depends on a choice between Dio's desire to see the worst in Seneca and Tacitus' more mixed appraisal—the same choice that faces us at many turns. We know Seneca lent money at interest and managed a far-flung financial empire; we also know that rebel Britons were hard pressed by debt. Whether there was a link between the two is ultimately a judgment call.

In his extant works, Seneca makes no mention of the disasters in England. But in his *De Beneficiis,* a work possibly composed after the rebellion had begun, he seems unusually concerned with the topic of moneylending.

Lending at interest, Seneca makes clear in *De Beneficiis,* is a special kind of giving-receiving relationship, subject to its own fixed rules. At certain points, he stresses the fairness of those rules or insists on the rights of the lender. He sounds content to be one of those lenders and, if necessary, to withdraw credit. But at other points, he castigates the whole project of lending at interest, using the voice of a newly created persona, Demetrius of Sunium.

Demetrius was a Greek philosopher of the Cynic school who had come to teach at Rome in Seneca's day. With his ready wit and fierce asceticism, he made a deep impression on Seneca, and the two became friends. (*Demetrius noster,* "our Demetrius," is how Seneca often refers to him.) Seneca seems to have regarded Demetrius as a latter-day Socrates or Cato—a model for his own best self to aspire to, or else a sad reminder of the self that might have been.

Near the end of *De Beneficiis,* Seneca assigns Demetrius two long speeches, using him as a mask the way he had earlier used Socrates. The second speech mounts a harsh attack on the evils of wealth, especially on riches got by lending. "What are these things—what is 'debt,' 'ledger-book,' 'interest,' except names supplied to human coveting that exceeds the bounds of Nature?" the outraged Cynic demands. "What are 'accounts' and 'calculations'? And time put up for sale, and a blood-sucking rate of one percent of capital? These are evils we choose for ourselves . . . the dreams of useless greed."

Seneca's use of masks and personae presents problems throughout his prose works, but nowhere more so than here. Demetrius, a man widely admired for contempt of wealth, viciously attacks a practice by which Seneca had increased his riches. Yet it was Seneca who had brought Demetrius onstage and given him voice. The choice of mouthpiece seems self-punitive, like the choice of Socrates, another famous pauper, in Seneca's defense of his wealth in *De Vita Beata,* or the stretch of that work that trumpets the charges of Seneca's enemies as if through a megaphone.

How much does the rebellion in Britain, and the role that usury had played in it, stand behind the strange ending of *De Beneficiis*? The question puts us at the crossroads of politics and psychology, uncertain which path to go down. Was Seneca dodging blame by seeming to disdain moneylending just as much as his worst critics? Or was he giving himself a highly public flogging, to salve a conscience weighed down by two hundred thousand deaths?

· · ·

The British rebellion passed, and peace was restored in the empire—for a while. Only four years later a new uprising would flare, in the East this time, among Jews fed up by the abuses of Roman overseers. But by that juncture, most of Nero's senior staff would be dead. The first to go was Afranius Burrus, prefect of the Praetorian Guard, who fell ill and began to fail in 62.

For eight years, Seneca had worked hand in glove with Burrus, a political ally who esteemed his judgment and shared his values. It is easy to forget this partnership while reading Seneca's prose works, for he mentions Burrus only once, in *De Clementia,* and then only tangentially. But Burrus was, without doubt, Seneca's close collaborator in the palace. By supporting each other in conclaves with Nero, Seneca and Burrus had been able to manage the princeps, check his worst impulses, and in the estimation of some historians, run the empire in his name.

Burrus became ill with a painful throat swelling, perhaps a tumor, that threatened to choke off his breathing. Nero sent a doctor to smear the swelling with a salve, a medicine it seemed, though some ancient sources charge that it was poison. They report that Burrus applied the drug and instantly recognized its toxic effect. When Nero came into his sickroom and asked after his health, Burrus turned his face away and answered gravely, "All's well with *me*"—an implicit contrast with the depraved condition of his sovereign.

Nero ended up the owner of Burrus' house, which perhaps supports the poisoning theory. His need for cash to subsidize the empire, and his own extravagant lifestyle, made it difficult for him to wait for his testators to die a natural death. Dio and Suetonius report that he had done much the same three years earlier in the case of a wealthy aunt, Domitia. Old, frail, and suffering from a blockage of her digestive tract, Domitia had lingered on, until Nero ordered the doctor treating her to give her a lethal overdose. Her estate would have come to him soon enough, but his expenses were mounting swiftly.

Whether or not Nero caused it, Burrus' death was a disaster for Seneca. Command of the Praetorian Guard was split in two, as it had been under Claudius, and awarded to Faenius Rufus and Ofonius Tigellinus.

The first was an honorable public servant with a spotless record, but the second was a man Seneca had reason to fear.

A former horse trader of questionable character, Tigellinus had risen in favor because he shared Nero's flamboyance, self-indulgence, and love of the chariot track. Playing up both to the emperor's love of pleasure and to his dread of usurpers, Tigellinus demonized Seneca and other Stoics as high-minded scolds whose arrogance made them dangerous. In Tigellinus, Seneca had a new enemy at court, one who was allied with the emperor's libido, against those who embodied his superego.

Emboldened by this change of prefects, Seneca's enemies roused themselves for fresh attacks. The charge brought ineffectually by Suillius four years earlier, that it was unseemly for Seneca to get so rich, now gained more traction. Seneca's wealth was set in a larger portrait of political and personal ambition, a desire to rival Nero himself. Was not Seneca a poet, just as Nero now hoped to be? Did he not advance his own art while trying to quash Nero's singing? Did he not beautify his gardens and estates so that they outshone those of Nero?

Seneca's position at court was eroding badly—but so was Nero's capital. The emperor's constant need for cash suggested to Seneca a way out of his palace prison.

Seneca's estate *was* huge, far bigger than he needed, given his modest lifestyle. It was more of a danger now than an asset, for it offered a fat prize to accusers. Seneca would lose at least half in the end anyhow, for men of his station customarily deeded that portion to the princeps, in hopes he would allow the rest to pass, unplundered, to their heirs.

Rather than wait for those outcomes, Seneca chose preemptive action. He could cash in all his chips—offer Nero his *entire* fortune—in exchange for a trouble-free exit from the imperial household. He could buy his way out of politics, even if it cost him half a billion sesterces.

The conversation in which Seneca proposed this bargain has been narrated by Tacitus. What source Tacitus drew on, and how much he embellished that source, are impossible to know. The entire scene might have been invented out of whole cloth. But Tacitus in any case made something unforgettable out of the encounter. The cold formality of both men, the cautious flattery employed by Seneca and the feigned deference of Nero, the mistrust lurking behind every word—these elements combine into a brilliant piece of political theater.

Seneca began, in Tacitus' account, by invoking historical precedent. Augustus had allowed Agrippa and Maecenas, his two closest adjutants, to retire from his service. *They* had performed great deeds on an emperor's behalf and earned great rewards; "but what else can *I* give, in return for your generosity, but learning, a thing trained in the shadows?" Then Seneca surveyed all he had gained in Nero's service: an equestrian from Corduba, he had risen to the first ranks of power and wealth. But, he said, he had grown old, and his fortune was a wearisome burden. The hours he gave to gardens and villas would be better spent on care of his soul. Nero's rule was secure, his strength equal to any challenge. He could afford to let Seneca go.

Nero began his reply by deferentially noting that he owed his eloquence to Seneca, his former tutor. But he did not accept Seneca's reasoning. Agrippa and Maecenas, the retirees from Augustus' court, had outlived their ability to serve, unlike Seneca, who still had much to offer. And they had *never* given back Augustus' bequests. Nero modestly claimed to still need his tutor's help: "Why not call me back, if the path of my youth anywhere descends and gets slippery?"

Then Nero turned to a more salient point. "If you return money to me, it won't be your moderation spoken of by every mouth, but my greed; if you leave your princeps, it will be chalked up to fear of my cruelty. Your self-restraint would earn great praise; but it doesn't befit a wise man to get glory for himself while bringing ill repute on a friend."

If Nero really did speak like this, he expressed what had been implicit from the start: Seneca's dignity and stature were vital assets to his regime. Seneca could not now withdraw those assets, or buy them back with cash, without doing the regime grave harm. He was shackled by chains forged of his own moral virtue. He must see the drama through.

The interview ended as it began, according to Tacitus: with insincere efforts to keep up appearances. Nero embraced and kissed the man he had just condemned to a joyless old age. Seneca, says Tacitus, with chilling insight into the courtier's predicament, "expressed his thanks, as he did at the end of every conversation with his master." Then the two men parted. Their friendship, if any of it was still intact before this, had come to an end.

Tigellinus had already taken Burrus' place as head of the Praetorian Guard. Now he also replaced Seneca as *amicus principis,* the unofficial post that combined the roles of top adviser, chief of staff, and best friend. The shift was to have grave consequences, not only for Seneca but for Nero's long-suffering and unloved, nearly discarded wife, the daughter of Claudius, Octavia.

Nero hated his marriage to this high-minded woman, now in her early twenties. For three years, he had made love to Poppaea instead, a woman far better suited to his tastes. But his senior advisers, adopting the line once taken by Agrippina, had always forbidden him to switch wives. Whenever he had consulted Burrus about divorcing Octavia, the blunt-spoken soldier only scoffed. "Sure, and be certain to give back her dowry," he said, meaning the principate itself. Marriage to Octavia, as Burrus had understood, brought Nero precious legitimacy.

Octavia had by this time attained new luster in the eyes of the Romans. The girl's plight won sympathy from onlookers, as did her temperament, which conformed to their standards of virtuous womanhood. Unlike other imperial brides, Octavia had sought neither power nor adulterous lovers but seemed content to stick to her role—thus far unfulfilled—of begetting an heir.

Seneca too urged Nero to stay in the marriage, if we can judge by *Octavia,* the anonymous Roman play that centers on the young girl's tragedy. The author offers startling insight, perhaps based on firsthand knowledge, of what was going on behind closed doors in the palace in 62. A crucial scene brings Seneca and Nero onstage together, for an intimate, even tender, exchange.

Nero has begun to detest Octavia, but he admits to Seneca that he had not always done so. Speaking with surprising candor, he reveals that

Octavia, wife of Nero.

his hatred was born of rejection, while Seneca attempts to move him past his hurt feelings.

> NERO: *Never was my wife joined to me in her heart.*
> SENECA: *But devotion is hard to spot in childhood years,*
> *when love, vanquished by shame, conceals its fires.*
> NERO: *So I too believed, for a long time—but no.*
> *Her cold, rejecting heart, the looks she gives,*
> *Have one clear message: she despises me.*
> *But the burning pain I feel will have its vengeance.*

Seeing the danger of an irreparable breach, Seneca tries gamely to champion Octavia's cause. But the lure of Poppaea, whom the playwright links to primal forces of fertility and lust, proves too strong for his arguments. The two women are contrasted like the two roads to happiness in a famous philosophic allegory, one steep and arduous but leading to lasting rewards, the other smooth, easy, and ephemeral. Nero never was one for choosing the harder path.

As the scene ends, the petulant princeps rejects Octavia and Seneca in the same breath. He has had enough of restraint:

> *Stop pressing me; you're too severe already.*
> *What Seneca condemns, let me enjoy.*

The dialogue is invented, but the insights ring true. Seneca had always defended the *gravitas* of the principate, keeping Nero out of chariots and off the stages of theaters. Octavia, with her sober bearing and high birth, represented the same *gravitas,* especially by contrast with Poppaea. Seneca is bound to have stuck by her, but doing so put him on the same side as the ghost of Agrippina. Nero had already shucked off his mother; he was done listening to his surrogate father as well. And that spelled danger for his beleaguered wife.

In the spring of 62, at about the time of the death of Burrus, Nero learned that Poppaea was pregnant. The news jolted the princeps into action. He was now determined to get rid of Octavia and enthrone Poppaea as empress. The Romans hated Poppaea, as he well knew, but once she had borne a future princeps, they would accept her—and have new regard for him as well.

But before he could divorce and remarry, Nero had some dynastic business to take care of.

> *Do as I order. Send someone to bring me*
> *the severed heads of Plautus and Sulla.*

These are the words Nero utters as he comes onstage in *Octavia,* an entrance that rivals Richard III's in Shakespeare for boldness of characterization. Nero was hardly as resolute a leader as he is shown in these lines, if we credit the account of Tacitus. Nonetheless, assailed by the urgings of Tigellinus, he decided in the spring of 62 to do away with his two most prominent cousins. It was to them that Romans would turn, as Nero knew, should he lose support, as he might well do by divorcing the adored Octavia.

Rubellius Plautus, a descendant both of the emperor Tiberius and of the sister of Augustus, had long been regarded by Nero as a threat. In 55, as has been seen, a rumor that Agrippina was preparing to marry him had sent the princeps into a panic. Five years later, when a comet appeared, heralding (as Romans believed) a change of ruler, all eyes looked to Plautus. Nero wrote to Plautus then, asking him to leave Italy and go to his family's estates in Anatolia. Plautus had obligingly complied. So he was off the scene by 62, but hardly off of Nero's mind.

Faustus Sulla was also descended from Augustus' sister, as well as from the great Lucius Cornelius Sulla, a military legend whose surname was still potent more than a century after his death. Sulla too had long aroused Nero's suspicions and, like Plautus, had been banished for it. He had lived at Massilia (Marseilles) for the past four years, exiled on a trumped-up charge. While abroad, he had done nothing to arouse alarm. But his lineage made him dangerous, Tigellinus now argued to Nero. The Gallic legions might feel inspired by this new Sulla and rise up.

Nero had already watched a brother die at close range, and he had put his mother aboard the ship meant to kill her. The task of ordering assassinations from afar was comparatively easy, especially with Tigellinus as his new Praetorian prefect. A hit squad was sent to Massilia, on a ship fast enough to outstrip any forewarning. The soldiers covered the four-hundred-mile journey in only five days. Sulla was reclining pleasantly at his banquet table when they arrived, not expecting any harm. They struck him down and severed his head for shipment to Rome.

The elimination of Plautus was harder, since the road into Asia was longer and the element of surprise was lost. Plautus' father-in-law somehow got wind of the coming attack and sent a message to Plautus to take action. The armies of the East would rally to Plautus' side, the message said—that is, by overthrowing Nero. It was a barely plausible scenario, but in the end, Plautus merely waited for death—a band of 60 armed men—to arrive. Perhaps he thought in this way he could safeguard his wife and children, or perhaps his Stoic preceptors, among them the great Etruscan sage Musonius Rufus, convinced him that a quiet end was better than a desperate and hazardous struggle.

With two sword strokes, Nero dramatically strengthened his hold on power. He sent a report to the Senate that Sulla and Plautus were both dangers to the state; he did not say they were already dead. The senators pretended not to know more than that and voted the two men expelled from their ranks. Nero was once again given a free pass for murder.

Now at last, after four years of waiting, Nero was ready to change wives. But he had not reckoned with the depth of popular sentiment on Octavia's side. The empress he detested had become a kind of cult figure in the streets of Rome. In the minds of the crowds, she stood for a purer, nobler principate that might have been—or might be again.

Nero justified divorce by leveling a charge of adultery. He had extorted, with help from Poppaea and Tigellinus, sworn testimony from an Egyptian flutist that he had slept with the empress. But mobs of Octavia's outraged supporters began to gather in the public squares.

Nero wavered. He appeared even to change his mind, or was rumored to have done so, and grateful throngs went wild, setting up statues of Octavia in the Forum while destroying those of Poppaea. Some revelers even approached the palace and had to be pushed back by Praetorians. This allowed Poppaea to argue that a revolution was at hand. Octavia's continued survival, she insisted, was a danger to the state.

Nero, it seems, was doomed to perform his crimes twice, so that no one could fail to observe them. Anicetus, the Greek freedman who commanded the naval base at Misenum, had had to attack Agrippina twice before finishing her off. Now Nero needed a second indictment of Octavia, and he turned again to Anicetus, most loyal of thugs. All Nero needed this time was a confession from Anicetus that he had shared Octavia's bed. Anicetus would have to be punished, but Nero vowed to deliver only a mild rebuke, banishment to some comfortable place, and to soften it with a vast, covert reward.

Because of Anicetus' position, Octavia's alleged infidelity was portrayed as a bid for power—an attempt to suborn the Misenum fleet. With blithe disregard for plausibility, Nero cast his wife as a usurper, a second Agrippina. It was enough to secure from the Senate a sentence of banishment.

Octavia was sent to Pandateria, a wave-swept Pontine island only a mile square. Her best hope was to live out her life there, under house arrest in a sumptuous villa. But other imperial women who had landed on that grim rock had been killed, far from the eyes and ears of supporters. It was a place for the quiet disposal of wayward females.

The author of *Octavia* ends his play with his heroine's deportation. It is a stirring scene, modeled on Euripides' famous portrait of Iphigenia, a young woman unafraid to die. As the ship arrives to bear Octavia away, she embraces her fate:

> *Why do I tarry? Take me to my doom. . . .*
> *Rig the mast, spread sails to the winds*
> *and waves, hold the rudder straight*
> *and seek Pandateria's shore.*

Octavia exits cursing neither Nero nor her captors but, strangely enough, her father Claudius. She seems to see, at the threshold of death, that Claudius, by marrying Agrippina, had set in motion the events that led her to this pass.

Tacitus' *Annals* provides a grimmer denouement to the drama. Executioners arrived on Pandateria only days after Octavia did. The sight of the troops made the girl desperate. As they bound her, she pleaded piteously, insisting she was no longer Nero's wife but only his adoptive sister. She invoked her descent from the clan of Germanicus. Finally she begged the soldiers in the name of Agrippina, now three years dead.

All entreaties were in vain. The soldiers opened Octavia's veins, hoping to preserve the fiction of suicide. But she did not bleed out quickly enough. In the end they sealed her in a steam-filled room until she suffocated.

At the request of Poppaea, the new empress of Rome, Octavia's head was taken off with a sword and sent to join those of Plautus and Sulla in Nero's palace.

CHAPTER 6

Holocaust

(A.D. 62–64)

Few were left from the clan that had gathered for Claudius' marriage to Agrippina on New Year's Day 49. Claudius himself was dead, as was his son Britannicus and now his daughter, Octavia. Agrippina too had gone to the underworld, to be forever tormented by the husband she had killed (or so her ghost declares in the play *Octavia*). Nero had stripped himself of immediate family, and with the assassinations of Plautus and Sulla, he had made inroads into the ranks of cousins—though two distant ones, Decimus Silanus Torquatus and his young nephew Lucius, still remained alive, the last direct descendants of Augustus besides Nero himself.

The freedmen who had run the palace fourteen years earlier were also gone from the scene. Narcissus and Pallas had both been killed, the former by Agrippina, the latter poisoned for his estate by a cash-hungry Nero. Even Doryphorus, a special favorite with whom the princeps enjoyed playing rough sex games, was dead, executed for showing too much favor to Octavia. New court pets had arisen to fill the empty places by Nero's side: Spiculus the gladiator, Menecrates the lyre player, Pelagon the eunuch.

The most consequential departure was that of Burrus, the stalwart

Praetorian prefect, recently dead. The gruff old soldier had been one of few who stood up to Nero, speaking his mind and then, if asked to reconsider, saying to the princeps: "I've told you already, don't question me twice." But Burrus' replacement, Tigellinus, had taken the opposite tack, indulging all Nero's vanities and delusions. Tigellinus spent vast sums for the emperor's pleasure and used his cruelty to serve the emperor's power. Above all, he supported Poppaea, the bride whom Burrus had resisted and the people hated, but who made Nero happy, and was about to bear him a child.

Seneca alone remained, of the old guard who had helped usher in Nero's age of gold. Isolated and vestigial, he lingered on, with no clear role to play in the regime but no hope of leaving it. The job Agrippina had given him long ago, that of *rector,* "steersman," of the emperor's youth, had ended. So too had the roles he had subsequently taken on—senior counselor, speechwriter, caretaker of government, voice of Nero's conscience. He lived now in twilight, a prisoner chained to the palace by the very moral stature that had brought him there to begin with.

There was no precedent for this plight amid the galleries of historical exempla in which Seneca often roamed. In the Greek world, philosophers had been banished, outlawed, or even killed by rulers they had sought to instruct; none had been retained at court against his will. Only Octavia, before her fall, furnished an analogue to Seneca's situation: an outsider whom the princeps did not like or trust yet could not set free. But Octavia's grim end did not bode well for Seneca. And her absence now made it harder for him to withdraw, for Nero could ill afford to lose *both* his most visible badges of moral authority.

Escape was out of the question; Seneca had no place to hide. Besides, he had his brother Gallio and his nephew, the adored Marcus Lucanus, to think of. Lucan, the young poet so full of promise, was especially vulnerable. By this time, he had published the first three books of his epic poem *Civil War,* but the brilliant debut was having a strangely adverse effect on Nero. Since the princeps, too, now fancied himself a bard, the luminous talent of his protégé no longer inspired pride but jealousy and mistrust. Lucan was going to need his uncle's protection—if Seneca still could provide any.

The danger that now lurked for the Annaei, and for all the political elite, had been made clear earlier in 62. Abandoning his restraint toward the Senate, Nero had come close to executing a Roman praetor, Antistius Sosianus, for a minor offense. That offense, as Seneca and his nephew must have noted, had been a literary one—composing poetry of the wrong kind.

The "crime" took place at a dinner party given by a certain Ostorius Scapula. Antistius, no doubt emboldened by drink, recited some scurrilous verses poking fun at the emperor. He had no reason to fear retribution; Nero had thus far preyed only on his own family. But now Nero had Tigellinus at his right hand, a man who believed in the principle *oderint dum metuant,* "Let them hate, as long as they fear." It was Tigellinus' son-in-law, Cossutianus Capito, who in the aftermath of the dinner party brought a charge of *maiestas,* treason, against Antistius. The authorities who screened such charges allowed the case to proceed.

Not since the bad old days of Claudius had a trial on *maiestas* charges gone forward. The very word evoked memories of that regime's abuses and of the far worse predations of Caligula before that. *Maiestas* had served those emperors as a catchall with which to destroy their enemies, or to allow their adherents to destroy *theirs.* Almost any gesture or word could be portrayed as treasonous if a princeps was willing to listen. Once, under Tiberius, a senator had been indicted for picking up a chamber pot while wearing a ring on his hand that bore the emperor's image.

Ostorius, host of the "treasonous" dinner party, made a brave effort to protect Antistius, swearing he had heard nothing untoward. This effort was in vain. To the horror of official Rome, Antistius was sentenced to die by an ancient and cruel method, his neck to be fixed in the fork of a tree and his naked body beaten with rods.

Under the hierarchical structure of the principate, no such sentence could have been passed without the emperor's approval. Tacitus says that Nero agreed to the death penalty because he planned to step in and prevent it, thereby winning points for clemency. The story is plausible, but it's also just what an emperor *would* say when caught overplaying his hand. As things turned out, it was not the princeps but a senator who intervened to save Antistius' life, in a move that had large implications.

Thrasea Paetus at last broke the silence with which he had thus far snubbed Nero's excesses. He argued before the Senate that Antistius deserved exile and loss of property, not death. Moved by his courage, the entire Senate fell in behind Thrasea, voting to rescind the death penalty and impose exile instead. The consuls feared to ratify the decision without Nero's consent, so they asked the emperor what to do. Nero sent a petulant letter telling the Senate to act as it pleased; he would not interfere. His pride had suffered a blow, whether his own plan to show leniency had been usurped, or whether—perhaps more likely—he had been denied his show of force.

It was not entirely a heroic moment, for Thrasea carefully larded his Senate speech with praise of the princeps. Nonetheless a threshold had been crossed. The calm that had prevailed in politics thus far in Nero's reign, the compact between Senate and ruler proclaimed in the inaugural speech, had been broken. *Maiestas* had again been unsheathed as an instrument of repression. But the thrust had been parried; Nero's will had been thwarted. The princeps began to look with greater mistrust on the Senate, and it upon him.

Whose side was Seneca on, as he watched this drama unfold? Thrasea was a kindred spirit, a committed Stoic like himself, yet the two men stood on opposite sides of a constitutional chasm. Seneca had embraced the absolutism of the principate, had virtually proclaimed Nero a king, while Thrasea was a senator to the core. Thrasea celebrated the birthdays of the tyrant-slayers, Brutus and Cassius, as though they were independence days. Both Seneca and Thrasea revered Cato, the steely-spined Stoic who had chosen suicide over surrender a century earlier. But Thrasea seemed more inclined to take Cato as a guide for action.

Seneca and Thrasea, two moral men who might have been close allies either in politics or in philosophy, were bound on separate paths, headed toward separate perils. Both would surely have been surprised to learn that those paths would converge and that a single cataclysm would one day consume them both.

For Nero, Thrasea Paetus had begun to loom as an enemy, and he put the Roman world on notice, in early 63, that he regarded him so. In January of that year, he celebrated the birth of his first child, a daughter whom he named Claudia. Brimming with exuberance, Nero brought the entire Senate to Antium, some twenty miles south of Rome, where Poppaea was caring for her newborn. True to his free-spending ways, he staged athletic games and laid out elaborate banquets for all present. He excluded only one senator—Thrasea Paetus—from the celebrations.

The prospect of an heir—Poppaea had not yet borne a son, but the couple had proved they were fertile—had greatly strengthened Nero's position, and a *maiestas* charge against Thrasea might not have been long in coming. Tigellinus, the new Praetorian prefect, no doubt urged such a move, for his family bore a long-standing grudge against Thrasea. Five years earlier Tigellinus' son-in-law, Cossutianus Capito—now serving the regime as a *delator* who brought legal charges against enemies—had incurred a rebuke from the Senate for mismanaging an eastern province. Thrasea had aided the prosecution.

Cossutianus was to have his revenge, but not yet. Claudia, Nero's adored daughter, did not survive past her fourth month. Thrasea's fate took a different turn. Nero was overcome with grief and also humbled by his loss of a trump card. He suddenly felt the need to shore up relations with the Senate. In a deferential gesture, he reached out to Thrasea Paetus. The two men agreed to a rapprochement—for the moment.

This prompted a bitter exchange between Nero and Seneca, recorded by Tacitus in one of his many snapshots of this tortured relationship. Nero boasted at court of his new entente with Thrasea, making certain that Seneca would hear. It was a cruel taunt, suggesting that the princeps would now bestow his favors elsewhere, even on another Stoic sage. But Seneca did not take the insult lying down. He replied that Nero deserved congratulations for this new friendship—as though the princeps, not Thrasea, was the one who gained by it.

"Thus increased the glory, and the danger, of these exceptional men,"

Tacitus observes, looking ahead to the parallel dooms that would end the unparallel lives of Seneca and Thrasea Paetus.

Unable to resign even at the price of his huge estate, Seneca had nonetheless withdrawn from court to the degree that was safe. He no longer kept up the routine of a powerful statesman, no longer saw crowds of *clientelae,* friends in need of favors, in his chambers each morning. He rarely went out in public, and when he did, he no longer had a large retinue of attendants. He was trying, within the limits Nero had set, to reduce his visibility.

His pace of writing increased. He had more time now for moral reflections and a greater need to publish them, for his reputation had suffered badly as Nero had spiraled downward. From 62 on, he produced an astounding body of work, some of it now lost, much still extant. His longest and most ambitious prose works were composed at this time and, almost certainly, his most harrowing tragedy, *Thyestes.* Seneca, now at the peak of his literary powers, was writing like a man running out of time—as indeed he was.

Seneca was in his midsixties and feeling his age. Constantly cold, depleted by lifelong respiratory disease, he claimed to be "among the decrepit and those brushing up against the end." Everywhere he looked, he saw reminders that he had passed into the last phase of life, his *senectus.* Making the rounds of his estates, he found that a stand of plane trees had become gnarled and withered; he scolded a caretaker for failing to irrigate them. The man protested that the trees were simply too old to be helped. Seneca did not reveal to the caretaker, but did to his readers, that he himself, in youth, had planted those trees.

Seneca was often on the move, whether checking on his properties or following the emperor and the court through Italy. He was in Campania much of the time, sometimes visiting the wealthy resort towns of Baiae and Puteoli. He went at least once to Pompeii, as he eagerly wrote to his old friend Lucilius, a native of that town. Seneca felt closer to Lucilius as the years advanced, perhaps because so many other friends were dead.

A man slightly younger than Seneca, a fellow member of Nero's staff—caretaker of the emperor's estates in Sicily—Lucilius shared Seneca's literary tastes and philosophic concerns. He was also a fellow survivor, having undergone torture at the hands of Messalina and Narcissus, Seneca's persecutors as well.

Wherever Seneca went in these years, he carried on work on his magnum opus, a remarkable set of short moral essays framed as letters. Ostensibly addressed to Lucilius, these letters were in fact aimed at a wide audience. But the fiction of an intimate correspondence gave Seneca latitude in the structure of the essays, as well as unusual freedom to vary voice, tone, and technique. The melding of ethical inquiry with epistolary style produced a breakthrough for Seneca. He carried on the *Letters to Lucilius* at far greater length than anything else he had written and with greater candor about his life and thoughts—or at least, what *seems* to be candor.

A typical letter begins with a moment from daily life, then goes on to explore insights arising from that moment. In one of the letters, for example, Seneca describes a trip to a friend's vacation home, a wealthy estate house in Puteoli (modern Pozzuoli).

To reach this house from Baiae, his point of departure, Seneca needed to cross a three-mile bay. He set out on a small hired ship, although dark clouds loomed in the distance. Hoping to beat the storm, Seneca told his steersman to save time by taking a direct route rather than hugging the shore. But that only put him in deep, open water when the winds began to pick up. Halfway across, when there was no longer any point in turning back, Seneca found himself in a pitching, heaving swell. Seasickness, a condition he found intolerable, began to torment him, though he found he could not relieve his distress by vomiting.

Panicking, Seneca urged the steersman to change course and head for the nearest shore, but that was a rough coastline without anchorage. The steersman argued that the ship could not go near those rocks, but Seneca was by now in agony. He forced the crew to bring the ship as near to land as they could. And then he leaped into the sea.

Noting that he had always been a good swimmer, Seneca describes to

Lucilius how he got himself to shore and hauled himself painfully onto the rocky beach. Somehow he located a faint path leading to the villa he was seeking. He now understood, he writes whimsically, that the sufferings of Odysseus, driven about in his ship for ten years as described in the *Odyssey,* must have stemmed more from seasickness than from sea monsters.

Later, washed and changed, with the villa's slaves giving his body a rubdown to restore its warmth, Seneca reflected on how nausea had driven him to desperation. "I endured incredible trials because I could not endure myself," he writes, using a typically pointed turn of phrase. Then he let his thoughts wander down their usual path, toward the search for a virtuous life, a life of moral awareness. Discomforts overwhelm the body, Seneca muses, in the same way that vice and ignorance overwhelm the soul. The sufferer may not even know he is suffering, just as a deep sleeper does not know he is asleep. Only philosophy can rouse souls from such comas. Philosophy, Lucilius, is what you must pursue with all your being. Abandon all else except philosophy, just as you would neglect all your affairs had you fallen gravely ill.

The letter lands its readers at a very different place than where it appeared to be headed. The retching, desperate man who pitches himself into the sea turns suddenly into a serious thinker. Seneca's portrait of his own folly in taking a shortcut, and his description of embarrassing physical distress, draw us in with their frankness and closely observed detail. Once we have been hooked by Seneca the man, Seneca the sage reels us in.

But Seneca was not only a man and a sage; he was also a politician. His mastery of image making during his decade at Nero's side, his many efforts to manipulate public opinion, make the task of reading his *Letters to Lucilius* a complicated one. Is it the real Seneca we see before us—a man of profound moral earnestness, whose every third thought is of philosophy—or an *imago,* a shape conjured by the wordsmith's arts? Did Seneca himself, after fifteen years in which his every written word was a political act, even know the difference?

Seneca explores in one of his letters how an author's style reflects his character. He seems not to have considered that style might *shape* character—that constant, prolonged engagement in "spin" might make it hard for an author to stop spinning. In the *Letters,* Seneca is often spinning himself, performing himself as philosopher. "Philosophy is such a sacred thing that even that which resembles it wins approval by means of deception," Seneca writes to Lucilius. There are times in the *Letters* when he too deceives, though just how often is very hard to say.

Seneca describes in one of the *Letters* the course of a typical day, but the description is only partial. His morning is consumed with reading and thinking, interrupted for a spot of exercise—a footrace against a young slave boy, Pharius, whom Seneca, on that particular day, had managed to tie. Then a tepid bath, with water heated only by the sun; for Seneca, who throughout his life kept up a habit of cold-water bathing, no longer has the fortitude he once had. Then comes a spare lunch: dry bread and other simple fare, requiring neither the use of a table nor the washing of hands afterward. Then a nap—brief, for Seneca claims not to need much sleep.

It is the ideal portrait of a sage in retirement, tranquil, ascetic, serene. But the description takes us only to the midpoint of Seneca's day. The letter turns to other topics, leaving afternoon and evening a blank. As in much of what he wrote, Seneca has contrived to have it both ways. He wins our trust with his willingness to expose himself. But then he leaves gaps in the record, keeping important moments veiled.

The *Letters* contain no mention of Seneca's political career. The deeds he took part in, the crises he managed, the people he had watched, or helped, Nero kill—none of them even entered his thoughts, if we judge the *Letters* to be their record. Perhaps he could not mention these topics without provoking the princeps; perhaps silence was the price he paid for freedom to publish. Whatever the reason, the *Letters* form a strangely partial self-exploration. Seneca examines himself from every angle, seeks the truth at every turn, seems willing to confide all—yet he says nothing about the most consequential part of his life, still ongoing at the time he was writing.

A few vague statements in the *Letters* seem to imply regret for the past or to admit failure. "I show the right path to others; I myself spotted it only late, after wearing myself out with straying," he says. He compares his moral condition to that of a patient with skin lesions that have at last stopped spreading, though they also are not healing. He claims to have found an unguent for these sores, a medicine he will record and transmit for posterity: the *Letters* themselves.

Not for the first time, Seneca portrays his moral self as suffering from incurable illness—a trope that allowed him both to acknowledge shortcomings and to disclaim responsibility. Coming from a man who colluded in the murder of Agrippina, the metaphor suggests special pleading or even an apology. Not all readers of the *Letters* have been willing to accept it.

Seneca had begun his literary career by pondering the omnipresence of death. "We are dying every day," he had written to Marcia to console her for the loss of her son. Now, as he neared the end of that career, the theme of death, and especially suicide, occupied his mind more than ever. He saw death drawing ever nearer, and the thought of hastening it by his own action was becoming very real.

In the *Letters,* Seneca anticipates death as a great philosophic challenge, the ultimate test of character and principle. Seneca's moral heroes, Socrates and Cato, had had their finest moments when they met that test. Socrates had calmly drunk a cup of lethal hemlock, then vowed an offering to the gods for having healed him. Cato had resolutely torn out his own bowels rather than have his wound stitched up. Seneca had chosen the compromises of the court over the absolute quest for virtue, yet he glimpsed a final chance to join these sages. His death might in the end redeem his complex, imperfect life.

All around him, Seneca encountered premonitions and foretastes of the coming crisis. His respiratory illness caused him attacks in which he could not draw breath and lingered in a state of near-asphyxiation. Referring to these moments by the medical term *meditatio mortis,* "rehearsal for death," he describes to Lucilius how he had ceased to dread them.

"Even while suffocating, I did not stop resting serene in brave and cheerful thoughts," he proclaims. "Take this as a guarantee from me: I will not tremble when I reach the brink; I am already prepared."

Examples of suicide also surrounded Seneca, reminders that the path of "freedom," as he had called it in *De Ira,* was always open. Two cases greatly impressed him, both involving enslaved gladiators forced to fight in the arena. Finding their plights intolerable, both men resolved to die, despite being constantly under guard. One man contrived to visit a privy and force the lavatory sponge down his throat, choking himself to death. Another, while being driven to the arena on a cart, drooped toward the ground as though falling asleep, then inserted his head between the wheel spokes so that its rotation broke his neck. Despite almost total powerlessness, these men had found release.

Meditating on these examples, Seneca takes on the gloomy question of whether one should commit suicide to preempt a death that is certainly coming. To endure torture or wasting disease is brave, he concludes, but to do violence to oneself and end these conditions is also brave. He cites arguments on either side, then admits, uncharacteristically, that he cannot make up his mind.

Seneca had reason to dwell on such topics. His relationship with Nero had become a kind of captivity, or else a wasting disease, likely to kill him in the end. He was dying every day, just as surely, and even more slowly, than the rest of suffering humanity. But his plight was not wretched enough to call for the final solution—at least, not yet. Indeed there are passages in the *Letters,* and in his other late prose work, *Natural Questions,* that suggest he was doing his utmost to stay alive.

In one of the *Letters,* Seneca appears to offer Nero a mutual nonaggression pact. The topic he has chosen to discuss with Lucilius is whether philosophers are the enemies of monarchs. Of course they are not, Seneca opines. Rulers preserve the peace that allows sages to think great thoughts; the sage should revere the ruler as a child does a parent, or a student his teacher. Seneca quotes two obsequious lines of verse, originally addressed by the poet Vergil to the emperor Augustus:

He is a god who made this serenity for us,
A god—such he will always be, to me.

The quote suggests a continuing effort to cut a deal with the princeps, a deal Nero had already once refused. Seneca will go quietly into retirement and not defame the regime, in exchange for being left unharassed. If Nero will become an Augustus and provide safety, Seneca will become a Vergil and give praise.

A parent, a teacher, a god—Seneca, in his midsixties, could not have relished giving these roles to Nero in his midtwenties, his own former pupil. He kept the discussion general and left the analogy implicit. But in another work composed at the same time, *Natural Questions,* he was more direct. Here, in a treatise dealing with meteorology and earth science, Seneca again dared to make mention of *Nero,* a name he had not set down in writing for nearly ten years.

Seneca knew that *Natural Questions* would have powerful readers, probably including Nero himself. He took care to mention the princeps, at several points, in ways designed to show amity and win favor. In one passage, he praises Nero for his poetry—an arena in which Seneca's talent had, according to Tacitus, posed a threat—and even quotes a line he claimed to especially admire. In a second passage, he discusses an expedition (otherwise unknown) that Nero had sent to the upper Nile. There, in a phrase that drips with insincerity, he characterized the princeps as "a man passionately devoted to truth, as he is to the other virtues."

In a third passage of *Natural Questions,* Seneca confronted his Nero problem by way of historical analogy. As was well known to Seneca's readers, the Macedonian king Alexander the Great had brought a philosopher to his court to elevate its moral standing—much as Seneca had been brought to Nero's. For years that sage, Callisthenes, had dutifully played his part, until one day, for unknown reasons, he shook off subservience. He stood up at a banquet and, before the assembled high command, denounced Alexander's pretensions to godhood. Within a few months, he was dead, on Alexander's orders.

Seneca recalls this notorious murder in the following way: "This is an eternal charge against Alexander, that no virtue, no success in war will redeem. Whenever someone says, 'He killed many thousands of Persians,' there will come a reply: '. . . and Callisthenes.' Whenever it is said 'He killed Darius, who ruled the greatest empire of that time,' there will come a reply: '. . . and Callisthenes.' " The reminder of Alexander's stained legacy carries an implied warning for Nero: if he too kills a philosopher, the crime will darken his name forever.

But even while touting the lessons this episode held for Nero, Seneca ignored the lessons it might have held for himself. Perhaps Alexander had incurred eternal reproach—but Callisthenes, at the same time, had won eternal glory. Some inner voice had prompted that sage to stand up and denounce a tyrant. The effort had cost him his life, but Callisthenes, if he shared the outlook of Socrates and Cato, the one all Stoics professed to admire, must have felt the sacrifice was worth it.

Had Seneca ever tried to emulate Callisthenes, or did he now hope to? With all his eloquence and inside knowledge, he could have done much to harm Nero's regime. Nothing suggests he felt tempted to use those weapons. Rather, he sought to keep writing, keep mum about the crimes he had seen, and keep alive. He would take a different path than Callisthenes. He would make himself too respected a sage for even Nero to kill.

While Seneca was composing *Natural Questions,* in 62 or 63, Campania was shaken for a number of days by severe earthquakes. Though Romans could not have known it, their sumptuous resort region straddled an active fault line; thus comes the vulcanism (ongoing today) of Mount Vesuvius. Pompeii and Herculaneum, wealthy resorts on the Bay of Naples, were hardest hit by the temblors. A stone frieze recovered from Pompeii gives one artist's record of the event, depicting cracked and collapsing buildings in the public square.

Seneca reflected on the disaster in *Natural Questions,* one portion of which deals with earthquakes. Curious details caught his interest: a flock of hundreds of sheep inexplicably dropped dead; a bronze statue was split down the middle; a man taking a bath watched his bathwater disappear into cracks that appeared between tiles, then surge up again as the cracks reclosed. Residents wandered away from the scene, some babbling insanely, some in a catatonic trance. Many, Seneca noted, vowed to leave Campania and never return to the stricken region.

The fact that destruction had arisen from the sudden instability of solid ground impressed Seneca mightily. To his philosophic mind, earthquakes offered a paradigm of greater instabilities, the evanescence of life itself. Death is stalking us everywhere, he mused, playing on his favorite theme. How useless to fear or dread death, still more useless to flee it! We panic over natural disasters, though the smallest things—a gangrenous cut, an accumulation of phlegm—can do us in just as easily. We fret over oncoming floods, when a drink of water that goes down the wrong way can be every bit as lethal.

This refusal to lament Campania's fate exemplifies the Stoic approach to misfortune. Happiness comes not from one's circumstances but from cultivation of Reason, the Stoics taught; a true sage, a *sapiens,* would be unharmed by torture or loss, even loss of life. But such acceptance can translate all too easily into passivity, especially in an autocracy where death often arrives by imperial order. By insisting that death is everywhere and cannot be escaped, Seneca seems to relieve himself of the burden of action. For indeed, Seneca was taking very little action in these years to help himself or others.

History supplies an ironic footnote to Seneca's discussion of the Campania quake. The refugees he scoffed at for leaving Campania were

A frieze depicting the devastation caused by the Campanian quake.

in fact, as time would tell, saving their lives. Seventeen years later the region would be enveloped by ash and hot gases, in the volcanic eruption that entombed Pompeii and Herculaneum. The earthquake had been not a disaster so much as a warning. Seneca, his eyes fixed on the ubiquity of death, had not seen that Nature was offering escape.

In August 64, Romans again faced sudden ruin, this time in Gaul, in the regional capital Lugdunum (Lyons). A fire raged through the town, virtually annihilating it in a single night. Again Seneca preached acceptance and calm, expressing his views this time in one of the *Letters to Lucilius*. His point of departure is the grief of his friend Aebutius Liberalis, a native of Lyons who had, in all likelihood, lost everything in the fire. It is pointless to grieve, Seneca reminds Liberalis, when disaster is the common lot of humankind. Far better to practice *praemeditatio malorum* and imagine doom before it arrives, mentally embracing it until it ceases to terrify.

"Exile, torture, disease, war, shipwreck—think on these," Seneca counsels. "Let us take in with our mind the worst thing that can possibly happen, if we don't want to be mastered by it"—for it will eventually come to pass. The rise of cities only portends their fall; we should greet that fall with untroubled minds. Besides, he remarks—changing tack and offering multiple solaces—new buildings will sprout from under the ashes. A better city will rise than the one destroyed by the flames.

This last idea strikes the keynote of apocalypse, another theme that had haunted Seneca from his earliest writings. His Stoic training taught that all humankind would be wiped out, then reborn in a primitive state, in an endless cycle designed to renew the tired world. But Seneca imagined the scene more vividly than any Stoic before him. And he was more certain that the last days were near.

"There won't be long until the destruction," he writes in *Natural Questions*. "Already *concordia* [the harmonious balance of the cosmos] is being tested and torn apart." The certainty and imminence of the collapse seems to have given him a kind of comfort. All would meet the same fate. All action—attempts to flee, to find remedies, to help others—would be equally useless.

Earlier Stoics had theorized that flames would cause the world's end, the fiery cosmic exhalations they called *ekpyroseis*. But Seneca, in *Natural Questions*, imagined, as he had before in *Consolation to Marcia*, a universal flood. With grim foreboding, he notes that water is everywhere on earth—collecting in every hollow, flowing down every mountain, pooling beneath every acre of ground. "Nature has put moisture everywhere—so that, when she wishes, she can attack us from all sides," he writes in *Natural Questions*. In a special-effects spectacular, he imagines each source breaking its bounds, each aquifer bursting forth from beneath its crust, until earth itself is liquefied.

"All boundaries will be sundered," he foresees, in the same ecstatic tone he had used in *Consolation to Marcia*. "Whatever Nature has split into separate parts will be merged together. . . . Waters will converge from East and from West. A single day will serve to bury the whole human race. All that fortune's favor has preserved for so long, all that it has raised above the rest—the noble, the glorious, the kingdoms of great peoples—all will plunge alike into the abyss."

The twilight of the world, it seemed to Seneca, was coinciding with the twilight of his own life. Soon, he foresaw, virtue and vice would no longer matter; such distinctions would be swallowed up by the cataclysm. Perhaps he told himself that the same was true of autocracy and freedom, passivity and defiance, action and inaction.

Seneca was not the only leading figure trying to withdraw from political life. Thrasea Paetus, the senator whose Stoic beliefs mirrored Seneca's in many ways, had suddenly stopped attending Senate meetings, at some point in 63.

This absence was remarkable and, to many no doubt, discouraging. Thrasea had thus far been a lone example of bravery in a servile body. It was he who had stirred the Senate to reduce the sentence of Antistius, the man whose only crime had been to recite risky verses at a dinner party. More recently, he had again led the Senate in asserting itself. He introduced a motion to ban state commendations, which, as he pointed out, were being used simply to advance the careers of corrupt administrators. His plea for honesty in public discourse was warmly welcomed—though the presiding officers, fearing Nero's disapproval, at first would not allow it to come to a vote.

Thrasea's dissent had often, up to now, taken the form of nonparticipation. He had walked out of the Senate, without a word, on the day in 59 when it heard, with approbation, the letter justifying Nero's killing of Agrippina. A short while later, when others had cheered Nero's first singing performance, he had withheld applause. Under the reign of Nero, where servile conformity was regarded as loyalty, mere absence and silence could be forms of protest. Now Thrasea had decided to employ them on a broader scale.

But was his departure from the Senate an act of courage or cowardice? By his absence, did he advance the cause of autonomy or deprive it of a leading voice? The dilemma must have troubled him, as it has troubled many others—righteous people whose political participation has helped bad rulers. Is withdrawal from the fray an act of conscience or mere self-protection?

However Thrasea answered these questions, he soon showed official Rome that his absenteeism would be total. On New Year's Day 64, when the Senate gathered to beseech the gods on behalf of the Roman state, Thrasea did not attend. Two days later he skipped another annual rite, at which the senators swore loyalty to the princeps and prayed for his safety. These breaches of protocol were unmistakable in their import: Thrasea was gone for good.

Like Seneca, he turned increasingly to his writing and to his study of Stoic precepts. It was probably in these years that he produced a biography of Cato, the exemplar of Stoic courage whom both he and Seneca revered. Perhaps he was inspired by Seneca's nephew, Lucan, who by this time had begun circulating his *Civil War,* an epic poem about the conflict in which Cato had died. For all three men, Seneca, Thrasea, and Lucan, Cato provided a powerful symbol of integrity in an age of autocracy—a symbol that could still be safely held aloft, thanks to a century of intervening time.

Thrasea had begun studying with Demetrius of Sunium, the Cynic guru whom Seneca also frequented and whom he had lionized in *De Beneficiis*. This man was said to go about "semi-nude," wearing only a threadbare cloak that left one shoulder exposed, or even to lie naked on the ground, showing both contempt for social mores and indifference to discomfort. In Demetrius, the virtues of the great Cato, who had also practiced self-exposure as an ascetic discipline, seemed to be reincarnated. This hardy Cynic provided both Thrasea and Seneca with a spiritual refuge—an escape from the cares of the palace, in Seneca's case, and from those of the Senate in Thrasea's.

Meanwhile in Sicily, Seneca's friend Lucilius was also seeking *otium,* retreat from political involvement, in the early 60s, as is clear from Seneca's advice in the *Letters*. To judge by the urgent tone of this advice, and the many different forms it took, the decision to leave the public sphere, for a thinking Stoic, was a complex one. How far into retreat should Lucilius go? Seneca wonders at various points in the *Letters*. How should he protect himself from the incursions of politics and business? How ought he to disguise his retreat—for to make it openly, Seneca is quite certain, would incur ill will or actual danger. At one point, he advises Lucilius to feign illness rather than openly withdraw. "Some animals mix up their own footprints around their lair so as not to be found," Seneca writes, metaphorically casting the seeker of *otium* as a hunted beast. "You must do the same, or there will be no lack of men to chase you down."

Seneca wrestled all his life with the issue of *otium* or nonparticipation, expressing different views in different works and even in different sections of a single work. He devoted an entire treatise to it, *De Otio,* only part of which survives. In a modern scholarly study, an analysis of Seneca's views on *otium* runs to fifty dense pages and even then comes to no firm conclusions. "It is difficult, if not impossible, to give an account of Seneca's views which, while remaining faithful, would produce a consistent and coherent system," concedes Miriam Griffin, the author of that study.

The problem that the principate presented to Stoic men of morals was indeed insoluble. The Stoic creed, with its emphasis on service to the common good, required involvement in political life, unless the regime was hopelessly evil or the Stoic's own life was in danger. But what if the Stoic's life was more endangered by leaving politics than by staying? And what if, by his departure, he made an evil regime more evil? The let-out clauses posed perils of their own. And the question of when to invoke them—at what point a regime's malady became incurable, or one's own risks rose unacceptably—was a thorny one.

Seneca's own career exemplified the dilemmas, yet he could not safely write from experience. He had to frame all discussions of withdrawal in general, even hypothetical, terms. This gives many of his works a strangely detached quality. He tells his father-in-law Paulinus, his brother Gallio, and his friend Lucilius to chuck political office and devote themselves to philosophy. But Seneca himself, when he addressed those men, still clung to political office. He spoke often as though he *would* withdraw, was doing so, or had already done so, never acknowledging the bonds that kept him at court.

The leading men of Nero's age made their way, as best they could, through the moral thicket of the participation problem. Thrasea chose to depart the arena, while Lucan, as will be seen, remained intensely engaged. Seneca, less free than these two to do as he wished, took the middle path, the hardest of all. He withdrew only part of himself into a serene world of philosophic contemplation. The other part, the part that had chosen politics to begin with, remained chained to Nero—even though the emperor was rapidly becoming Seneca's worst nightmare.

Now in his midtwenties, Nero was growing fat. He had already lost the graceful lines and angles that his youthful portraits reveal. His jowls were heavy, his brow doughy and soft. Soon he would grow a chin beard, the first facial hair yet seen on a princeps, perhaps as a way to disguise the fleshiness of his thick neck.

Nero had many opportunities to add to his girth, for everywhere he went, he found courtiers and social climbers eager to provide what he most enjoyed: banquets that stretched from noon to midnight, inter-

An official portrait of Nero
in his early twenties.

rupted perhaps by refreshing dips in snow-cooled pools. By offering such
hospitality, an aspiring parvenu could rise higher in Nero's favor than any
senator or noble. For it was on the *equites* and even lower social classes
that Nero relied for support. One such was Vatinius, a cup maker from
Beneventum, who pleased the princeps with an oft-repeated joke: "I hate
you, Nero—*because you're in the Senate*!" Both men enjoyed the camara-
derie of this quip, the illusion that they belonged to the same class and
could together scoff at their betters.

By May 64, Nero's mind was bent on music. He was determined
to build an audience for his singing and lyre playing, arts to which he
had given intense efforts. Thus far, obeying the restrictions imposed by
his senior counselors—principally Seneca—he had taken the stage only
once, in a private setting, on his own palace grounds. Now he wanted
to go public. He chose to begin in Neapolis, a largely Greek city in
Campania—the Hellenic spirit being more receptive, he thought, to the
mixing of musicianship and rule.

Even at Neapolis, Nero took cautious measures to ensure a large audience. His Augustiani accompanied him, well paid to applaud in rhythmic

patterns for their princeps, along with a few thousand recruits from the lower classes. But he wanted a full house, which at Neapolis meant more than 8,000. His troops and advance men collected farmers and herdsmen from surrounding villages to fill the benches. Finally the Praetorians themselves took up any empty seats. Spectatorship was a new kind of military service, imposed by a new kind of emperor.

Nero had trained his singing voice throughout his reign and always took care not to strain it. At the suggestion of Terpnus, his Greek lyre teacher, he had kept on a rigorous diet heavily weighted with leeks and had purged himself frequently with emetics and enemas. When he had to address the army, he avoided shouting but whispered instead, and subordinates soon learned they could avoid a dressing-down by reminding him to spare his throat. Terpnus had stayed in his service throughout his reign, coaching what was reportedly a thin and hoarse voice into one worthy of the stage.

Nero sang for the crowds at Neapolis over the course of several days. No reports have survived of those historic performances, except a notice that the stands at one point collapsed due to a seismic tremor. Fortunately the crowds had all gone home before this occurred. In nearby Pompeii, gladiatorial games were held in thanks "for the safety of Nero in the earthquake," as one resident inscribed on a wall. Those words were preserved when the town was buried in volcanic ash, fifteen years later.

Seneca might well have been among Nero's audience, for several of his *Letters to Lucilius* place him in Neapolis at this time. But if he did attend the performances, he tried his best to disguise that fact. In one letter, he complains to Lucilius that he had found the theater of Neapolis full while the philosophers' lecture hall—his own destination—was empty. This was among the riskiest things he said in all his written works, since it could be taken as a jab at Nero's artistic ambitions. But it also showed, perhaps quite pointedly, that Seneca had no part in them.

Nero's launch of a public singing career deeply disappointed Seneca. He had long tried to prevent such a spectacle, finding it unsuited to the gravity of the principate, but he could no longer rein in Nero's will. Conceivably he had played a role in the choice of Neapolis, not Rome, for the debut, just as earlier he had persuaded Nero to move his chariot racing outside city limits. But it was now Tigellinus, not Seneca, who shared Nero's counsels, and Tigellinus was urging the princeps to pursue whatever mad fancy he pleased.

In the ancient battle between philosophy and poetry, the lines of which had been drawn by Plato four centuries earlier, Nero and Seneca had ended up on opposing sides. While Seneca focused on moral self-examination in *Letters to Lucilius,* Nero moved further than ever from this pursuit—toward passion, fantasy, and the ecstasy of Greek music. Reaching out in their different media toward different audiences, Seneca and Nero were vying for the hearts and minds of Rome, one exalting the power of reason, the other channeling strong emotion.

Those who now surrounded Nero, in particular Tigellinus, saw an opening in this temperamental divide. They whispered in Nero's ear that the moral gravity of the Stoics was somehow a threat to his regime. In months to come, they would openly allege that mere gloomy looks, or ascetic ways of life, were treasonous in that they implied disapproval of Nero's exuberance. To be "schoolteacherly"—to go about with a superior or censorious air—became a crime against the state. Nero would rely on such prejudices to brand the Stoics his enemies and to destroy some of the best men of his time.

From Neapolis, Nero intended to make a crossing to Greece and begin a full concert tour, but his movements became halting and uncertain. He got only as far as Beneventum before canceling his Greek trip and returning to Rome. There he announced an intention to sail for Egypt but immediately abandoned that journey, too, claiming that adoring Romans would not want him absent for long.

This change of heart prompted Tigellinus, who was vying to add the post of master of revels to his brief, to pull out all the stops. He arranged a fantastic soiree to celebrate Nero's decision to stay near Rome. On the Lake of Agrippa, a reservoir near the Pantheon, he floated a vast barge and had it towed about by rowers in gold-and-ivory-adorned ships. The lake was stocked with exotic fish brought from afar, while rare animals and birds ringed the shore. In the center of the barge, Nero, Tigellinus, and other high officials dined while lying on purple pillows. The rowers meanwhile took them on a sexual pleasure cruise: on every bank stood women, from high classes and low, beckoning Nero to enjoy their favors in specially built lakeside brothels.

After this grand fete, Nero left Rome and headed to Antium, about twenty miles south. His intentions at this point are unclear, and from his rapid pace of movement, it seems he had become agitated or uneasy in mind. That summer had been thick with portents. At the start of May, a comet had appeared in the night sky, and it had continued to move slowly through the heavens, week after week.

Nero looked for advice about the comet's meaning, but not, significantly, from Seneca—though the sage had discussed comets in *Natural Questions* and had used "the comet we saw for six months in the most fortunate reign of Nero" (in A.D. 60) to prove that they did not portend the fall of rulers. Instead Nero turned to Balbillus, a former prefect of Egypt who had become adept in astrology. Balbillus did not question the dire significance of this new comet but suggested a ruse to avert the danger. If Nero contrived to kill off some high-ranking aristocrat, the intent of the heavens would be fulfilled and the princeps spared.

Probably Balbillus meant to give a pretext for the murder of Lucius Junius Silanus, the last male member of Augustus' sacred line—other than Nero himself. But on July 17, it seemed that no such measure would be needed, for the comet was no longer seen. The baleful star had shone for more than two months without incident. Rome, and Nero, were able to breathe a sigh of relief.

But the very next night began a disaster as terrible as if the comet had hurtled to earth and struck the city dead center.

Nero was at Antium in mid-July of 64, the place of his daughter's birth and his own, when messengers from Rome told him of a fire in the city. It had begun near the Circus Maximus, a racecourse built of stone but surrounded by wooden shops crammed with flammable goods. Winds were driving the blaze into several adjoining regions, and thousands of residents were fleeing. Nero elected to stay where he was, trusting in the *vigiles,* the corps that oversaw fire fighting and civic safety, to handle the problem. Later, though, when he learned that his own grand construction, the Domus Transitoria, was being consumed, he made haste to return to Rome.

By the time he arrived, the city had become a cauldron. The flames had moved at breakneck speed and were attacking four of Rome's seven hills. The primary weapon of the *vigiles,* buckets of water, was utterly useless. A fallback strategy, destruction of buildings to form a brake, was failing as well: by the time battering rams could be brought into position, the blaze had already raced past the line of defense, or else the intense heat—estimated at 1100 degrees Fahrenheit—simply jumped any barrier. Those who escaped their tinderbox homes had become a throng of seared, scarred, and panicked refugees. They jammed the narrow streets and blocked one another's paths, clogging escape routes with heaps of goods they had saved from the flames, or looted.

Nero could not save Rome, but he did what he could for the Romans. He threw open his own properties, imperial gardens in untouched places like the Vatican hill, to survivors and ordered shelters built. The Field of Mars, thus far out of the path of the fires, was converted into a refugee camp. Emergency grain supplies were brought up from Ostia and sold at a subsidized price. Those still able, and willing, to live would have the means to do so.

After six days the fire was apparently stopped by a brake, but it flared up again and burned for three more days. Finally it died out for good, mostly for lack of fuel. Perhaps two-thirds of the city had been destroyed. The only regions spared were those fenced off by barriers: the Tiber River had protected the Vatican, while the Field of Mars and the Quirinal and Esquiline Hills were shielded by a set of old ramparts called the Servian Walls, originally built around a much smaller Rome to guard against Gallic invaders.

In the camps that now sprawled in these places, stories began to spread, many demonizing Nero. Some said that torchbearers had been seen setting the blaze, who, when accosted, claimed they were acting on

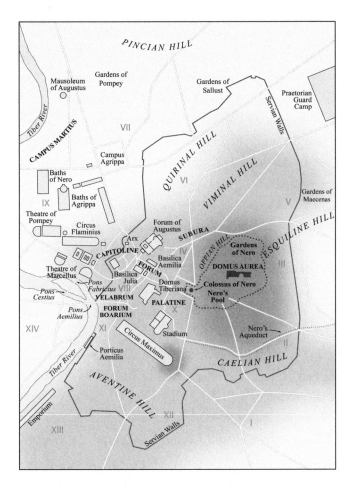

Map of Rome showing the extent of fire damage.

high authority. Others said that *vigiles* attempting to douse the blaze had been prevented. The most damning rumor of all claimed that the princeps had stood on his palace battlements and strummed his lyre while the city burned, reciting his own verses about the destruction of Troy. The ingenious lampoon allowed the public to feel both rage over the fire and disgust at Nero's artistic delusions, a devastating mixture. The image thus created continues to define Nero, in popular lore, to this day.

Was Nero far enough gone in mind to torch his own city? Or to treat its destruction as an occasion for song? What would have been his purpose in setting the fire—to build a new Rome in his own image, a Neronopolis, as Suetonius says he planned to do? Or to lash out at disapproval of his new persona and at the Stoics, whose scowls hurt him so deeply? Rome was his conscience, the city he dreaded to enter after killing his mother, the city that had, briefly, made him ashamed to reject Octavia. If, as psychologists tell us, arson often springs from buried rage and a quest for revenge, then Nero *did* have motives. Whether he actually set the blaze is a question that, for Tacitus, could not be resolved, and it remains unresolved today.

What mattered to Nero was that people believed him guilty. He threw himself into the reclamation of the city and of his battered reputation. He poured fortunes from the treasury and from his own funds—the two were hard to distinguish—into relief and reconstruction. And he began a campaign to shift blame from himself to others.

The sect the Romans called Christiani, and their founder Christus, appear first in Latin literature in Tacitus' account of the great fire. According to this famous passage, the Christians were arrested on spurious charges and brought to Nero's palace grounds for horrendous ordeals. They were dressed in animal skins and then were set upon by wild beasts; they were wrapped in pitch-soaked cloth and set on fire; or with a significance Nero could not have intended, they were nailed to crosses to suffocate to death. Perhaps Peter or Paul, or both, met their deaths in this savage purge—though evidence is strangely lacking, in both Roman and Christian sources, on the fates of these apostles.

Rage over the fire, and the violence it spawned, slowly died away, along with the heat trapped in the smoldering ruins. Nero began to rebuild. He made certain that the new Rome would be more fire-resistant than the old; he widened streets and introduced flat porch roofs from which the *vigiles* could do their jobs. He paid for much of the construction himself, since most homeowners had been wiped out. The princeps, and the state, were spending on an unprecedented scale, reconstructing Rome while supporting perhaps 200,000 displaced and suffering Romans.

In such a crisis, any sane princeps would have scanted his own needs. The flames had spared many imperial properties; Nero was comfortably housed. But his precious Domus Transitoria, not yet fully complete before the fire began, had been destroyed. Nero set out to replace it with a building that would beggar Rome's imagination—and break its bank. He began work on the Domus Aurea, the Golden House, an immense pleasure grounds occupying more than a hundred acres. At the entrance to the main building—a three-hundred-room architectural fantasy, designed largely for entertainment—he erected the Colossus Neronis, a bronze statue of himself, over one hundred feet tall.

Money had to be found. Imperial agents scoured the provinces, squeezed taxpayers, and ransacked the treasuries of Greece and the Near East. Not even temples of the gods were spared, for many contained precious statues clad in gold and ivory. The hoard of art stolen from the Greeks during Rome's eastward expansion, two and three centuries earlier, had been largely lost in the fire. Replacements were ripped from their shrines by Acratus, one of Nero's trusted freedmen, and Carrinas Secundus, a lackey who had been trained in Greek philosophy and could sweet-talk his way through the East.

It was the greatest transfer of wealth since the conquests of Alexander the Great. It pained all those who admired the beauty of the Greek world, or who wanted Rome's empire to be more than merely a global shakedown. Among them was one who, despite his earnest efforts and dearest wishes, was implicated in the squeeze.

Seneca felt, as he watched the Golden House rise on mountains of loot, that he must get clear of politics without delay. Nero had become an offense to all Stoic principles, an embodiment of luxury and excess. The icons of the gods themselves were being smelted into the emperor's tableware. The twilight realm in which Seneca dwelt had grown gloomier than ever.

The fire of Rome had destroyed part of Seneca's property, but he was still vastly wealthy. Two years earlier, when he had tried to buy his way out of politics, Nero had refused. Now, with imperial funds draining away as never before, Seneca saw a second chance. He once again sought to surrender his wealth to the princeps. This time his offer was accepted—but on Nero's terms. The princeps took possession of Seneca's wealth and lands, but would not allow the sage to absent himself from court. The regime was too badly weakened to withstand a high-level defection.

Seneca's last stratagem was the course he had urged on Lucilius, his friend in Sicily, when advising him how to practice *otium*. He feigned illness and stayed in his chambers. He must live a lie, if he was to live at all.

Tacitus reports that at this point Seneca discovered from his loyal freedman, Cleonicus, that Nero was trying to have him poisoned. There is no reason to doubt the information, though Tacitus indicates it did not have solid authority. Nero had the means for such a crime, thanks to Locusta, and plenty of opportunity. Simple dislike would have served for a motive, or the fear that Tigellinus had drummed into him, that serious and sober men—"schoolteachers"—meant him harm.

Seneca had already watched as Claudius and Britannicus were felled by Locusta's poisons. He began eating simple, uncooked foods, plucking fruit off the trees on his estates, scooping water from running streams. Earth itself would nurture him, with victuals even Nero could not taint.

Death was looming all around. The question Seneca could not answer in *Letters to Lucilius* haunted him every day: whether to await a doom that was sure to come, or by suicide take charge of his own fate. With his actions, he gave his answer. While the fruit trees burgeoned and the streams ran pure, he would do his best to stay above ground.

CHAPTER 7

Suicide (II)

(A.D. 64–66)

Rome prepared for the second Neronia, the arts festival instituted by Nero on a five-year schedule, in a very different mood than it had celebrated the first. In 60, the city had just completed what a later emperor, Trajan, termed the *quinquennium Neronis*, "Nero's half-decade," claiming it was the high-water mark of Roman history. By 65, the city was a burned-out shell and a construction site, above which towered a monstrous pleasure palace with a colossal statue of Nero at its entrance. In that intervening *quinquennium*, Rome had become Neronopolis, as Nero reportedly intended, in all but name.

Prompted by Trajan's comment, historians have seen in Nero's reign a diptych of good government followed by bad, and they have studiously sought the dividing line. For some, the murder of Agrippina in 59 forms the downturn; for others, it was the death of Burrus; for still others, including Tacitus, it was the first, partial retirement of Seneca in 62. But the path of Nero's decline was less a V-shaped turn than an arc, paralleling the arc of his own maturation. In his teens, Nero deferred to his elders, but as he grew, he took the reins in his own hands—at times quite literally, by indulging his passion for chariot driving. He finally drove Rome's chariot, and his own life, into the ditch.

Any Romans who still in 65 read Seneca's *De Clementia,* ten years after it was written, had occasion for a bitter laugh. "That which is undergirded by truth, and grows out of solid ground, becomes better and greater with passage of time," Seneca had proclaimed, reassuring his readers that their new *princeps* was innately good and could not deteriorate. It turned out that age seventeen had been a bit early for such certainty. Seneca must not have believed his own words, but perhaps he thought his influence could *make* them true. Over time he had lost that influence. Now only one of the restraints he had imposed was still in force: Nero had not yet sung in a public theater within the bounds of Rome.

Nero's inaugural speech to the Senate, written by Seneca and later posted proudly on silver tablets, might also have evoked laughter a decade later—or tears. The emperor's early reverence for the Senate had dissolved into paranoia and contempt, following a spiral pattern set by his two predecessors, Caligula and Claudius. Imperial anxiety had begotten senatorial fear, fear had bred opposition, and opposition had spawned cruelty. Seneca had tried to prevent the cycle from starting, and indeed he had succeeded in delaying its onset. Without his moderating influence, the *quinquennium Neronis* might have been a three-year span, or two, or only one.

But was the time he had bought worth the price he had paid? Nowhere in his prose works does Seneca reflect on his political successes or failures, beyond a few vague mutterings in the *Letters* suggesting the failures weighed on him heavily. Nowhere does he say, as the author of *Octavia* has him say, that he should have stayed on Corsica, beneath the benign stars of the open sky, and never seen Nero's palace—now being fitted with a ceiling depicting that sky, a mechanical wonder that could be wheeled around by laboring slaves. Seneca tried, on at least two occasions, to leave that palace, realizing it had become his prison. But he had first entered it of his own free will. Unlike his great role model, Socrates, he had felt the pull of ambition, and he still felt it to the end of his life, if we believe an analysis he made in the *Letters* of his own moral state.

What could have prompted a committed Stoic, a man who thought happiness came from Nature and Reason, to also pursue wealth and rule? Seneca never referred this question to himself, but he pondered it in a mythic parallel, in his greatest verse tragedy, *Thyestes*.

Seneca almost certainly composed this play during his time at Nero's court, or afterward in retirement. It is the most self-referential of his dramas, so much so that one doubts it could have been published in his lifetime. Here Seneca used the conflict between two royal brothers—Atreus, a bloody autocrat possessed by spirits of Hell, and Thyestes, a gentle sage trying to stay out of politics—to wrestle with questions that his own strange journey had raised.

When the drama begins, Atreus sits on the throne of Argos, enjoying sole power, though he and his brother Thyestes were meant to rule by turns. Thyestes has gone into an exile that Seneca depicts as a philosophic retreat, a communion with Nature such as he himself had claimed to enjoy on Corsica. But Atreus, infected by the demonic spirit of his grandfather Tantalus, is bent on destroying his brother, whom he regards as a threat. He sets out to lure Thyestes back to Argos, then enact a diabolic plan: to feed his brother a banquet of his murdered children's flesh.

The conflict is neither a coded version of Seneca's relationship with Nero, nor an allegory contrasting political ambition with philosophic detachment, but it contains elements of both. Atreus is challenged by a henchman to say how he will ensnare Thyestes from such a great distance. Atreus replies:

> He could not be caught—unless he wants to be caught.
> He yet covets my kingdom.

With the omniscient insight of the criminally insane, Atreus seems to look straight into the heart of his brother—and Seneca's heart too. The will to power, Atreus implies, lurks in even the most detached, self-contented sage.

Thyestes now enters the scene, walking toward the trap we know is waiting. Seneca portrays him as a virtuous Stoic, disgusted by the world he long ago renounced:

How good it is
to be in no one's way, to eat safe meals
stretched out on open ground. Hovels don't house crimes;
a narrow table holds a wholesome feast;
it's the gold cup that's poisoned—I've seen, I know.

It is as if Seneca has turned back the clock on his own life and given Thyestes the same choice he faced on Corsica, but also given him knowledge of what awaits. Thyestes lingers agonizingly on this precipice, unwilling to go forward, sensing danger ahead, unable to make up his mind—but then takes the fatal step.

Why does Thyestes return to Argos, while claiming to hate what he will find there? He makes his choice passively, almost fatalistically. As his children urge him onward, he appears to surrender: "I follow you, I do not lead," he tells them. He has resisted long enough to satisfy his own conscience. He will resist further when Atreus offers him the scepter, but he accepts this as well; it was, as Atreus had divined and as Seneca finally makes clear, what he had wanted all along.

Accepting tainted power rather than staying in virtuous exile—this was Thyestes' sin, and one familiar to Seneca. The impulse behind it was deeply rooted in Thyestes' nature, perhaps in all human nature. "All of us have done wrong," Seneca wrote in *De Clementia;* "some have stood by our good designs not firmly enough and have lost our guiltlessness, unwillingly, while trying to keep our grasp on it." *Trying* is what Seneca depicts Thyestes doing, but not hard enough.

Seneca's prose works offer forgiveness, but in the bleak world of the tragedies, the sin of weakness comes back on the sinner's head a thousandfold. In a gruesome messenger speech, we hear how Atreus butchered, fileted, and stewed Thyestes' children. Then we watch as Thyestes unknowingly consumes the horrid casserole.

In the play's final act, a gleeful, drunken Thyestes revels over his meal and, significantly, curses his former poverty; he has gone over to the world of pleasure and power that he once renounced. Atreus now enters to deliver the crowning blow. He reveals the severed heads of the sons on whom Thyestes has feasted. No deities have intervened to prevent this atrocity, and none care that it happened, as Seneca suggests in his nightmarish closing lines:

> THYESTES: *Gods will come to avenge me;*
> *To them I entrust your punishment.*
> ATREUS: *And I entrust your punishment—to your children.*

Thyestes can pray for justice as long as he likes, but the noisome contents of his guts are all that the play endorses as real.

There is nothing left for a cosmos that has beheld such horror except to fall and cease. In *Thyestes,* Seneca once again imagines the advent of apocalypse, the theme that had haunted his written works from their inception. In this case, a new kind of disaster is at hand—the disappearance of the sun, bringing darkness to Argos at daytime. No one in the play understands this phenomenon, but all are aware it portends something dire.

After Thyestes' cannibal banquet, not only the sun but the stars, too, seem about to vanish. The play's chorus members, the citizens of Argos, envision the zodiac tumbling into the sea, leaving only black void above:

> *Are we, out of all generations,*
> *deserving of the sky's collapse,*
> *its axis knocked from beneath its dome?*
> *Is it on us the last age comes?*
> *A harsh destiny has brought us to this:*
> *Wretches, either we lost our sun,*
> *Or else we drove it away.*

In these words we seem to hear Seneca's own voice, speaking about his own time. *Thyestes* is a bleak cri de coeur, the most despairing Seneca ever allowed himself to utter. For him, the benign stars of Corsica had been extinguished. His sky had become blind, black, untenanted.

Death was the only route out of the diseased world in which he dwelled, yet he lived on. The last words of the play's apocalyptic chorus sound the theme that preoccupied him in his last years, suicide:

> *Greedy for life is he who declines*
> *to die, along with the dying world.*

It is perhaps Seneca's exhortation to himself—or his self-reproach.

While Seneca was writing *Thyestes,* Lucan was working on a masterpiece of his own, the epic poem *Civil War*—but writing in a very different spirit than his uncle. Lucan was not ready to despair or withdraw into fatalism. He was certainly not ready to die. The young lion of the Annaeus clan was in his midtwenties and at the height of his extraordinary literary powers. As the second Neronia approached, he began to employ the potent weapon of his poetry toward a goal that most thought out of reach: standing up to Nero.

It had been otherwise five years earlier, when Lucan first arrived in Rome. He had recited *Praises of Nero* at the first Neronia, and in the prologue to *Civil War* had—apparently without irony—cautioned Nero to step carefully when he took his place among the constellations. He had eagerly adopted the ways of the court, where poets rose in stature the more highly they exalted the princeps.

Adored by both Seneca and Nero, gifted with prodigious talent, Lucan had then seemed destined for political or literary glory, or both at once. But talent, at Nero's court, was not always a blessing. The princeps, the more his own artistic ambitions grew, had become more jealous of his protégé. Relations went downhill, and Seneca's fall from favor accelerated the decline. Lucan continued to publish and read sections of *Civil War* but no longer with Nero's approbation. Indeed, the princeps broke up one recitation by abruptly calling the Senate into session, forcing most of the auditors, and Lucan himself, to go directly to the Senate house.

Lucan resented the emperor's small-mindedness, and resentment began to infect his verse. The subject matter of *Civil War*—the era of

Roman history that had brought Julius Caesar to power—was politically sensitive, though Lucan initially sought to avoid provocations. But as the poem progressed, its view of the house of Caesar became darker. By the time Lucan reached book seven—he completed ten books and intended at least two more—his verses had begun to border on sedition.

Acting either out of anger or envy, Nero banned Lucan from giving readings or publishing. Lucan only made his *Civil War* more polemical than ever. In book ten—the last book he was to complete—the murder of Julius Caesar was openly hailed as an *exemplum* for future generations. In private circles, Lucan began to circulate harsh verse lampoons of the princeps—the same crime, as he surely knew, that had nearly gotten Antistius condemned to death two years earlier.

Most likely it was now that Lucan uttered a bon mot that later became legendary. While using a public lavatory, he heard the sound of his own flatulence echoing through the hollow privy beneath him. His quick literary mind seized on an apt quotation—from the poetry of Nero. *You might think it had thundered beneath the earth,* Lucan intoned, gleefully spoofing the emperor's verse about an eruption of Mount Aetna. Those who heard him hastened to leave the latrine, fearing that their presence there put them in danger.

Lucan finally chose a direct line of attack. He unleashed his *De Incendio Urbis,* "On the Burning of the City," a work dealing with the still perilous topic of the great fire. It is now entirely lost, and its content is barely known—we cannot even say whether it was a poem or an essay—but one scant reference suggests that it held Nero to blame. In any case, merely to write publicly about the fire, an event that had deeply damaged Nero's reputation, was certain to offend the princeps. Seneca, in all the reams of prose he wrote in 64 and 65, never once mentioned it.

Could Lucan, or any writer, hope to escape with his life after exercising such license? Was the young genius courting arrest? It seems rather that Lucan was hopeful that the current regime would soon be over and that he would emerge into the next era as a hero of the opposition. For by late 64 or early 65, he had become a leading member of a plot to assassinate Nero.

. . .

Nero's assumption throughout his reign was that only a member of the Julian or Claudian family could rule Rome. Starting with his brother Britannicus and proceeding through Agrippina, Plautus, Sulla, Octavia, and most recently, Decimus Silanus, he had systematically killed off those who shared the blood of Augustus or of Augustus' wife, Livia. Now there was only one potential rival left: Junius Silanus, last scion of the doomed Silani, the great-great-great-grandson of Augustus. He remained untouched for the time being, but Nero watched him with unease.

Nero had tried to safeguard his rule by leaving Rome no alternatives. He, and the son he hoped to father with Poppaea, would be the only eligible members of the once-crowded imperial house. But the strength of this dynastic strategy had never been tested. The principate, after all, was not a monarchy. It was not clear that every princeps had to come from a single line. Acclamation by the Praetorian Guard was the best authority a new ruler could claim, and this potentially could be obtained by anyone.

Lucan and his fellow conspirators decided to test that possibility. They chose an amiable, flamboyant aristocrat, Gaius Calpurnius Piso, to be put in Nero's place, should they succeed in killing the princeps. Strangely, they bypassed Junius Silanus, the only male Julian left. Perhaps they regarded him as too young to rule; other young men who had taken the throne, first Caligula and now Nero, had been driven by it into self-absorption, delusion, and fantasies of omnipotence. That pattern, it was felt, could not be repeated.

A dynastic marriage was arranged for Piso, such that the Julio-Claudian house would not be wholly extinguished. It was planned that he would divorce his wife, a commoner ill suited to the throne, and marry Antonia, Claudius' daughter from an early marriage. Still in her midthirties, recently widowed by Nero's execution of her husband Sulla, Antonia had shown she was capable of bearing children, though the son she had borne to Sulla had not survived.

No one among the band of plotters dreamed of restoring the republic. Lucan was glorifying that long-ago world in his *Civil War,* but the values of epic poetry did not often carry over into political reality. Most in the Roman elite accepted the view that Seneca had expressed in *De Clementia*: autocracy had won. To imagine otherwise was to court a *new* civil war and social chaos. The best Rome could hope for, as the men behind Piso judged, was a milder, saner autocrat and a return of dignity to the Senate.

The conspiracy gained strong military support. Faenius Rufus, coleader—with Tigellinus—of the Praetorian Guards, was a crucial convert to its ranks. Rufus had fallen from favor as Tigellinus rose, since he declined to feed Nero's appetites and flatter his vanities as Tigellinus did. Nero had begun to treat Rufus with mistrust, even accusing him of having shared the bed of the hated Agrippina. A fall from grace, perhaps even a death sentence, was likely coming, unless Rufus struck first.

Other Praetorians joined the plot because Nero offended their soldiers' honor. Some were disgusted by a stagestruck princeps or one who raced as a charioteer. Others suspected Nero of having set the fire that destroyed Rome. Still others resented him for the murder of Agrippina, daughter of the great Germanicus, or for the deepening bankruptcy of the Roman state, provider of their generous salaries.

On the civilian side, adherents of the plot spanned the social scale. At the top were senators, among them consul-designate Plautius Lateranus, son of a hero of the conquest of Britain. Among the *equites,* Claudius Senecio, who had long been one of Nero's closest friends, vowed his support. At the bottom of the ladder was Epicharis, a clever Greek freedwoman and courtesan, at this time apparently the concubine of Annaeus Mela, Lucan's father and Seneca's brother. Despite her low station, Epicharis was among the most zealous conspirators, as the rest would soon learn—to their woe.

The plotters hoped to enlist Seneca in their cause. On several occasions, Piso, who had three years earlier been so close to Seneca as to bring suspicion on them both, wrote to the great sage requesting a parley. But Seneca put him off, claiming ill health and a desire to not be disturbed. Piso finally sent a go-between, Antonius Natalis, to persuade Seneca to meet with him in person.

The arrival of this messenger raised difficult questions for Seneca. At stake was the fate of a man whose life had intertwined with his own for nearly two decades. He had helped raise Nero from age thirteen and had been the closest thing to a father the princeps had. Clearly he had failed to instill in him any part of his own moral code. But had Nero become such a monster that Seneca wished him dead? Or would help kill him?

And what would become of the Roman state should the plot succeed? Seneca knew Piso well enough to see that he was no Augustus. Piso too might fall from favor, and the pattern of dislike leading to abuse, abuse leading to assassination, would set in all over again. In *De Clementia*, Seneca had described the Roman people as a mob needing to be controlled, liable to do itself much harm if it threw off its "yoke." Perhaps the harm even Nero might do was less grievous than the alternative.

Then, too, Seneca faced the ethical questions surrounding regicide. In *De Beneficiis*, he had written that a ruler who went utterly insane could be justly removed; assassination would in effect be a mercy killing. But such cases, Seneca went on to say, were freaks of nature, as rare as fires mysteriously spewing forth from underwater caverns. Even Caligula, he elsewhere implies, did not meet this threshold; still less then did Nero. Was the princeps so far gone in mind, in his late twenties, as to deserve death?

Finally, Seneca had to consider his own fate, his tenuous hold on life. Were his chances of survival better if he joined the plot or stayed out of it? Nero, if we trust the report in Tacitus, had already tried to have his former tutor poisoned. If the plotters succeeded in killing Nero, Seneca had nothing more to fear, but they might well fail. If so, Nero would seize any evidence as a reason to arrest Seneca—something he had thus far been unwilling to do. The death that would follow would be more painful than any poison.

Throughout his political career, Seneca, a practiced diplomat, had hedged bets and navigated between extremes. Now, at his most important crossroads, he once again temporized. He would neither join the conspiracy nor oppose it. His reply to Piso was this: it would not be in his own interest or in Piso's to meet or have further communication. But, he added, his own well-being depended on Piso's safety. The remark was an elaborate pleasantry, but it carried a tone of approbation; he seemed to be signaling he would not stand in the plotters' way. It was a sentence he would come to regret.

Perhaps one other consideration led Seneca to hold aloof. Tacitus reports a rumor that some of the Praetorians, led by one Subrius Flavus, intended to install Piso, then kill him in turn and put Seneca in his place. They regarded Seneca as a virtuous man who would command the respect of the public, while Piso, in their eyes, was a moral lightweight—a man who had demeaned himself by performing in tragic dramas. How would it ease Rome's shame, they asked, if a lyre player were removed from power but replaced by an actor? Tacitus states, but again only as a rumor, that Seneca was aware of this subconspiracy.

Of all the tantalizing but ambiguous clues to the mind of Seneca, this is surely the most tantalizing and the most ambiguous. It has no more substance than a story heard and recorded, several decades after the fact, by a man who was not sure he believed it. Yet Tacitus was not willing to dismiss it; nor are many modern historians. It raises the awesome possibility that Seneca, while holding back from action, had hopes of ending up the new princeps, the Western world's first philosopher king.

But it remains only that, a possibility, not subject to proof or refutation. Here is the greatest measure of how little, in the end, we understand Seneca, the man who tried his whole life to reveal his soul yet left so much opaque. After all his discussions of how and why to withdraw from political life, we cannot declare that the rumor Tacitus reported was groundless. We cannot know that Seneca, if Rome had acclaimed him, would have declined to rule.

Though it had many notable members, the conspiracy against Nero lacked leadership. Piso, with his charm and affability, stood high in the group's affections but proved unable to guide it toward action. Much time passed as the plotters debated when and where to carry out their deed. They had complacency on their side, for Nero had no cause to suspect an attack, but the odds of detection increased each day. In the end, it was Epicharis, the Greek freedwoman belonging to Seneca's brother's household, who, in an excess of zeal, forfeited the element of surprise.

Epicharis, weary of the constant debates and delays of her fellow conspirators, took it upon herself to push the plot forward. While in Campania on other business, she visited the naval squadron at Misenum, the sailors who had served Nero loyally and killed his mother for him. One of those assassins, a midlevel officer named Proculus, felt he had not gotten the rewards he deserved. He grumbled loudly about Nero to all who would hear, including Epicharis. She seized on the chance to recruit him. If Proculus would bring his sailors into the plot, she said, he would get his just rewards and more.

But Epicharis had misjudged Proculus' disaffection. He had only meant to vent his grievances, not avenge them. Appalled at Epicharis' suggestion, he took word of the interview straight to Nero.

Epicharis was brought in for questioning but denied everything. She had given Proculus no evidence of the plot nor disclosed any names, so the investigation went no further. But Nero had been put on alert. He kept Epicharis in his custody.

The plot that had moved so slowly now went into high gear, for the plotters expected to be betrayed. It was the middle of April; a yearly planting festival sacred to Ceres was set to begin. Though reclusive at other times, Nero would attend the closing ceremonies in the Circus Maximus, a structure already rebuilt after the fire nine months earlier. It was planned that Lateranus, a consul-designate who could get close to Nero, would take the emperor's knees as if making an appeal on some personal matter, then immobilize him. A similar strategy had been used against Julius Caesar more than a century earlier, with devastating effectiveness.

A senator named Flavius Scaevinus asked for the privilege of striking the first blow. He was hardly the obvious choice, as his life to that point had been marked by self-contentedness and soft living. But Scaevinus felt that his moment was at hand. He even procured a sacred dagger with which to stab Nero, an ancient relic that had been enshrined in a nearby temple, and he cherished this object with fetishistic care. On the night of April 18, just before the close of Ceres' festival, Scaevinus asked his freedman Milichus to sharpen and polish the dagger for him, and also to procure bandages and tourniquets for stanching blood.

Imperial freedmen had played many consequential roles over the past decades, but never before a *senator's* freedman, still less a senator's freedman's wife. The wife of Milichus, a woman whose name has gone unrecorded, became alert to Scaevinus' preparations. She convinced her husband that something was afoot, and that the rest of the household knew it. Milichus would lose a great reward if he were not first to give information to the palace, she argued. Indeed, merely by sharpening the dagger, Milichus had put his own life in danger.

At dawn on April 19, Milichus and his wife, bearing the sharpened dagger as evidence, made their way to the emperor's residence and gained an audience with Nero. Scaevinus was immediately seized and brought in to explain himself. Scaevinus defended himself with such vehemence that Milichus almost retracted his charge. But his wife was not going to let slip the prize that Fortune had dropped. She produced new information: that she had often seen Scaevinus in parleys with Antonius Natalis, a known associate of the doubtful Piso.

Now Natalis too was brought to the palace for questioning, and he and Scaevinus were taken to separate rooms. Both were asked for details of their recent conversations, and the details did not agree. Both were put in shackles, and implements of torture—used routinely on slaves and noncitizens, but only illegally, and in crises, on men of senatorial rank— were made ready. Following a pattern that has served tyrants well in every age, both men quickly confessed, each fearing that the other, when flayed or burned with hot irons, was bound to do so.

The most urgent task of the interrogation was to obtain names of accomplices. The accused gave them selectively, hoping to betray only enough confederates to secure their own safety. Scaevinus implicated Lucan and Senecio, both members of Nero's inner circle, along with several others. Natalis was the first to name the ostensible leader of the plot,

Gaius Piso. Then, in an effort to gain Nero's favor—for he knew how the princeps would be pleased—he named Seneca as well. Natalis himself had carried Seneca's strangely florid message to Piso, and he now repeated it to Nero: *My well-being depends on your safety.*

Meanwhile, word had leaked out to Piso and the other plot leaders that their plan had been betrayed. Piso's associates urged him to go at once to the Praetorian camp, or mount the speaker's platform in the Forum, and rally the city to his cause. Hatred of Nero was widespread; Piso might succeed in igniting an uprising. In any case, what did he have to lose? His life was forfeit; he could at least go out as a martyr, making a public show of resistance.

Piso wandered out into the streets of Rome, where, for most citizens, the day had begun like any other. The quiet and unconcern he found there must have struck him as cruel indifference. The effort needed to rouse this inert populace, the risk that torture might be inflicted on himself or his beloved wife, were too much to contemplate. He went back inside his home and waited for soldiers to arrive, then opened his veins. Like so many others of his class, senators whose will to fight had been ground down by a century of autocracy, Piso found it easy to give up. The slow oblivion of blood loss overcame him, and then all was peace.

In his will, composed in an effort to save his wife and family, Piso left behind exorbitant praise of Nero.

As he supervised the questionings and watched the list of accused grow, Nero saw his deepest misgivings confirmed. The political elite of Rome, high-minded senators and aristocrats, hated him as he had always sensed they did, hated him enough to kill him. Their moralizing had oppressed him for years. They seemed to share a single disapproving mind, a mind nurtured by the severe Stoic school that taught men to scowl and scold— the school of his former high counselor, Seneca.

Nero resolved to hit back with full force. He would sweep the board clean of his critics, the guilty along with the innocent. For as the circle of suspects widened, the line between guilt and innocence became blurry. Huge numbers of the upper class were known to be friends of those accused or had conversed with them recently. Even Seneca, though he had carefully avoided direct contact, had sent a message to Piso that seemed, to Nero at least, to imply collusion. Nero dispatched a Praetorian tribune, Gavius Silvanus, to find Seneca and confront him with this message.

Nero did not at this point realize that much of the military, including this same Gavius Silvanus, was involved in the plot. He still trusted the Praetorians, even their coprefect Faenius Rufus; he had assigned this man, who was in fact a conspirator, to head important interrogations. Faenius, clinging to the hope of evading detection, maintained a pretense of loyalty and cruelly abused his fellow plotters. Those he was now obliged to torture declined to denounce him, thinking Faenius could engineer their release, or even carry out the planned coup, if he stayed undercover.

That second goal was very nearly achieved. During one torture session, Faenius was assisted by another closet conspirator, Subrius Flavus, while Nero himself looked on. At a certain point, Flavus realized the absurdity, the bizarre futility, of what was taking place: of three men in the room who wanted Nero dead, two were attacking the third, while Nero stood by and watched, unarmed and outnumbered. Flavus used covert gestures to suggest to Faenius that they kill Nero then and there; he even began to draw his sword. But Faenius passed up the plot's unexpected second chance. He shook his head to Flavus and turned back to his work. The crackdown had gone too far, and he had too little nerve, for a sudden reversal of direction.

Meanwhile guards were spreading through the city to put the populace in a chokehold. Watches were posted on the old Servian wall, their presence visible to everyone, and at points along the Tiber where ships might try to enter—or leave. Squads of Praetorian toughs, their ranks strengthened by strapping Germans, shouldered their way through the Forum and broke into private homes, dragging away those wanted for questioning. Shackles and chains were no longer held in reserve but were slapped instantly onto all suspects. A great stream of manacled men surged toward Nero's residence, so many that the suspects had to be detained outside, near the gates, for lack of rooms to torture them in.

Immunity was promised to those who would implicate others, and many grasped at the slender hope that this bargain would be honored. The poet Lucan was one of them. Though he had been among the fiercest of the plotters, even offering Nero's head as a gift to several of his friends, the chance to preserve his own life, so young and full of promise, turned him compliant. He confessed his guilt and gave names of several accomplices, even throwing in that of his own mother, Acilia. If we believe Suetonius' cruel analysis, he hoped to please Nero, the killer of Agrippina, by joining him in matricide. Luckily, as Tacitus reports, Acilia was forgotten in the confusion and ultimately left alone.

One brave holdout refused to implicate anyone.

The freedwoman Epicharis, a member of Lucan's household and a fellow firebrand, was still in custody after denying her recruitment of Proculus at Misenum. Now Nero ordered torture—burning with red-hot plates and stretching on the rack—trusting that a woman's resolve could be easily undone. Epicharis, however, endured her ordeal in silence for the better part of a day. The next day her body was so badly broken that she had to be carried into the torture chamber on a chair. Nonetheless she managed, when left alone in the locked room, to undo her breastband, tie it in a noose, and hang herself, half naked, from the bars supporting the chair's canopy.

It was an episode that Seneca might have enshrined in *Letters to Lucilius,* amid his galleries of heroic suicides. A concubine and former slave, seemingly the lowest thing of Fortune, had found the ultimate freedom and power, the choice of her own death. Perhaps Epicharis' cause had utterly failed. But in Seneca's moral scheme, where self-destruction granted escape from oppression, this proud woman had *won,* defeating the aggregate might of the Roman state.

But Seneca was never to learn of Epicharis' end. Even as his brother's bedmate was being stretched on the rack, Praetorians, led by Gavius Silvanus, were surrounding the villa outside Rome where he was taking dinner with his wife, Paulina.

Seneca had arrived at this villa earlier in the day, returning from Campania to the outskirts of Rome. His movements, for once, are clear thanks to the detailed report of Tacitus, but his motives are as inscrutable as ever. Doubtless he knew the plot to kill Nero would go into motion that day. Was he hoping to be on hand to serve the new government, even to be hailed as princeps? Would he, like his mythic avatar Thyestes, have gone back to his Argos and drunk again from the poisoned chalice of power? Tacitus did not know and did not speculate. We too can only guess.

Seneca shared a simple meal with Paulina that night, for he had been avoiding foods that might conceal poison. Paradoxically though, even while he sought to elude Nero's toxins, he had collected some of his own, a cup of hemlock prepared as if for an Athenian state execution. One venom might have been thought as good as another, but the manner and mood of death mattered intensely to Seneca. For years he had contemplated and anticipated, in *Letters to Lucilius,* the last scene in the vivid drama of his life. Now his chance to play that scene, before an audience of friends and household staff, was at hand.

Fortunately for Seneca, a great dramaturge would immortalize that scene, using a report passed on by an admiring eyewitness. Tacitus, ever fascinated both by Seneca and by the ways great men met their dooms, made it one of the longest, most detailed, and most intense episodes of the *Annals.* He shaped it into a tour de force but left its tone ambiguous, reserving judgment on Seneca right up to the end. It is unclear whether he cast the man's final drama as tragedy or as satire, or as a modernistic melding of the two.

Among the scene's ironies was the fact that Silvanus, the captain of the squad sent to confront Seneca, was, like Faenius Rufus, an as-yet-undiscovered conspirator. That very morning, perhaps, he had anticipated coming to this villa to hail Seneca as princeps. But now, to avoid detection, he had to play his part, that of a steadfast Nero loyalist. On orders, he questioned Seneca about his recent exchange with Antonius Natalis. Had Natalis indeed tried to get Seneca to meet with Gaius Piso? And had Seneca sent him back to Piso bearing the strangely portentous message "My well-being depends on your safety"?

It mattered little how Seneca replied, for mere accusation gave Nero license to do as he liked. Nonetheless, Seneca gamely mounted a defense. He still might win clemency from the regime or at least respect from the two friends dining with him—witnesses who would transmit his last acts to the world. It was true that Piso had sought meetings, he told Silvanus, but he had rejected these requests. As for the fateful sign-off, Seneca had intended nothing by it, for he had no reason to so highly value the health of any man—except, he added significantly, that of a princeps. He had no reason to flatter Piso, for flattery was not his way, as Nero could himself attest. Indeed, he grandly claimed, the emperor had seen more of freedom than slavery in Seneca's behavior.

Silvanus returned to the palace and reported Seneca's words. Nero was closeted with his two closest advisers, Poppaea and Tigellinus. He asked whether Seneca was preparing to commit suicide. No doubt he hoped for a positive answer, for evidence was slight, and in the end evidence would be needed. Silvanus, however, said that Seneca showed no awareness of peril. Nero told him to return to the villa and deliver the emperor's verdict: death.

Silvanus did not obey. Though he knew the plot had collapsed, the actions required for Nero's reign to continue were more than he could endure. He made his way to his commanding officer and fellow conspirator, Faenius Rufus, to ask whether he should carry out his mission. Rufus ordered him to do so, but still Silvanus demurred. He could do nothing to save Seneca, but he could at least spare himself the taint of collusion. He asked another soldier to carry his fatal message and went on his way.

The double role Faenius Rufus was playing had helped none of the conspirators. They were getting weary of concealing it. Scaevinus, the first plotter to confess, was under interrogation by Faenius when his patience ran out. With witnesses standing by, Scaevinus replied knowingly to one of Faenius' questions: "No one knows better than you yourself; why don't you step forward and help out your great princeps?" Taken by surprise, Faenius turned white and began spluttering incoherently. The game was up, and he was soon under arrest.

After that, the military's huge role in the plot was unmasked. This led to some remarkable exchanges, as Nero questioned Praetorians who, with nothing left to fear, were blunt in their replies. Subrius Flavus explained to the emperor the origins of his disaffection. "No one in the army was more loyal to you than I—when you deserved our love," Flavus said. "But I began to hate you, after you became the murderer of your mother and wife, a chariot driver, an actor, and an arsonist." Tacitus remarks that nothing Nero heard during the crisis wounded him more than this terse catalogue of crimes.

A centurion named Sulpicius Asper was equally forthright in addressing Nero. Asper framed his defense in philosophic terms. Asked why he had joined the conspiracy, he replied, in Tacitus' account, "Because there was no other remedy for your atrocities" (or according to Dio, "It was the only way I could help you"). Seneca was not alone in seeking an ethical imperative for assassination.

One by one the soldier-conspirators were betrayed, arrested, and beheaded, willingly stretching their necks for their comrades' blades. Flavus is said to have looked impassively at his own grave as he went to the block, finding it too shallow. "Not even this is up to code," he sneered. The Rome he had been trained to serve, the Rome of Augustus and Germanicus, was gone. In its place stood Neronopolis, ruled by a megalomaniac brat.

The roll of accused civilians kept growing as well. Nero lengthened it by adding long-standing enemies, guilty or no. A sitting consul and close friend of the princeps, Atticus Vestinus, got onto the list, though he was implicated by no one. He had shown, with his abrasive jokes, that he knew too much about Nero and was not afraid of him. A squad of soldiers was sent to bring Vestinus in for questioning. Vestinus was feasting with friends when they arrived, making a good show of fearlessness. But one word of summons was enough to dispel the charade. He immediately opened his veins and retired to his bath to die. His dinner guests were detained at the table for hours, their terror furnishing sadistic amusement for Nero.

Soldiers bared their necks and senators slit their arms, all going passively, peacefully, resignedly to their dooms. Some even took their own lives *after* they were out of peril. Gavius Silvanus, who had refused to deliver Seneca's death sentence, was acquitted by Nero's inquisition but killed himself nonetheless. Perhaps the guilt of surviving a horrific purge was too much to live with, or else fear of retribution from the kin of the unlucky.

In the great catalogue of deaths that ends the extant text of Tacitus' *Annals*—a list so long that Tacitus fears it will bore and disgust his readers—only one man is said to have gone down fighting. Junius Silanus, the last male descendant of Augustus other than Nero himself, was in detention in the town of Barium when a soldier arrived to kill him. Though unarmed, Silanus fought back with all the strength he had, quipping to his assassin that he would not get a free pass for his job. He alone died in combat, wounds on the front of his body, rather than fading slowly away in the warm, languid waters of his bath.

In his prose treatises and in *Letters to Lucilius,* Seneca examined suicide from every angle, especially the question of when it was called for. Wasting disease might justify it, or the abuse of a cruel tyrant, or the certainty that death was coming soon in any case. As he awaited word from Nero's palace, Seneca might have reflected that though he was approaching a critical threshold in all three areas, he had not crossed it in any. He still might hope that banishment, not death, would be Nero's verdict. His philosophic stature might protect him, as it later shielded his fellow Stoic sage Musonius Rufus.

Seneca was also in mind of his wife, Pompeia Paulina, whose life in exile—if that was to be her fate—would be much harder without him. "Her *spiritus* depends on mine," he had written in one of the *Letters,* using the Latin word for the breath of life. "The *spiritus* must be called back as it flees—though in torment—out of reverence for our dear ones, and held on the tip of our lips. For a good man must live not as long as he wants, but as long as he ought." Those words might have recurred to him as he sat with Paulina, a woman who had never offended Nero but, if familiar patterns prevailed, would be considered guilty by association.

Then a centurion arrived from Rome, and all hope vanished.

Seneca asked the soldier if he might have access to his will. Apparently he wanted to deed part of his wealth—most of it was already in Nero's hands—to the two friends who were dining with him, sharers of his last hours. Nothing he might write now could stop Nero from seizing the whole estate, if he pleased, but the centurion nonetheless refused the request. Seneca explained to his friends, in the words of Tacitus, that he could thus leave them only the *imago* of his life, the one legacy over which he had control.

Imago is a multilayered word. Like its English derivative *image,* it can mean simply "shape" or "form." But it can also mean "illusion," "phantom," or "false seeming," something "imagined." Tacitus, a superb ironist and verbal artist, chose this word with care. Seneca, too, as Tacitus was aware, was a consummate ironist—an author who had painted his self-portrait in half a million words yet had never, in all his treatises, plays, and epistles, addressed the truths of his life in power. He had created an *imago* of himself since the day he began writing. He was shaping it still in his last hours, hastily revising an incomplete work and taking steps to ensure its survival.

But perhaps it was not too late to speak truth. In an effort to comfort his friends, who now had begun weeping and lamenting, Seneca pointed out that the current crisis had been predictable. "What was left to Nero, after the murders of his mother and brother, except to add that of his teacher and mentor?" he said. Seneca himself had helped conceal those two murders and had colluded in at least one of them. His blunt words,

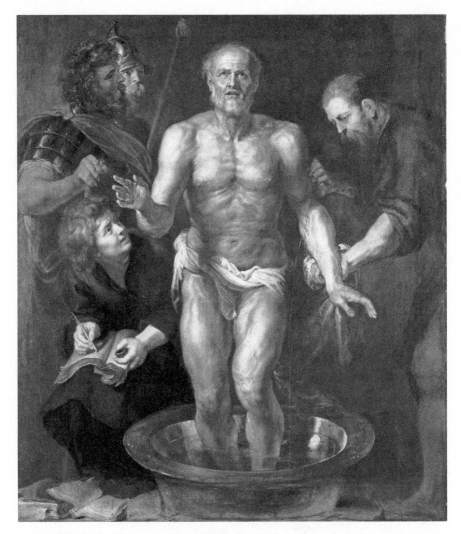

The death of Seneca, as depicted by Rubens in the early seventeenth century.
The philosopher's idealized features were taken from the bust
known today as Pseudo-Seneca (see pp. xiv–xvii).

spoken (in Tacitus' phrase) as if to Rome generally, seemed intended both
to expose them and to lay them squarely at Nero's feet.

Seneca had a cup of hemlock prepared for this moment, so that he
could die as Socrates had done five centuries earlier. But for some reason, he declined to use it, choosing instead a more Roman death, by

slow blood loss. Paulina, the wife who shared Seneca's peril, now said she wanted to share his fate, and he acceded to this. He and Paulina opened their veins, laying arms side by side so that one stroke of the knife could cross both. To one observer, this was a moment of moving marital harmony, but to another, it appeared that Seneca was forcing his wife to die. Thus do reports diverge, in this last and most extreme case, in the works of Tacitus and Dio.

When the blood didn't run fast enough from his arms, Seneca gashed himself behind the knees and around the ankles as well. He was in considerable pain, and he and Paulina dragged themselves to separate rooms to be spared the sight of each other's suffering. Attended by slaves, freedmen, and his two close friends, Seneca waited for death.

But death would not come. Seneca's aging veins, attenuated by meager diet, were not allowing enough blood to escape. His slow decline gave him time to dictate a last work to his scribes, presumably a moral essay, though Tacitus did not specify. Then he asked his friend Statius to bring him the long-reserved cup of hemlock, and swallowed it. The noxious drink had paralyzed Socrates within minutes, but somehow it had no effect in Seneca's case.

At last Seneca made his painful way to the baths of his villa and immersed himself in hot water. Still conscious enough to seek kinship with Socrates—who had died, according to Plato, vowing an offering to Asclepius, the god of healing—Seneca sprinkled some bathwater on the ground, saying he did so as a libation to Jupiter the Liberator. He was either beseeching, or thanking, the god for deliverance. Then, weakened by blood loss and sickened by hemlock but finally suffocated by hot vapor, Seneca breathed his last.

The most complex life of the Neronian age had ended fittingly, with the most complex death. Seneca's protracted, three-stage suicide had not gone at all according to plan, a plan he had contemplated for years. Yet it was his own distinctive construction, composed without interference from the soldiers. In the end, he must have been pleased with the autonomy and single-mindedness of his exit. It was the one thing he owned that Nero couldn't touch.

His body was cremated and the ashes interred without rites or ceremony, as he had requested in his will.

Miraculously, Paulina survived the night of April 19. Her arms were bound up by her slaves and her bleeding arrested. Some said it was on Nero's order, to lessen the infamy of Seneca's death; others said it was by her own wishes, after she realized Nero did not hate her and that her life as a widow might not be harsh. She survived a few years longer, pale and depleted by her ordeal.

She was, it would turn out, a rarity. All Seneca's other kin and associates were consumed in the inferno of Nero's wrath.

Lucan's death followed close on the heels of his uncle's. Though the young man had been promised amnesty in exchange for information, Nero was thoroughly sick of the poet who outshone him, and ordered his suicide. Lucan opened his veins and bled to death, retaining his literary gifts even as his limbs grew cold. It occurred to him at some point that he had written in *Civil War* about a soldier dying from blood loss, and as he expired he recited the verses from memory, perhaps these:

> *He fell, with all his veins burst open;*
> *No life ever fled by such a broad route. . . .*
> *The lowest part of his trunk surrendered its limbs to death,*
> *But where the lungs swelled, where organs were yet warm,*
> *the fates held on a long time.*

Lucan's father Mela, bereft now of his son and brother, soon found himself sucked into the fire's backdraft. The youngest of the Annaei had always steered clear of politics, preferring wealth to influence, but that preference led to his downfall. After inheriting Lucan's estate, he tried, perhaps too hard, to collect debts owed to his son. This irked a certain Romanus, probably one of the debtors, and Mela found himself denounced. A forged letter, tricked up to look like Lucan's, suggested that Mela had been part of his son's plot. Mela opened his veins as Lucan had done, after deeding most of his carefully hoarded estate to Nero's dreaded henchman, Tigellinus.

The oldest of the Annaei, Gallio, nearly escaped with his life, thanks to a sudden reversal of sentiment. The purge had almost run its course when Gallio was attacked by a senatorial foe, Salienus Clemens, as an enemy of the state. The senators present in the Curia sensed that things were going too far; public safety was being used as a pretext to act on private hatreds. Clemens was shouted down. Gallio got a reprieve but could not shake the ill fame that the charge had brought. He too became a victim of Nero's violence in the end.

Like the great fire that had preceded it, Nero's conflagration of killing appeared to die down but blazed up again with renewed force. A second round of executions, extending many months past the first, fell on men who could be tied to the Piso plot only by hearsay evidence. Gaius Petronius went down, according to Tacitus, merely because Tigellinus, jealous of a court rival, suborned testimony from a slave. This bon vivant made his death, like his life, that of an antiphilosopher, chatting merrily and trading light verse and jests with friends as he bled to death. His final composition, dictated in his last hours, was no moral treatise but an insider's guide to Nero's bizarre sex romps.

The fires raged on, consuming prose writer and poet, senator and soldier, moralist and merry hedonist. Rome was scorched clean of all whom Nero or Tigellinus considered threats. It was as though the *ekpyrosis,* the world-ending conflagration of the Stoics, had arrived but in a different form than expected. Rather than cleansing the world of a corrupt human race, the blaze claimed only the best and the brightest, the flowers of Rome's literary elite and military officer class.

Among the last to go into the inferno was Thrasea Paetus.

Noble Thrasea, so much revered for his effort to preserve dignity and avoid servility, had, like Seneca, stayed clear of the plot against Nero. Indeed, he had stayed out of public life entirely for the preceding three years. But that very withdrawal could be used against him. Cossutianus Capito, Tigellinus' son-in-law, caricatured Thrasea's proud solitude in a brutal Senate speech. The man was a new Cato, he claimed, a scowling secessionist using Stoicism to rally dissent. Moral gravity—the same quality that had helped bring Seneca low—could easily, in the carnival world of Neronopolis, be portrayed as a crime.

Thrasea was condemned by a Senate that met in the presence of Nero's armed troops. In a private room of his estate, accompanied by his son-in-law Helvidius and his Cynic guru Demetrius—the same man Seneca had admired and lionized in *De Beneficiis*—Thrasea had his veins opened. As his blood flowed onto the ground, Thrasea echoed Seneca's words—already well known by this time—and declared a libation to Jupiter the Liberator.

Tacitus quotes the final prayers of the two men in precisely the same language. Did he mean to link the two great Stoics, one who colluded with absolute power and one who opposed it, in an eternal bond of amity? Or was he contrasting a meaningful sacrifice, made in blood, with a more facile one done with bathwater?

Only one man, according to Tacitus, sought to stop the purge before it claimed Thrasea's life. An ardent young tribune named Arulenus Rusticus offered to use his power of veto to overturn Thrasea's conviction. But Thrasea himself forbade it. He pointed out that the veto would be overridden and would likely cost Rusticus his life. "You're only at the beginning of your career in office," he counseled the young man. "Consider well what path you will walk, in times like these, through politics."

After all the deaths he had witnessed, on the verge of meeting his own, Thrasea could advise only nonresistance. Rome was better off, he felt, with good men like Rusticus compromising their principles. Better they stay in public life, and lend it some shred of moral dignity, than hurl themselves into the flames.

The time of the second Neronia was at hand. The nightmares of April— the month now known, by decree of the Senate, as *Neroneus*—had passed, and Rome was slowly stabilizing. Nero had achieved an annihilation of his aristocratic opponents, guilty and innocent alike. But there was one victory he still hungered for, a prize that had eluded him for years, largely because Seneca had kept it from him.

Nero had by now sung in Neapolis and on other regional stages, but he longed for the acclaim that only Rome could grant. He planned to make his Roman debut at the Neronia, but the prospect horrified the Senate, even a Senate stripped of the noncompliant. The senators tried to forestall the debacle by voting the princeps first prize in advance. But Nero turned this diplomacy aside, vowing to defeat all comers in a genuine, unbiased musical contest.

Nero took the stage of Pompey's Theater and recited a poem of his own composition, a miniepic about the Trojan War. Then he tried to exit, but a faction of the crowd, coached in advance, shouted their demand to hear the "divine voice." Nero offered them a private performance in his gardens, but the crowd kept chanting, and Praetorians approached Nero to beseech him on its behalf.

Finally Aulus Vitellius—son of Claudius' most supple courtier, now following his father's profession—made himself spokesman for the crowd and, in a carefully choreographed sequence, demanded aloud that Nero enter the citharode contest.

Feigning reluctance, Nero cast his token into an urn, signifying he would compete. When his turn to perform arrived, the crowd beheld the strangest spectacle yet of the many Nero had provided. There was the princeps, dressed in a long flowing robe and high boots, with the two Praetorian prefects carrying his lyre, and a file of soldiers and senators behind them. An ex-consul, Cluvius Rufus, stepped onto the stage to announce the emperor's aria. The princeps, he said, would sing *Niobe,* the lament of mythology's most tragic woman, a mother bereft of her children.

With the focus and earnestness of a diva, Nero launched into his song. Observing competition rules, he declined to clear his throat, to use a cloth to wipe sweat from his brow, or to sit down, though the song went on for hours. When he finally concluded, late in the afternoon, he humbly bent down upon one knee in a gesture of deference. The crowd raised a mighty cheer, employing the applause cadences first introduced and now led by the Augustiani, the emperor's hired claque.

Among the crowd walked Nero's soldiers, newly confirmed in their loyalty. Some had helped execute their comrades, even commanders, in the recent purge; all had received a bonus of two thousand sesterces, plus a lifetime allowance of cost-free grain. The imperial treasuries were already exhausted, but Nero had to go deeper in debt if his regime was to stay in power.

The Praetorians observed carefully who in the crowd failed to applaud and who had fallen asleep while Nero sang. They beat and struck the commoners who did not clap loudly enough and those who disrupted the fine rhythms of the Augustiani by clapping out of time. Men of higher rank had their names taken down so that punishment could be enforced later on. At the theater entrances, panicked throngs were trying to shove their way in—now aware that absence from the performance might be a criminal offense.

Buoyed up by the wild cheering, Nero gazed into the stands and savored the fruits of victory. He was rid of Seneca, and the old moralist's tiresome restraints, forever. He had killed off his enemies and rivals, along with his mother, wife, and stepbrother; he had terrorized Rome into adoring him. He could at last take center stage in the greatest city on earth. His new golden age had begun.

Euthanasia

(A.D. 68 AND AFTER)

Seneca allegedly once told Nero—the occasion of the remark is not known—"No matter how many you kill, you can't kill your successor." But in this case, as in many others, Nero proved his teacher wrong. He had indeed eliminated all possible successors, men belonging to the Julian line, by the end of 65.

Even those outside the family who fancied themselves rivals had been done away with. Nero's stepson Rufrius Crispinus, the child of his wife Poppaea by a previous marriage, was killed after imprudently impersonating a princeps in some of his childhood games. Nero sent him on a fishing trip in an open boat, then had his slaves toss him over the side and leave him to drown.

While rubbing out successors whom he feared and dreaded, Nero also caused the death of one he desperately wanted. Poppaea was pregnant in the summer of 65, perhaps with the son who would cement Nero's rule. But just after the second Neronia, the princeps, riding high on a wave of acclaim for his singing, threw a tantrum at Poppaea. Suetonius says she had carped at him for coming home late from the chariot races—an endearingly domestic vignette. Whatever the cause of his rage,

Nero kicked his beloved wife hard enough to cause internal bleeding and the death of both mother and fetus.

Nero never fathered another child. He tried to wed Antonia, daughter of Claudius, but she would not have him, and he killed her for intransigence. Instead he married Statilia Messalina, a noblewoman in her early thirties, with whom he had already carried on an affair. But Statilia never became pregnant. Perhaps Nero missed Poppaea too much to make the effort; he allegedly had Sporus, his male castrato love pet, made up to look like the woman he had adored.

Nero tried to replace familial love with celebrity. He toured the Greek world as a citharode and competed for age-old musical prizes, winning every time. He staged a fantastic ceremony in Rome for the visit of Tiridates, an Armenian king who had come to pledge subservience. He received this pledge in the Theater of Pompey, the place of his earlier singing triumph, on a stage that had been covered with sheets of gold.

Nero spent wildly on such spectacles, bankrupting the state but winning the hearts of the masses. The aristocracy, however, whose fortunes helped fund his debauches, were not so easily impressed. Nor was the army, defenders of a stauncher, less decadent ethos.

In the spring of 68, three years after quashing the conspiracy against his life, Nero faced rebellion—not within Rome this time, but in the camps of the provincial legions. By summer, he had so lost control of events that he faced the question his teacher Seneca had once pondered: whether to wait, patiently and passively, for a death that is sure to come, or forestall it by taking one's own life.

At the time of the crisis, Nero had poison with him, since Locusta, his staff toxicologist, had prepared a special draught. In early June 68, when rebellion had swelled to the point that Nero was planning to abdicate, he placed this venom in a golden box and kept it with him, but only as a last resort. He had plans for his future—several conflicting ones that, in his panic, he pursued all at once. He would get the Praetorians to accompany him and take flight in a ship; he would seek asylum with the Parthians; he would go to Alexandria and devote himself to a performing career; he would appeal to Rome by making a public address in the Forum, begging for a second chance as princeps. While he pondered these alternatives and slept fitfully in his palace, his bodyguard removed the golden box from his room and deserted.

It is strange that the Praetorians, who had long propped Nero up but now turned against him, chose neither to kill him nor allow him access to Locusta's toxins. One of the soldiers supposedly asked Nero, as the princeps cast about desperately for a means of escape, "Is it as awful as that, to die?" The line is from Vergil's *Aeneid,* where it is spoken by the great warrior Turnus. The soldier was challenging Nero to live up to the martial code of that epic hero—to die by the blade, his own or another's, rather than by the gentle oblivion of poison.

Seneca, had he lived, would have appreciated the irony: his wayward pupil, in the end, became a student of his hardest lesson. The questions of when and how to die had preoccupied Seneca in his last years. Seneca too had stored up poison, the means to a clean, quiet end, but in the event he had preferred the blade and the shedding of blood. Even that had not killed him, but Seneca had suffered in death, a point he considered crucial. It was what set Cato, Seneca's great moral hero, apart from ordinary men.

Nero woke in the middle of the night to find the palace guard posts abandoned. He called out for a gladiator named Spiculus, one of his favorites, or some other *percussor*—expert swordsman—to come to his aid. He felt now that his life must end, but he wanted a capable executioner to end it. Instead two Greek freedmen, Phaon and Epaphroditus, answered the summons, and Sporus, the youth whom Nero had dressed to resemble Poppaea. Along with one or two others, they became Nero's last cohort and honor guard. They disguised the princeps and helped him sneak out of Rome, a city that was already at that moment declaring allegiance to Galba, one of the mutinous legionary commanders.

Huddled on a thin mattress in a villa outside Rome, aware now that the Senate had declared him a public enemy, Nero contemplated his choices. He had brought two daggers with him—not sacred objects, like the blade once sharpened for his murder, but adequate to their task. As his companions dug a shallow trench for his burial, Nero tested the daggers' points against his skin. The sensation was more than he could bear. He replaced them in their sheaths, telling his entourage, "The fated hour is not yet here."

But the pain he would undergo if he was captured was far worse than a knife thrust. His companions described for him the requisite punishment: Nero would be held immobile with his neck in the fork of a tree, then beaten to death with stout rods. His ravaged corpse would be flung from the Tarpeian Rock, in imitation of the death reserved for Rome's worst criminals. These were agonizing details, for Nero had become morbidly anxious about mutilation of his body. In his last hours, he several times begged his loyalists not to allow his captors to sever his head.

As mounted soldiers approached the villa, Nero begged piteously for one of his companions to "show by example how to achieve death." Staff members of other imperials had, out of devotion or desperation, followed their masters to the grave. Nero, uniquely, was asking that someone precede him. No one responded to his plea. Then hoofbeats were heard on the ground outside, and Nero could postpone his choice no longer.

As he picked up one of his daggers, he might have reflected on the writings of Seneca, if he had ever read them. The power to die, Seneca had promised, was present at every moment and transcended every oppression. Any vein in one's body, he had written in *De Ira*, furnished a high road to freedom. Even a German slave forced to fight in the ring, the lowest of the low in Roman society, had found this road, though guarded night and day. In the solitude of a privy, he had choked himself on a lavatory sponge.

Nero grasped a dagger firmly and struck it into his throat. It was a desperate move, for killing oneself in this way, by severing the carotid artery, was difficult. Perhaps he was afraid to attack his vital organs, or unsure that his dagger would reach them beneath layers of clothing and fat. Or perhaps he needed to punish his "divine voice," now that his singing career had brought ruin on Rome and on himself. Whatever his reasons, he made only a painful and bloody, but not fatal, incision. It appeared that the soldiers were going to take him alive after all.

The freedman Epaphroditus now stepped forward to perform a

last service for his master. He took hold of the dagger and enlarged the wound, opening the vital artery. Almost thirty years later, he would pay with his life for this act of mercy, when another besieged princeps, Domitian, wanted to make a point about assassination. Nero was still conscious enough to perceive that he was being euthanized. He was grateful and rasped out through his injured throat, "*This* is loyalty."

A centurion burst into the room and found Nero lying on the floor, still barely alive, blood streaming from his neck. The soldier made a desperate effort to stanch the wound with the edge of his cloak—seeking to preserve Nero's life, so that it could be driven out more painfully and publicly, in the center of Rome, with thousands taking part. But the princeps knew he had found freedom at last. "Too late," he said, as though in triumph, and died.

Nero was dead at age thirty-two, having ruled since before his seventeenth birthday. By his crackdowns of 65 and 66, the savage purge that took the lives of Lucan, Thrasea Paetus, Seneca and his brothers, and many more, he had bought himself less than three more years on the throne, time he had largely squandered on singing tours in the East. Rarely in dynastic history has such a small gain been won at such a steep price.

Nero was buried as he had lived, with extravagant expense. His first love, the freedwoman Acte, still devoted despite his stunning decline, oversaw the interment of his ashes in a coffin of fine stone, in the tomb of a father he never knew.

The Julian line had come to an end. Nero had survived in power long enough to eliminate all potential heirs. The principate was up for grabs, and many pairs of hands were reaching to grab it. Rome was destined for a four-way civil war, though mercifully it lasted only a year. A new imperial family, led by the general Vespasian and his son Titus, took over the palace, and a new dynasty was begun.

As Rome recovered stability, it looked back at the era of Nero and the curious man who had loomed so large in it, the philosopher Seneca. The long debate over who this man was, and whether he should be admired or hated, had begun. It has not yet ended.

Seneca's prose works were by this time all the rage among Roman youth. Quintilian, a literary critic, wrote that they were "in everyone's hands" while he was young himself (perhaps meaning in the 60s and 70s). The trend worried him because he disapproved of Seneca's epigrammatic style and feared that readers would be seduced by it. Fortunately, Quintilian remarks in his *Institutio Oratoria* (a work written in the 90s), the young men of Rome loved reading Seneca but did not want to write like him. Their more learned elders, he says, never went for Seneca's bait.

Seneca's tragedies too were attracting fans in the years after his death, whatever their diffusion in his lifetime. Someone living in Pompeii scrawled a half-line from his play *Agamemnon* on a wall: "I see the groves of Mount Ida" (*Idai cernu nemora*). The quote seems to have no particular reference; it was merely a phrase the graffitist admired or could not get out of his head. When Pompeii was covered in volcanic ash in 79, the inscription was preserved, along with many other scribblings on the town walls. Someone else in Pompeii wrote Seneca's name, slightly misspelled, perhaps in the way a modern fan might scrawl the name of a celebrity, and this too has survived.

Another admirer of Seneca's tragedies left behind a play modeled after them. That play, *Octavia,* stands as the greatest Roman tribute to Seneca—an imitation that attests to his stature as author, and a stirring portrait of his efforts to uphold moral politics. Whoever composed it followed Seneca's verse style so closely that the play was long thought to be the work of Seneca himself, as it is identified in manuscripts. One or two scholars still believe that today, though most agree it should be deattributed.

The author of *Octavia* gave his hero a star turn in one long scene of the play. He showed "Seneca" trying, earnestly but in vain, to correct Nero's abuses and guide him to a better path. He depicted this sage lamenting his departure from Corsica and longing to be back under the benign night sky. The speech suggests that the question of what had brought Seneca into Nero's palace—his own ambition, or forces beyond his control—was a cardinal one for the generation that had witnessed his rise and fall. This author holds *impotens Fortuna*, a fate that could not be resisted, to blame.

Other literary men who survived the reign of Nero paid their tributes to Seneca's memory, some of them hard to decipher. Pliny the Elder, who died in the volcanic eruption that buried Pompeii, awarded Seneca the admiring title *princeps eruditorum*, "princeps of the wise." In its literal meaning, the phrase merely proclaims Seneca wiser than his peers, but in common usage the word *princeps* of course had larger resonance. Pliny perhaps meant to throw a barb at Seneca's palace career with this ironic phrase, or perhaps he only intended a wry compliment. Perhaps he alluded to the rumor reported by Tacitus, which, if true, meant that Seneca had missed, by the slimmest of margins, the chance to become princeps himself.

The satirist Juvenal was a child during Nero's reign, but perhaps he could remember the strange political partnership that dominated it. He included a memorable passage in his eighth satire, a long rant on the follies of Rome's class prejudices: "If the people were given a vote, who is so far gone in vice / as to hesitate before picking Seneca over Nero?" And then came Tacitus, whose multilayered and ambivalent account of Seneca has been explored extensively in this book.

Seneca's critics were also active in the years after his death. Their names are largely unknown to us, but their views can be found in the pages of Cassius Dio. They restated the charges first made by Suillius in his Senate attack and rebutted by Seneca in *De Vita Beata*: it was sheer hypocrisy, they said, for a Stoic sage to gather a huge fortune, or for a lover of freedom to work hand in glove with a princeps. They tried to make *tyrannodidaskalos*, "tyrant teacher," Seneca's epitaph, rather than Pliny's *princeps eruditorum*. In the eyes of many today, they succeeded.

Perhaps the most apt judgment on Seneca's career can be taken from something Quintilian said in his *Institutio Oratoria*. On its surface the remark applies to Seneca's literary style, but it seems to reach beyond that and into the realms of morality, politics, and character—the arenas in which Seneca's strange drama played out.

"There is much we should approve in him, much that we should even admire," Quintilian wrote. Then he urged Seneca's readers to be selective in winnowing out good prose from bad, saying: "Only take care in making your choice." Finally he added, speaking this time of Seneca, "If only *he* had taken that care."

The Stoic movement at Rome, though deeply damaged by the deaths of Seneca, Lucan, and Thrasea Paetus and the exile of many others, was not defeated. Some important leaders survived the great purge of 65 and 66, including Helvidius Priscus, Thrasea's son-in-law and protégé, and Demetrius the Cynic, once guru to Thrasea and Seneca. Both these men, along with the famed Etruscan sage Musonius Rufus, hurried back to Rome after Nero's death, determined to continue their cause.

They were angry now at injustices that had been done. Helvidius tried to get revenge for his father-in-law's death by indicting one of those who engineered it; but so many senators had colluded in Thrasea's downfall that, he came to feel, any prosecution risked starting a new purge. Musonius, however, succeeded in gaining the conviction of Egnatius Celer, a Stoic turncoat who had betrayed his great teacher, Barea Soranus, in exchange for vast rewards. In the early days of the new princeps, Vespasian, it was Celer who was in disrepute, and a death sentence was easily procured.

Helvidius, who had stood by in silence when Thrasea opened his veins, had been made militant by the abuses of the Neronian age. He became determined not to knuckle under, not to allow Vespasian to believe that autocracy had won. He refused to address the new princeps by his imperial titles or to acknowledge his sovereignty over state finance. In verbal showdowns with Vespasian, Helvidius disregarded Thrasea's advice, once given to the headstrong tribune Rusticus, to bend himself to the temper of the times. Helvidius dared Vespasian to exile him or kill him, claiming those were the only ways to curb his tongue.

It was not long before the regime of Vespasian went down Nero's path with regard to the Stoics. *Delatores* seeking the emperor's favor again depicted the sect's solemnity as a kind of sedition. Vespasian took drastic action in 71, banishing all Stoics and Cynics from the city of Rome; he even sent some of the more extreme agitators to the Pontine Islands. Helvidius, of course, he had killed. For the first time in the principate, Rome saw the systematic repression of an entire school of thought.

For unknown reasons, Vespasian allowed one sage, Musonius Rufus, to stay in Rome during this diaspora and continue giving lectures. Attending these talks was a young man, a foreign-born slave, whose name would soon be known across the Roman world: Epictetus. Once a member of Nero's staff—he belonged to Epaphroditus, the freedman who had helped Nero die—Epictetus somehow obtained freedom and began giving philosophic lectures of his own, attracting even bigger crowds than those of Rufus.

As Vespasian's reign gave way to those of his two sons, first Titus and then Domitian, new crackdowns on Stoicism caused new heads to roll. One man died for writing an admiring biography of Helvidius Priscus; another, the still-unbowed Rusticus, for memorializing Thrasea Paetus. Helvidius' son, Thrasea's grandson, was executed for writing a mythic play that carried (in Domitian's eyes at least) political overtones. It seemed that each new generation of Stoics was destined to suffer new rounds of persecution, as each new princeps sought targets for his cruelty.

Domitian again, as his father had done, banished the Stoics from Rome, including Epictetus, whose magnetic personality had by now become a phenomenon. Epictetus landed in Nicopolis, in the Greek East, and began attracting new followers. His conversations and quips were written down by one of them, young Arrian of Nicomedia (later a famous historian), and began circulating as the *Discourses* and *Encheiridion* ("Handbook"). In time these writings, in Greek, filtered back to Rome, where they came under the eyes of an aristocratic youth named Marcus Aurelius Antoninus. One day, after his elevation to princeps, this Marcus would quote the sayings of Epictetus in his own writings—bringing Stoic philosophy back into the palace from which it had been exiled since the death of Seneca.

Marcus Aurelius achieved, a century after Seneca had sought it, the reconciliation of Stoic morality and Roman political authority, a development as pathbreaking as Nero's ill-fated fusion of the roles of princeps and performing musician. The record Marcus left behind of his thoughts and musings, *Meditations,* still inspires countless readers today. It has appeared in no fewer than six new editions during the year this book was written. It attests to the power of ethical teachings to enlighten even an autocrat, if only he is willing to listen.

Had Seneca lived a century later than he did, he might have sat at Marcus Aurelius' right hand, rather than serving as Nero's footstool. But at least history in the end bore out the thesis on which Seneca had based his life: that moral gravity was not out of place in the halls of imperial power. The Romans had at last gained what many of them, apparently, had hoped that Seneca, despite all his flaws, might be: a philosopher king.

Acknowledgments

I have many to thank for helping me through the moral thicket of Seneca's life. Among the scholars I consulted, Elaine Fantham, Miriam Griffin, Harry Evans, and Gareth Williams were generous with their time, as were Shadi Bartsch, Ted Champlin, Robert Kaster, and James Ker. Emily Wilson has been a comforting fellow laborer as we both worked on studies of Seneca (mine went to press before I was able to consult hers). Outside the academy, Dan Akst, Bryan Doerries, Pam Mensch, and Matthew Stewart helped me solve some of this book's problems, or at least offered solace when I could not solve them at all.

Much of this book was written at the Dorothy and Lewis B. Cullman Center for Writers and Scholars at the New York Public Library, and I want to thank the Center's marvelous staff, in particular Jean Strouse and Marie D'Origny, and NYPL generally. All of my Cullman colleagues encouraged this work, particularly Annette Gordon-Reed, Larissa MacFarquhar, and Andy Stott, to whom I am grateful.

Deep thanks go also to my agent Glen Hartley, cartographer Kelly Sandefer, art researcher Ingrid Magillis, bibliographer Cara Wasserstrom, illustrator Mark Boyer, editorial assistants Charlotte Crowe and Audrey Silverman, copy editor Janet Biehl, proofreaders Benjamin Hamiton and Bert Yaeger, and production editor Victoria Pearson.

Jim Ottaway, my friend and fellow philhellene, lent his expert eye and sharp pencil to the effort of improving an early draft.

My final thanks go to Vicky Wilson, an editor who can inspire the sense that writing books still matters, and writing them well matters intensely.

Notes

xiv *relied on earlier writers:* The sources Dio relied on, at least one of whom held a positive view of Seneca, are discussed by Miriam Griffin in *Seneca: A Philosopher in Politics* (Oxford, 1976), pp. 428–33. It has proven impossible thus far to determine just what these sources were. For more discussion, see T. D. Barnes, "The Composition of Cassius Dio's *Roman History,*" *Phoenix* 38 (1984): 240–55. One specialist on the play *Octavia* regards it as having been written to answer the critics cited by Dio; see p. 71 of Rolando Ferri, ed., *Octavia: A Play Attributed to Seneca* (Cambridge, 2003), p. 71.

xiv *Our most detailed account of Seneca:* A wide range of opinion has been expressed about Tacitus' views of Seneca, which itself is a testament to their ambivalence. The discussion prior to 1976 is summarized nicely by Griffin (*Seneca,* p. 441), who then lays out her own largely positive reading. More recent contributions to the discussion are Ronald Mellor, *Tacitus' "Annals"* (Oxford, 2011), pp. 165–70; James Ker, "Tacitus on Seneca," forthcoming in *The Blackwell Companion to Tacitus,* edited by V. Pagán; and many stretches of Ker, *The Deaths of Seneca* (Oxford, 2009), especially pp. 41–49. My own view falls closely into line with that of W. H. Alexander, "The Tacitean '*non liquet*' on Seneca."

xiv *the face of a businessman or bourgeois:* "The bust does not . . . leave the impression of a man weighed down by deep, introspective speculations. It is rather a likeness of a man occupied with less weighty matters." H. W. Kamp, "Seneca's Appearance," *Classical Weekly* 29 (1935): 50. The Penguin Classics edition of *Seneca: Letters from a*

Stoic (Robin Campbell, translator), which used to feature the Berlin bust of Seneca as its cover image, has recently replaced it with a bust of Pseudo-Seneca.

xv *a model for painters:* As discussed in Ker, *Deaths of Seneca,* pp. 299–310.

xv *especially in his relationship to wealth:* This has always been the primary arena of attacks on Seneca's "hypocrisy," starting with Suillius Rufus in Seneca's own day (see pp. 102–3 in this book) and continuing today. Miriam Griffin ("*Imago Vitae Suae,*" p. 55), whose view of Seneca is generally positive but highly nuanced, admits in her uniquely personal discussion that however one tries to rationalize Seneca's riches, "the discrepancy between words and deeds remains."

xviii *to "feel out" that influence:* The approach that Griffin (*Seneca,* p. 412) labels "positivism"—"the explanation of a literary work by its outward circumstances"— has been variously endorsed or rejected by interpreters of Seneca, and some of them will no doubt feel I have carried it too far in this book. But it seems to me that, once this approach is admitted at all—and very few dismiss it altogether—it is difficult to limit its application. Even Karlhans Abel, who strongly criticized the positivist approach in his *Bauformen in Senecas Dialogen* (Heidelberg, 1967), none-theless used it in the case of *Consolation to Helvia* and *Consolation to Polybius,* and Griffin expressed surprise that he had not added *De Vita Beata* to the list. Once one has accepted that "secondary purposes" intrude into Seneca's treatises, causing "oddities of emphasis and argument" (Griffin, *Seneca,* p. 407), one cannot easily say which passages are "odd" enough to qualify and which are not.

xviii *"Seneca was a hypocrite":* The opinion of the ever-provocative Robert Hughes in *Rome: A Cultural, Visual, and Personal History* (New York, 2011), p. 104.

xviii *a news item appeared:* The May 2013 graduation from Columbia of Gac Fillipaj, who credited Seneca as his inspiration, was covered by numerous news outlets.

CHAPTER I: SUICIDE (I) (A.D. 49 AND BEFORE)

3 *The most likely candidate was then twelve years old:* The date of Nero's birth is generally agreed to be December 15, A.D. 37, the date given by Suetonius (*Nero* 6.1). See the discussion by Barrett in *Agrippina,* p. 234. Suetonius has erred at *Nero* 7.1 when he says that Nero began lessons with Seneca at age eleven; he was in fact twelve. See Griffin, *Seneca,* p. 420.

4 *had dismissed her stepson's tutors:* Tacitus, *Annals* 12.41.8; see p. 42 in this book.

4 *or so she hoped:* The reasoning Agrippina used in arranging Seneca's recall is reported by Tacitus at *Annals* 12.8. There Tacitus mentions that Seneca's trustworthiness would be assured by his *memoria beneficii,* "recollection of a good deed," a phrase often thought to refer to some prior benefaction by Agrippina but possibly indicating the recall itself. G. W. Clarke has proposed in "Seneca the Younger Under Caligula" that the *beneficium* in question was the rescue of Seneca's life when, in an incident related by Dio, Caligula had decided to take it, but this is pure speculation.

5 *I was better off hidden away:* *Octavia*, lines 381–90, with the textual emendations accepted by Rolando Ferri. Seneca blames his change of status on Fortuna, a force to which (as Ferri points out, p. 229) the Stoics did not normally accord such high regard.

5 *he hoped to go to Athens, not Rome:* A report attributed to Probus by the scholium to Juvenal's *Satires,* 5.109, but treated with grave skepticism by scholars. It is noteworthy that Seneca, unlike other aspirants to philosophic wisdom (including his nephew Lucan), showed no desire to go to Athens in his youth, when he still had freedom of movement.

6 *at the feet of Attalus:* Attalus was the most prominent of several teachers whom Seneca remembered fondly later in life; he was also praised by Seneca's father (*Suasoriae* 2.12). The debt Seneca felt he owed to Attalus is elucidated at *Letters* 9.7 and 67.15 as well as in long sections of *Letter* 108, the source of the passage quoted here.

6 *Seneca briefly adopted their practice:* Seneca's flirtation with Pythagoreanism is discussed in *Letter* 110, sections 17–23.

6 *Quintus Sextius:* Seneca recalled the influence of this Roman philosopher at *Letters* 73.12–15, 98.13 (which notes Sextius' rejection of senatorial office), and 59.7 (which contains the passage referred to on p. 7 in this book, on virtue as a military struggle). In *De Ira* 3.36, Seneca took Sextius as his model for a famous exercise in self-examination, discussed in this book in Chapter 3, pp. 68–69.

6 *almost hurled himself out a window:* Anecdote related by Plutarch, *Moralia* 77e.

7 *avoiding mushrooms and oysters:* Self-reported by Seneca at *Letters* 108.15: "These are not foods but spurs to compel those already full to eat more." In the same passage Seneca declares that "my stomach lacks wine," sometimes interpreted to mean that he was a lifelong teetotaler, but this is surely pressing the statement too hard. It is

difficult to imagine that the man who spent sixteen years at the imperial court, and who owned and managed some of Rome's most productive vineyards, had never taken a drop.

7 *entered the Senate:* The evidence on which to date this crucial turn of events is slim. Most likely Seneca reached the Senate in the late 30s, when he was around forty years old. That is a late start for a Roman political career. Griffin (*Seneca*, p. 46) thinks that the timing suggests "simple disinclination" toward politics. Her view is approved by Brad Inwood ("Seneca in his Philosophical Milieu," *Harvard Studies in Classical Philology* 97 [1995], pp. 64–66), who further speculates that Seneca was pressured into a political career he didn't want (while also admitting that "we shall . . . never know" his true motivations). The desire to see disinclination in this delay is indicative of the view that both Griffin and Inwood (and others) hold of Seneca, exemplified by the subtitle to Griffin's book, *A Philosopher in Politics*—which defines Seneca as a moral thinker first and foremost and characterizes his political career as something secondary, perhaps accidental. My own approach puts Seneca's political and philosophic/literary selves on an even footing and even at times subordinates the latter to the former. I am almost prepared to invert Griffin's formulation and characterize Seneca as "a politician in philosophy."

7 *His clan, the Annaei, were* equites: Attested by Tacitus, *Annals* 14.53, and implied by Seneca the Elder in the preface to *Controversy* 2, section 3. In the early principate, equestrian rank required an estate of more than 100,000 *denarii,* though property alone was not sufficient to ensure appointment to the order.

7 *the elder Seneca gave a qualified blessing:* Preface to *Controversy* 2, section 4. One gets a glimpse of Seneca the Elder's parenting style in this preface, which is addressed to all three sons yet clearly marks out the youngest as his father's favorite.

9 *the portent she saw at her son's birth:* Suetonius, *Nero* 6.1.

9 *a spirited, beautiful twenty-two-year-old:* Agrippina's beauty is attested by Tacitus (*Annals* 12.64.4) and Dio (60.31.6). Both authors report an anecdote (Tacitus skeptically) that after Agrippina died at age forty-three, Nero viewed his mother's corpse and remarked on its attractiveness.

9 *Agrippina formed a bond of friendship:* This must be assumed given Agrippina's recall of Seneca in 49, even if we do not identify the *memoria beneficii* referred to by Tacitus (see note to p. 4 on previous page) with an event in Caligula's reign. The section of

Tacitus' *Annals* dealing with Caligula's reign is lost. But his first mention of Seneca in the extant portion of the work shows that he had already introduced him earlier.

10 *"Sand without lime":* Suetonius, *Caligula* 53.2. On the thin evidence for this period of Seneca's life, see especially Clarke, "Seneca the Younger Under Caligula," 62–69.

10 *"There is hardly a sentence":* *The Life and Letters of Lord Macaulay,* ed. Sir George Otto Trevelyan (London, 1875), p. 1:339.

11 *"It seems that Nature produced him as an experiment":* *Consolation to Helvia* 10.4. In some translations, the emperor whom we usually call by his nickname, Caligula, is instead referred to as Gaius, the name by which Seneca knew him. For Seneca's horrific remembrances of Caligula, see Griffin, *Seneca,* pp. 213–15, and Anthony A. Barrett, *Caligula: The Corruption of Power* (London, 1989), pp. 156–58.

13 *family was linked to the* Seianiani: The degree of Seneca's family's involvement with Sejanus is disputed, but it is clear that there was some. Zeph Stewart has perhaps overstated it in "Sejanus, Gaetulicus, and Seneca," *American Journal of Philology* 74 (1953): 70-85, as Griffin (*Seneca,* pp. 48–50) has pointed out, but Griffin also agrees that Seneca's uncle, Galerius, and the close family friend Lucius Junius Gallio (later the adoptive father of Seneca's brother Novatus) had close Sejanian associations. Barrett (*Caligula,* pp. 112–13) has made the case that Lucilius, a close friend of Seneca, also had strong ties to the Sejanus conspiracy.

13 *written about* A.D. *40:* The dating is uncertain, but the reading advanced here, first put forward by Stewart ("Sejanus, Gaetulicus"), assumes that the work was published after the Lepidus conspiracy had come to light in the fall of 39. Griffin (*Seneca,* p. 397) rejected Stewart's reading, partly on the basis of uncertainty about the publication date, but then, in a separate discussion, leaned toward "a date after 39." In an extensive study of the work, *On Seneca's Ad Marciam* (Leiden, 1981), C. E. Manning opted for a date of 40, whereas Abel (*Bauformen in Senecas Dialogen,* p. 159) argued for 37. Since no certainty is possible on other grounds, the cogency of Stewart's interpretation is itself an argument for a post-39 publication date.

14 *a pattern of opportunism:* Stewart ("Sejanus, Gaetulicus," p. 85) speaks insightfully of "the spirit of opportunism which is so often present and so offensive in [Seneca's] writings," though he sees this spirit diminishing as Seneca ages. My own view is that over time Seneca merely got more adept at weaving his opportunistic stratagems into the weft of his philosophic discourse.

15 *largely obsolete by Roman times:* The leaders of the so-called Middle Stoa, in the second

and first centuries B.C., especially Panaetius, had abandoned the scheme of cyclical destruction in favor of Aristotle's hypothesis that the cosmos was eternal.

16 *Caligula awoke from a strange dream:* Reported by Suetonius, *Caligula* 57.

17 *more likely well briefed on what was to happen:* This is the opinion of Levick (*Claudius,* pp. 32–8).

17 *a precedent that was to endure for centuries:* The role of the Praetorians in determining when a princeps had failed, and who was to be his successor, increased over time. In A.D. 193 the guardsmen assassinated the reigning emperor, Pertinax, and then held a notorious auction in which the office of princeps was literally sold to the highest bidder.

17 *he kept a cool distance from the conspiracy:* At *De Ira* 1.20.9, Seneca speculates as to what motivated the conspirators who struck Caligula down, making clear that he himself does not know. He uses the assassination as a moral exemplum in *De Constantia Sapientis* 18 and *Letters* 4.7, both times indicating only a general knowledge of the circumstances.

17 *In one hypothetical discussion:* The passage in question, *De Beneficiis* 7.20.3, is often taken as an oblique justification for the murder of Caligula, for instance by Griffin (*Seneca,* p. 214). But the wording of the passage is obscure, and Griffin acknowledges in the note to her recent translation of the work—*Seneca: On Benefits* (University of Chicago, 2011), p. 208—that Seneca might have been advocating helping a mad tyrant kill *himself.* Seneca also qualified his advice: he said that such a final remedy would be appropriate only if the mad tyrant had no hope of recovery. Would that scenario include Caligula, whose madness had gone on for only two years?

18 *the defining problem of Seneca's age:* Vasily Rudich, with his firsthand experience of repression and covert dissent in Soviet Russia, has contributed enormously to our view of the Neronian era in his two studies, *Dissidence and Literature Under Nero* and *Political Dissidence Under Nero.* Rudich, it should be noted, takes a rather dim view of Seneca's solutions to the problem of autocracy.

19 *Pastor, a wealthy* eques: Pastor's story is related at *De Ira* 2.33.3–4. Nothing is known of the incident, or of Pastor, beyond what Seneca tells us.

20 *for Seneca, it became a kind of fixation:* Griffin (*Seneca,* chap. 11) reviews the wide array of Senecan texts with admirable thoroughness and carefully distinguishes "the notion that Seneca exalted suicide" from "the truth . . . that he exalted martyrdom"

(p. 386). Choosing to accept a painful or arduous death, for Seneca, carried many of the same moral virtues as inflicting it on oneself. Nonetheless Griffin agrees that "Seneca used suicide frequently to preach contempt of death," tracing this focus to the prevalence of political suicide in his own day. Paul Plass, in *The Game of Death in Ancient Rome: Arena Sport and Political Suicide* (Madison, Wisc., 1998), is more inclined to regard Seneca's treatment of suicide as obsessional. See also Catharine Edwards, *Death in Ancient Rome* (New Haven, Conn., 2007), especially chapters 4 and 5. Robert Kaster makes the interesting observation that Seneca's "hymn to suicide" in *De Ira* "seems to owe more to traditional Roman thought than to Stoic doctrine." See Kaster and Martha C. Nussbaum, trans., *Anger, Mercy, Revenge* (Chicago, 2010), p. 123 n. 300.

20 *the Latin phrase* se necare: James Ker (*Deaths of Seneca*, p. 200) traces the etymology as far back as Domenico da Peccioli, a fourteenth-century humanist.

21 *an exemplary act of lived philosophy:* The full account of this tradition is given in R. J. Goar, *The Legend of Cato Uticensis from the First Century* B.C. *to the Fifth Century* A.D. (Brussels, 1987). A shorter version can be found in the introduction to Edwards, *Death in Ancient Rome,* the cover of which sports a superb French canvas depicting Cato's death. The philosophic background is discussed by Miriam Griffin in her two-part article, "Philosophy, Cato, and Roman Suicide," *Greece and Rome* 33 (1986): 64–77 and 192–202.

21 *it glows incandescent:* The major passages are found at *De Providentia* 2.10–13; *De Constantia* 2; and *Letters* 24.6–8, 67.13, 95.70–72, 104.29–34. An intriguing but unprovable thesis by P. Pecchiura in *La figura di Catone Uticense nella letteratura latina* (Turin, 1965), pp. 69–71, holds that Seneca only glorified Cato's suicide during the times he was out of political power.

21 *A bizarre compact:* Discussed in Edwards, *Death in Ancient Rome,* pp. 116–21, and Plass, *Game of Death,* chap. 7. The terms of the compact are stated most explicitly by Tacitus, *Annals* 6.29.1–2, in a passage describing practice under Tiberius. Edwards notes that at some later time, the guarantee that a suicide's legacy would pass to his heirs was revoked, but it seems to have been in place throughout the Neronian era.

22 *two notebooks of enemies' names:* Attested by Suetonius, *Caligula* 49.

22 *was rushed as he expired to a place of execution:* As described by Tacitus (*Annals* 6.40); see Plass, *Game of Death,* p. 95. An even more absurd example is found at *Annals*

16.11, where Nero intercedes to block an order of execution passed against victims who were already dead.

22 *to embarrass the princeps:* Tiberius, according to Tacitus (*Annals* 6.26), felt discomfited by the suicide of Cocceius Nerva. Significantly, though, this discomfiture arose because Nerva killed himself while he was under no charge or suspicion. True "political" or "forced" suicides do not seem to have been interpreted as an act of protest, *pace* Edwards, *Death in Ancient Rome,* pp. 122–23.

22 *the sequel to the story:* Related by Herodotus, *Histories* 3.202.

23 *a cathectic spell:* See Catharine Edwards, *The Politics of Immorality in Ancient Rome* (Cambridge, 1993), and Susan E. Wood, *Imperial Women: A Study in Public Images, 40 B.C.–A.D. 68* (Leiden, 1999). Judith Ginsberg's analysis of Roman "rhetorical stereotypes" evoked by Agrippina the Younger is also very illuminating: *Representing Agrippina: Constructions of Female Power in the Early Roman Empire* (Oxford, 2006), chap. 3.

23 *some mixture of these frightening roles:* Wood (*Imperial Women,* p. 261) remarks on the illogic of the blends: "The elements of the stereotype are unbridled ambition, bloodthirstiness, sexual flagrancy, yet at the same time an ability to retain the loyalty of her husband. . . . Attackers of such women routinely accuse them both of unfeminine frigidity and of promiscuity."

25 *to take the title* Augusta: The Senate had offered her this title in A.D. 41, after the birth of Britannicus (Dio 60.12.5).

26 *alleged partner in crime:* The charge is variously given as adultery pure and simple (Dio 60.8.5) or as something vaguer but still primarily sexual, "immoral relations" (scholium to Juvenal 5.109; see Stewart, "Sejanus, Gaetulicus," p. 83 n. 86). It is pointless to speculate whether there were any grounds to the charge.

26 *Corsica had two Roman towns:* As attested by Seneca himself, *Helvia* 7.9. One of these two *coloniae,* Mariana, has been the subject of recent radar surveys revealing the remains of streets, houses, and a public bath. The ruins of Aleria, a Greco-Roman city that once had an estimated population of 20,000, can be visited in Corsica today.

27 *his first essay written there:* The date often given for *Consolation to Helvia* is A.D. 42, on the basis of its psychology; Seneca wants to assuage his mother's grief before it has gone past a reasonable limit of time. In *Consolation to Marcia,* he judged two years too long, and that was for a son who had died. That dating would place it

well before *Consolation to Polybius*. But it should be noted that Griffin (*Seneca*, pp. 397–98) does not accept this reasoning and in her chronological table lists *Helvia* after *Polybius*.

27 *the case of Apicius: Helvia* 10.9–10. Apicius lived in the early first century A.D. His taste for high living was known to Tacitus, Pliny the Elder, and Aelian, but only Seneca preserved the anecdote about his death. A cookbook of Roman delicacies survives to this day under the name Apicius, but it dates from much later in time. The name Apicius had become so closely associated with fine dining that it was attached pseudonymously to the cookbook.

28 *in the play* Octavia *and elsewhere:* The opening monologue of the character Seneca in *Octavia* (quoted on pp. 16–17) attributes his departure from Corsica to the influence of a capricious Fortune. Rolando Ferri's comment (p. 229) on the line points out its incongruity: "This plaintive address to Fortune is at odds with Seneca's own doctrine." The scholium to Juvenal 5.109 asserts, in a similar vein, that Seneca had wanted to go to Athens, not Rome, on leaving Corsica. Griffin (*Seneca*, p. 62) is willing to admit that this may have been a wish Seneca actually expressed, but if so, it was probably in retrospect after Rome had become a prison.

28 *probably written a year or two after the first:* The dating of *Consolation to Polybius* is fairly secure, given that in it Seneca celebrates Claudius' recent conquest of Britain.

28 *The poet Ovid, banished from Rome:* Ovid's exile (for unknown reasons) to Tomis on the coast of the Black Sea, starting in A.D. 8, was immortalized by the poet's own *Tristia* and *Letters from Pontus,* collections of wheedling, fawning, and bitterly plaintive poems presented to Augustus. Seneca would have known these works. Two of the poems attributed to Seneca by the collection *Anthologia Latina* (236–37) describe the rigors of life on Corsica in distinctly Ovidian terms and meter, but the attribution is doubtful.

28 *Borrowing a trick from Ovid:* The parallels between the closing words of *Polybius* (18.9) and Ovid's *Tristia* (3.14 and 5.7.57–58) seem too close to be coincidental. See Griffin, *Seneca*, p. 62 n. 3, and John J. Gahan, "Seneca, Ovid, and Exile." For both Seneca and Ovid—writers famous for style and prolixity—the plaint that command of Latin was being eroded constituted a powerful appeal for clemency.

29 *"When you wish to forget all your cares": Consolation to Polybius,* sections 7–8 and the far more effusive passage at 12–13. The flattery contained in these passages is so grotesque that an apologist has argued that they should be read as satire: W. H.

Alexander, "Seneca's *Ad Polybium*: A Reappraisal," *Transactions of the Royal Society of Canada* 37 (1943): 33–55. That view is nicely dismissed in Griffin, *Seneca*, pp. 415–16.

29 *Seneca sought to have them suppressed:* Dio (61.10.2) claims that Seneca scuttled—or perhaps repudiated, as Griffin (*Seneca*, p. 415) interprets Dio's language—a work, sent to Rome from Corsica, containing flattery of *both* Claudius and Messalina. *Consolation to Polybius* flatters only Claudius, but most scholars accept that it is the work to which Dio refers.

30 *Messalina felt her position deteriorating:* There is considerable bewilderment over Messalina's motives in 48, but I have assumed that they were dynastic and power-based rather than purely emotional. Ancient sources portray Messalina as a nymphomaniac driven by bizarre sexual impulses, and there may have been some truth to this. But the marriage to Silius seems to have been part of a coup attempt, possibly plotted in collusion with a faction of the Praetorian Guard. That at least is the view of Susan Wood (*Imperial Women*, pp. 252–55) as well as Barbara Levick (*Claudius*, London, 1990), pp. 65–67. Richard Baumann, by contrast, is inclined to trust Tacitus' account and see Messalina as acting on emotional impulses: *Women and Politics in Ancient Rome* (London, 1992), pp. 176–79.

30 *on orders issued by the palace:* Tacitus states that Narcissus, a leading palace freedman, gave the death order, while Claudius himself vacillated and considered pardoning his wife. But Tacitus' whole portrait of Claudius is a caricature of passivity and uxoriousness. It seems likely, given the rapidity with which Claudius married Agrippina and adopted her son, that he was glad of the pretext to rid himself of Messalina.

30 *As had often been true in the Julian clan:* The pattern is nicely sketched out and diagrammed in Mireille Corbier, "Male Power and Legitimacy Through Women: The *Domus Augusta* Under the Julio-Claudians," in *Women in Antiquity: New Assessments*, edited by Richard Hawley and Barbara Levick (London and New York, 1995).

30 *A decree had to be obtained:* Tacitus (*Annals* 12.6–7) describes with characteristic irony how Lucius Vitellius spearheaded this piece of legislation. It remained legal in the Roman Empire for a man to marry his niece until the fourth century A.D.

30 *now perhaps eight years old:* There is confusion about the date of Octavia's birth, since Tacitus (*Annals* 14.64) declares that she was twenty years old in 62. But most

scholars accept the evidence that she was born in 41, not 42, and was thus slightly older than Britannicus.

31 *high expectations for Silanus' future:* Dio 61.31.7. Dio then gives the very honor that Claudius had bestowed on Silanus as a reason the regime later wanted him dead.

31 *The allegation of incest:* That the principal charge against him was incest is the view of Tacitus (*Annals* 12.3–4) and Seneca (*Apocolocyntosis* 8). Dio (61.31.8), by contrast, speaks of a plot against Claudius.

31 *soon after their marriage:* Probably in A.D. 50; see Tacitus, *Annals* 12.26, and p. 42 in this book.

32 *he took his own life:* The sources diverge concerning the manner of Silanus' death. Tacitus is quite certain it was a suicide, and he is seconded by the author of *Octavia* (lines 148–49); but Dio (61.31.8) and Seneca (*Apocolocyntosis* 8) both claim (Seneca in vaguer terms) that he was executed. I believe, with D. McAlindon, that "the authenticity [of the suicide story] is almost certain in view of the expiatory rites in Tacitus." "Senatorial Opposition to Claudius and Nero," *American Journal of Philology* 77 (1956): 116.

CHAPTER 2: REGICIDE (A.D. 49–54)

33 *Seneca adapted the cyclical scheme:* Seneca's is the first known attempt by a Stoic to frame the cyclical destruction of the earth as a flood rather than an *ekpyrosis,* though Thomas Rosenmeyer notes that Cornutus, a Stoic writer roughly contemporaneous with Seneca, gives two alternatives, fire and flood, as the ways the world might end; see *Senecan Drama and Stoic Cosmology* (Berkeley and Los Angeles, 1989), p. 149. The extensive discussion by A. A. Long does not even mention the possibility of a world-ending flood: "The Stoics on World Conflagration and Eternal Recurrence," *Southern Journal of Philosophy* 23 (1985): 13–33.

33 *the fatal waters could arise:* In a later apocalypse-by-flood passage (*Natural Questions* 3.29.4), Seneca took this immanence a step further, imagining the solid earth itself dissolving into water.

34 *a practice Seneca deplored:* The long diatribe against luxurious use of snow at *Natural Questions* 4b.13 is the most prominent of several passages.

35 *quoted these lines as a prophecy:* For a survey of the evidence, see my "New World and

Novos Orbes: Seneca in the Renaissance Debate over Ancient Knowledge of the Americas," in *The Classical Tradition and the Americas,* edited by Wolfgang Haase and Meyer Reinhold (Berlin, 1993), pp. 1:78–116.

35 *does not end there:* My reading of this famous *Medea* passage is very much at odds with that of Anna Lydia Motto, "The Idea of Progress in Senecan Thought," *Classical Journal* 79 (1984): 226. It is troubling that Motto cites the Renaissance readings of this passage, badly distorted by the tendency to regard it as prophetic of Columbus, as support for her interpretation. I follow closely the view of Gilbert Lawall that the second, "triumphal" ode of the play cannot be understood without reference to the catastrophic third ode that forms its sequel. Lawall, "Seneca's *Medea:* The Elusive Triumph of Civilization," in *Arktouros,* edited by G. W. Bowersock (Berlin and New York, 1979).

35 *when Seneca wrote* Medea: The dating of the tragedies is perhaps the greatest and least soluble problem impeding efforts to chart Seneca's evolution. Miriam Griffin (*Seneca,* app. A) did not include the tragedies in her otherwise comprehensive chronology of Seneca's writing and chose not to discuss them at all in her study of Seneca's life. Abel (*Bauformen*) took a guess and listed them as "ca. 50–60" in his chronological table. John G. Fitch has made good progress by comparing the metrical and stylistic features of the plays in "Sense-pauses and Relative Dating in Seneca, Sophocles and Shakespeare," *American Journal of Philology* 102 (1981): 289–307, and I accept his conclusions as a general guide for ordering the plays and assigning them to a large span of Seneca's life.

36 *turn the cosmos itself into an enemy:* Seneca's jaundiced view of imperial expansion is discussed in connection with *Natural Questions* in Harry Hine, "Rome, the Cosmos, and the Emperor in Seneca's *Natural Questions,*" *Journal of Roman Studies* 92 (2002): 42–72.

36 *even less pleased by* Phaedra: The problem of *Phaedra's* topicality is mysteriously not discussed by Michael Coffey and Roland Mayer in their edition of the play (*Seneca: Phaedra* [Cambridge, 1990]), though they note that "Seneca was aware that the Greek myth could be applied to a Roman political context with perilous results" (p. 4) and that the incestuous union of Claudius and Agrippina bore an uncomfortable resemblance to Greek mythic tales (p. 26). R. G. M. Nisbet, by contrast, has tentatively dated *Phaedra* before 49, based on the fact that its condemnation of stepmothers was "difficult for a courtier to say at the exact moment when Agrip-

pina was displacing Britannicus with her own son Nero." Nisbet, "The Dating
of Seneca's Tragedies, with Special References to Thyestes," in *Papers of the Leeds
International Latin Seminar: Sixth Volume,* edited by Francis Cairns and Malcolm
Heath (Leeds, 1990), p. 353.

36 Phaedra *would have raised uncomfortable associations:* The close link between Phaedra's character and that of Agrippina has been noted by many commentators; a list
has been compiled by Eckard Lefèvre in "Die politische Bedeutung von Senecas
Phaedra," *Wiener Studien* 103 (1990): 109–22. Lefèvre's opinion is that the play must
have been written after Agrippina's death, though the dating scheme established by
Fitch's analysis suggests it is earlier ("Sense-pauses and Relative Dating," 289–307).

37 *addressed this concern in the Senate:* Tacitus, *Annals* 12.5.

37 *it seems more likely that, in the matter of succession, the two were in cahoots:* This is
almost guaranteed by the fact that the breakup of Octavia's engagement to Silanus,
a preparatory step to getting her engaged to the future Nero, preceded the marriage of Claudius and Agrippina. That is, the emperor and incoming empress were
already, in late 48, planning for a merged Julio-Claudian line that would carry
their dynasty forward. It is hard to imagine that Agrippina, even if possessed of the
seductive charms that the sources attribute to her, had already besotted Claudius
at that early stage. Levick (*Claudius,* p. 70) and Barrett (*Agrippina,* p. 111) con-
cur that Claudius acted with deliberation and forethought in preferring Nero to
Britannicus.

37 *contrary to Roman law:* Previous imperial adoptions, including those of Tiberius by
Augustus and of Germanicus by Tiberius, were done by fathers who had no sons.
See M. H. Prévost, *Les adoptions politiques à Rome* (Paris, 1949).

38 *February 25, A.D. 50:* The date is known through an inscription, number 224 in the
collection *Inscriptiones Latinae Selectae,* from the records of the Arval brethren,
a priestly caste at Rome. Tacitus (*Annals* 12.25) specifies that the Senate acted
after hearing a speech delivered by Claudius himself. Different versions of Nero's
full name after adoption are recorded; he sometimes appears in inscriptions as
"Tiberius Claudius Nero Caesar."

38 *more than three years before Britannicus:* The exact date of Britannicus' birth is
not known. Tacitus (*Annals* 12.25.2) states that Nero was three years older than
Britannicus.

39 *so unfeeling toward his own flesh and blood:* Aristotle, in a theoretical discussion of

monarchic succession (*Politics* 1286b25–28), says it would be beyond what one could ask of human nature for a king to prefer some other heir over his own progeny.

39 *Narcissus had feared Agrippina:* See Tacitus, *Annals* 12.2, where Narcissus argues against making changes in the dynastic order by bringing Agrippina into the imperial house.

40 *effused over the young Britannicus:* The relevant passage, from which the quote is taken, is *Consolation to Polybius* 12.5. Seneca goes on to advise Claudius to make Britannicus "consort" even before his accession, perhaps diplomatically alluding to Claudius' ill health.

41 *perhaps involuntarily:* Suetonius (*Nero* 7) says that Britannicus was merely speaking out of habit, but that rings false since the adoption had taken place more than a year earlier.

42 *Only the most revered imperial women:* Livia, wife of Augustus, had been the first to receive the title *Augusta* but did so only after her husband's death. Antonia, grandmother of Caligula and the ancestor who connected him most closely to Augustus, was the second *Augusta,* and Agrippina was the third.

42 *share the front face with him in jugate profile:* Susanna Braund points out that "this was the first time the wife of a reigning emperor had been portrayed with her husband on an imperial coin." See Braund, *Seneca's De Clementia* (Oxford, 2009), p. 432. For further discussion, see Walter Trillmich, *Familienpropaganda der Kaiser Caligula und Claudius: Agrippina Minor und Antonia Augusta auf Münzen* (Berlin, 1978), pp. 55–63.

43 *"This was a new thing":* Tacitus, *Annals* 12.37.

44 *power unprecedented for her gender:* Wood (*Imperial Women,* p. 259) notes that "Agrippina II was the first and only woman in Roman history to demand real, and official, power as opposed to influence."

44 *bring back her severed head:* Tacitus (*Annals* 12.22) says that Lollia was forced to commit suicide, not that she was executed; and he says nothing of beheading. Dio (61.32.4), on the other hand, adds the gruesome detail that Agrippina had trouble recognizing the head, distorted as it was by decomposition, but that she finally assured herself by examining the teeth. Dio strongly implies that Agrippina's main motive was to amass wealth for Nero.

44 *an enormous undertaking:* For details, see M. R. Thornton and R. L. Thornton, "The Draining of the Fucine Lake: A Quantitative Analysis," *Ancient World* 12 (1985):

105–20. Suetonius (*Claudius* 20) reports that the project occupied eleven years. The lake was only partially drained in antiquity; it finally disappeared through drainage conduits in the nineteenth century.

45 *Agrippina beside him in a* chlamys: As described by an eyewitness, Pliny the Elder (*Natural History* 7.46), as well as by Tacitus (*Annals* 12.56). The only other instance I am aware of in which a woman wore a *chlamys* is Vergil's Queen Dido (*Aeneid* 4.137), precisely because she occupies what would ordinarily be a male political station.

45 *an ingenious rumor was spread:* Reported by Dio 61.33.5; other details of the story come from Tacitus, *Annals* 12.56–57.

45 *Pallas rose to heights:* The story that follows is taken from Tacitus, *Annals* 12.53.

46 *fulsome praises be inscribed on a brass plaque:* They were later moved to a monument on the Via Tiburtina, where Pliny the Elder, a later Roman official, saw them and mocked them in his letters (*Epistles* 7.29 and 8.6).

47 *just when Paul arrived there:* The encounter between Paul and Gallio is carefully dated to the late summer of A.D. 51 in Jerome Murphy-O'Connor, *Paul: A Critical Life* (Oxford, 1996), pp. 18–22. Paul had apparently been in Corinth since spring of the previous year.

47 *The head rabbi of Corinth, Sosthenes:* He is possibly, but not necessarily, the same Sosthenes as the one mentioned as coauthor of 1 Corinthians in the opening sentence of that epistle. See Murphy-O'Connor, *Paul,* p. 264.

47 *recorded in Acts of the Apostles:* Acts 24:1–27.

47 *a ruthlessly effective technique:* Josephus, *Jewish War* 2.254–57.

47 *An insurrectionist known as "the Egyptian":* His brief but tempestuous career in Judaea is recounted in Josephus, *Jewish War* 2.261–63, and *Jewish Antiquities* 20.170–72.

48 *it must be the Egyptian:* As is clear from Acts 21:38.

49 *allowed enough freedom of movement:* The picture painted by Acts 28:16–30 is of a man under house arrest, able to receive students and acolytes and to teach freely. Rome did not as yet have any prohibitions on Christian doctrine nor any ideological complaint against Paul.

49 *Paul's life in Rome:* In particular, it is unclear whether Paul left Rome at some point during the 60s to travel in Spain and elsewhere, a question that hinges partly on the authenticity of the so-called Pastoral Letters.

49 *Seneca a kind of proto-Christian:* For a survey of the history of this notion, see Arnaldo

Momigliano in "Note sulla leggenda del cristianesimo di Seneca," *Rivista storica italiana* 62 (1950): 325–44. Lorenzo Valla, the great Italian humanist, first challenged the authenticity of the letters in the fifteenth century.

49 *did not think much of philosophy:* Suetonius, *Nero* 52. Suetonius also supplies the less credible report that Seneca prevented Nero from reading any oratorical works other than his own.

50 *"You taught me not only how":* Tacitus, *Annals* 14.55. For the circumstances of this colloquy, see pp. 136–37 in this book.

50 *a new thing in the history of the principate:* Attested by Tacitus, *Annals* 13.3.

50 *a passionate fan of the chariot races:* Suetonius (*Nero* 22) reports that Nero's earliest teachers had to scold him to stop talking about this sport.

50 *stopped being able:* The source of this rather cryptic statement is *Letters to Lucilius* 49.2.

51 *"You nurtured my boyhood":* The source is again Tacitus, *Annals* 14.55.

51 *"for the sake of improving":* *Letters to Lucilius* 108.6–8. Mark Morford has attempted to use the advice on teaching in *De Ira* (2.18–21) as a template for reconstructing Seneca's lessons. See Morford, "The Training of Three Roman Emperors," *Phoenix* 22 (1968): 57–72. But it is generally assumed that *De Ira* (or at least its first two books) was composed prior to Seneca's appointment as tutor. The practical needs of the situation in the palace would have required a very different approach than anything Seneca could have envisioned as general guidelines.

51 *"laid siege" to Attalus' classroom:* Recollected by Seneca at *Letters to Lucilius* 108.3, with a characteristically pointed military metaphor.

51 *if only by way of his presence:* Seneca was a strong believer in the power of social conditioning. "Those who frequent the perfume sellers and stay there for even a short time will carry away some of the scent of the place," he wrote in a discussion of philosophic education (*Letters* 108.4), meaning that proximity to philosophy would cause it to rub off on even those not interested in its teachings.

51 *under a bloodred sky:* Reported by Dio 61.33.2.

52 *show his wife more affection:* Suetonius, *Nero* 35.1, the sole source. In the following section (35.2), Suetonius also provides unique information that Nero several times tried to strangle Octavia.

52 *"The soul of my wife":* *Octavia*, line 537. See pp. 137–38 in this book for more discussion of this remarkable exchange.

52   *"Her life's breath depends":* Letters to Lucilius 104.2. Elsewhere Seneca's references to Paulina are rare and tangential. At *Letters* 50.2, we learn that he tolerated having her female clown Harpaste in the house, though he disliked clowns.

52   *possibly a good deal earlier:* Griffith (*Seneca*, pp. 57–58) reaches the conclusion that the question of whether Paulina was his first wife or his second cannot be resolved.

53   *at around the time Seneca became Nero's tutor:* The date of c. 49 for Paulinus' appointment has been convincingly argued in Miriam Griffin, "*De Brevitate Vitae,*" *Journal of Roman Studies* 52 (1962): 104–13.

54   *Miriam Griffin, a leading Seneca scholar:* Griffin's interpretation, advanced in the article cited in the previous note, seems to me the only good explanation for the treatise's anomalies, just as that advanced by Zeph Stewart in the case of *Consolation to Marcia* (see pp. 13–14 in this book) alone explains the unique relationship there of author and addressee. However, Griffin's critics jumped on her argument and caused her to take a more cautious approach in *Seneca,* where she explains at length (pp. 401–7) that she still believes in a date of 55 for *De Brevitate Vitae* but cannot prove it. Gareth Williams, in his introduction to a recent edition (*Seneca: De Otio, De Brevitate Vitae* [Cambridge 2003]) calls Griffin's interpretation "highly speculative" (3 n. 7) and "intriguing but inconclusive" (20), and refuses to date the treatise.

54   *do two things at once:* Griffin (*Seneca,* p. 407) speaks in terms of a "primary" (philosophic) and "secondary" (political) purpose to several of the prose works, a position mischaracterized by Williams (introduction to *Seneca,* p. 2) as "ulterior motive."

55   *His great wealth:* Narcissus was credited with an estate of 400 million sesterces (Dio 61.34.4). Jeffrey Winters has estimated the average wealth of the ten richest Roman senators as only a quarter of this amount: *Oligarchy* (Cambridge, 2011), p. 92.

55   *a maimed hand:* Agrippina refers to the hand (Tacitus, *Annals* 13.14) in a context clearly signifying that she perceived it as a political liability. The historical evidence on Burrus is nicely collected in W. C. McDermott, "Sextus Afranius Burrus," *Latomus* 8 (1949): 229–54.

56   *a farce written by Seneca: Apocolocyntosis* 3, discussed on pp. 62–64 in this book.

56   *"the palace is being torn apart":* The campaign is described by Tacitus (*Annals* 12.65). Other sources (Suetonius, *Claudius* 43) give some of the actions attributed to Narcissus (less plausibly) to Claudius.

58   *Tiberius removed the signet ring:* Suetonius, *Tiberius* 73. The source of the anecdote is a work subsequently lost.

58 *a similar quandary:* Griffin, who is usually quite circumspect in dealing with historical evidence, concurs that in 54 "Claudius began talking about [Britannicus'] advancement." See her *Nero: The End of a Dynasty* (London, 1984), p. 32. Levick (*Claudius,* p. 76) speaks of "increasingly sharp rows" between Claudius and Agrippina over Britannicus' future and believes that Claudius intended Nero and Britannicus to be joint heirs.

58 *some scholars do not believe:* Neither Barrett (*Agrippina,* pp. 141–42) nor Griffin (*Nero,* p. 32) is willing to take a position on whether Claudius was murdered; Levick (*Claudius,* p. 77) inclines "on balance" to think that he was. See, however, the argument against this view by John Aveline, "The Death of Claudius," *Historia* 53 (2004): 453–75. R. W. Pack points to malaria as a possible cause of death in "Seneca's Evidence in the Deaths of Claudius and Narcissus," *Classical Weekly* 36 (1953): 150–51.

59 *the perfect time to strike:* The same reasoning has persuaded T. E. J. Wiedemann, "Tiberius to Nero," in *Cambridge Ancient History,* p. 10.241, that Claudius probably was murdered.

59 *contradicted on details by other ancient historians:* Suetonius (*Claudius* 44) notes that there was disagreement in his day about who administered the poison and what followed. Suetonius gives one account that says, as Tacitus does, that a mushroom poisoned the princeps at a family dinner, but also cites a second in which Claudius' taster, a eunuch named Halotus, poisoned him while he was dining with a caste of priests. Dio (61.34) agrees with Tacitus up to the point where Claudius ingests the poisoned mushroom, but he has no report of the second poisoning by Xenophon. Josephus (*Jewish Antiquities* 20.151) reports a rumor that Agrippina caused Claudius' death but gives no details and does not endorse it.

59 *a dish of mushrooms:* This is the position of Aveline in "Death of Claudius," who goes so far as to correlate Claudius' reported symptoms with the effects of a particular species of mushroom. It seems to me paradoxical to rely on Tacitus as a source for Claudius' symptoms but not for the agent of his death. Nero reportedly (Suetonius, *Nero* 33; Dio 61.35.4) made a wisecrack later in life about mushrooms being "the food of the gods" because they had made Claudius a god, but this does not imply a deliberate poisoning.

60 *a troupe of comedians:* Seneca (*Apocolocyntosis* 4) refers to them as though they had arrived while Claudius was alive, and in general he contradicts the notion that

Claudius' death was concealed for some eight to ten hours, giving the time of death as noon or shortly after on October 13.

60 *Dio specifies that Seneca:* Dio 61.3.1. The information in the same chapter, that Seneca also wrote the speech given to the Senate that day, and that it was later inscribed on silver tablets, seems to confuse two different speeches; see pp. 67–68 in this book.

CHAPTER 3: FRATRICIDE (A.D. 54–55)

62 Apocolocyntosis Divi Claudii: Most scholars agree on the title *Apocolocyntosis,* but a few dispute it, feeling that the work referred to by Dio (61.35.3) under that title is not the one we have. In manuscripts, the work is titled "Satire on the Death of Claudius" or "Deification of Claudius the God Told Through Satire," neither of which sounds authentic.

62 *a mystery:* The problems are nicely outlined in the introduction to P. T. Eden's edition of the Latin text, *Seneca: Apocolocyntosis* (Cambridge, 1984).

63 *hauled up to heaven with a hook:* Dio 61.35, the same chapter that informs us about the title of Seneca's work.

63 *a colossal new temple in central Rome:* A small section of Claudius' massive temple on the Caelian can be seen today in Rome. It was not completed until the 70s, work having stalled under Nero.

63 *no one would ever think:* A few scholars continue to doubt the attribution despite Dio's testimony. G. Bagnani, in *Arbiter of Elegance* (Toronto, 1954), tried to assign it to Petronius.

64 *Seneca's motives:* The various theories are summarized by Eden in his edition of *Apocolocyntosis* and by H. Macl. Currie, "The Purpose of the *Apocolocyntosis,*" *Acta Classica* 31 (1962): 91–97.

64 *suggest he wanted revenge:* The 2010 volume issued by University of Chicago Press, edited by Robert A. Kaster and Martha C. Nussbaum, bears the title *Anger, Mercy, Revenge,* characterizing the principal thrust of the three works it comprises, *De Ira, De Clementia,* and *Apocolocyntosis.*

64 *like a martial anthem:* Underscoring the anomalous tone of this passage, Edward Champlin has argued that it is an insertion made five or more years after the rest of the work was written. See Champlin, "Nero, Apollo and the Poets," *Phoenix* 57 (2003): 276–83, and *Nero* (Cambridge, Mass., 2003), p. 116. It seems to me a dif-

ficult argument to make, and no other scholars have thus far endorsed it. Martha Nussbaum does not question the lines in her recent translation of *Apocolocyntosis* in Kaster and Nussbaum, *Anger, Mercy, Revenge*.

65 *tried to have it suppressed:* See p. 29 in this book and note.

65 *a single Saturnalian banquet:* Eden (*Apocolocyntosis*) endorses the idea in the introduction to her commentary.

65 *vigorous portrait statues:* Surveyed in Ulrich W. Hiesinger, "The Portraits of Nero," *American Journal of Archaeology* 79 (1975): 113–24.

66 *Seneca had had a dream:* Reported by Suetonius, *Nero* 7.

66 *widely disliked by the Senate:* As attested by *Apocolocyntosis,* which constructs a doppelgänger of the Senate in the form of an assembly of gods, then uses it to denounce and reject Claudius.

67 *both a writer and a courtier:* Very little is known of Tacitus' life or his role at the courts of various emperors, but he expresses (*Agricola* 44–45) what seems to be anguish at his own complicity in the crimes of Domitian (who reigned from 81 to 96). "Tacitus as a public servant during the reign of Domitian must have experienced many times the same kind of difficulties of conscience that beset Seneca, and on the whole he seems to have faced them in a similar way." Denis Henry and B. Walker, "Tacitus and Seneca," *Greece and Rome* 10 (1963): 108.

68 *"My youth was not troubled":* There is some confusion among our sources as to when this inaugural speech was delivered. Dio (61.3.1) inserts it into the events of October 13, the day of Nero's accession. Tacitus (*Annals* 13.4), more reliably, places it after the funeral of Claudius. That both historians refer to the same speech seems certain, since it was a landmark address setting out the program of the new regime. Such a forward-looking speech would have appeared presumptuous if delivered only hours after accession, as Dio would have it.

68 *Seneca quoted on three occasions: De Ira* 1.20.4, and *De Clementia* 1.12.4 and 2.2.2.

68 *certainly in circulation:* The terminal date for the composition of *De Ira* is established by the way it names its addressee. Novatus, Seneca's older brother, became known as Gallio by 52 at the latest. So *De Ira,* addressed to Novatus, must precede that date, just as *De Vita Beata,* addressed to Gallio, must follow it. The need to rely on such arcane clues in establishing the chronology of Seneca's works is a mark of how thoroughly their author avoided all mention of contemporary people and events.

68 *merely wiped his face:* The story, which turns on an untranslatable pun, is told at *De Ira* 3.38.

69 *practiced a Zen-like exercise:* On the famous passage (*De Ira* 3.36) in which Seneca describes this practice, modeled on that of the Roman philosopher Sextius, see James Ker, "Seneca on Self-examination: Re-reading *On Anger* 3.36," in *Seneca and the Self,* edited by Shadi Bartsch and David Wray (Cambridge, 2009).

69 *"Pull further back, and laugh!":* It is difficult to know at what point Seneca ceases to use "you" for himself talking to himself and applies it instead to a hypothetical member of the Roman upper class. By the end of *De Ira* 3.37, his "you" is certainly more than just himself, and I am assuming the same is true of the entire chapter.

69 *"The one to whom nothing was refused":* De Ira 2.21.6. As Robert Kaster's note to the passage (*Anger, Mercy, Revenge,* p. 115) makes clear, various social cues in the passage show that Seneca was thinking of childrearing among the elite.

69 *poked fun at her:* Agrippina's response to *Apocolocyntosis* has been variously assessed, but most scholars assume it could not have been positive. "The institutions to which she had dedicated herself were made to seem ridiculous. The blow to Agrippina's pride . . . must have been immense." Barrett, *Agrippina,* p. 165.

70 optima mater, *"best of mothers":* Tacitus, *Annals* 13.2, and Suetonius, *Nero* 9.

71 *sculpture found in Aphrodisias:* Discussed in Rose, *Dynastic Commemoration,* pp. 47–48, and in Wood, *Imperial Women,* pp. 301–2.

71 *new format:* The closest parallel was a coin issued several decades earlier in the time of Drusus II, showing the heads of Drusus' two sons facing each other atop cornucopias. See Charles Brian Rose, *Dynastic Commemoration and Imperial Portraiture in the Julio-Claudian Period* (Cambridge, 1997), pp. 47 and n. 17.

72 *Nero was not involved:* Tacitus (*Annals* 13.1.1) explicitly says that Nero did not even know of the plan to murder Silanus; at the end of the same chapter, he says that the killing of Narcissus was "contrary to his wishes," which seems to imply that Nero found out about it only after the fact. Agrippina evidently had the right to issue orders to the Praetorians on her own authority.

73 *compared a leader's handling of the state:* The passage referred to, *De Ira* 1.6.3, is extended at 1.16.2 of the same work, where the gradations of remedial punishment are once again laid out, progressing from least (private reproof) to greatest (mercy killing).

74 *appeared on the emperor's dais:* See pp. 42–43 in this book.

74 *Some Romans fretted:* The report of sentiment in the Roman street is given by Tacitus, *Annals* 13.6.

74 *Seneca and Burrus sat beside Nero:* The scene that follows incorporates details of Tacitus' account (*Annals* 13.5) and Dio's (61.3.3–4). The assumption that the move to block Agrippina was preplanned, not spontaneous, is my own.

75 *"You did not make use of our influence":* Consolation to Helvia 14.3.

76 *"womanly and childish vice":* De Ira 1.20.

76 *composed concurrently:* If the view advanced in this book (p. 34) is correct, *Medea* was written not long after Claudius' invasion of Britain, in the mid-40s. *De Ira* is dated by most between 41 and 49.

76 *only a single volume:* The work in question is James Ker, Ronnie Ancona, and Laurie Haight Keenan, eds., *A Seneca Reader: Selections from Prose and Tragedy* (Mundelein, Ill., 2011).

76 *Interpreters have struggled:* The literature on how Senecan tragedy relates to Senecan philosophy is vast and varied. Martha Nussbaum gives a brief rundown of some important recent discussions in *Therapy of Desire: Theory and Practice in Hellenistic Ethics* (Princeton, 1994), pp. 448–49 n. 13, and her own reading of *Medea* in that book contributes to them. More recently, articles in Shadi Bartsch and David Wray, eds., *Seneca and the Self* (Cambridge, 2009), especially part 3, and in Katharina Volk and Gareth D. Williams, eds., *Seeing Seneca Whole* (Boston, 2006), have tackled this time-worn dilemma. The Middle Ages and Renaissance believed that the Seneca who wrote the tragedies was a different Seneca from the author of the prose works, and it is still possible today to suggest that the tragedies come from a different hand; see Thomas D. Kohn, "Who Wrote Seneca's Plays?" *Classical World* 96 (2003): 271–80. The only evidence from antiquity linking "Seneca" (not necessarily Seneca the Younger) to one of the tragedies (*Medea*) is a single, and vague, sentence in Quintilian, *Institutio Oratoria* 9.2.9.

77 *inversions of his prose works:* "What was Seneca trying to achieve with these portraits of disturbed and even deranged personalities? The most likely answer is that he was exploiting the emotional directness of dramatic poetry to make his audiences feel the appalling consequences of passion, that the shock and revulsion aroused by his most effective scenes were meant to be the stimulus to moral awareness and growth," writes Richard Tarrant in *Seneca's Thyestes* (Atlanta, 1985), pp. 24–25; but

he immediately acknowledges the insufficiency of this approach to account for the power of the plays.

77 *"compartmentalized mind"*: The phrase comes from Henry and Walker, "Tacitus and Seneca," p. 108. Less generous interpreters have attributed to Seneca a neurotically disorganized or even schizoid personality.

78 *he craved the exotic and outré:* Nero's sex life was to take some bizarre turns in later years, such that it included bestial play-acting, cross-dressing, and a homosexual wedding ceremony. The evidence is collected and discussed in Champlin, *Nero,* pp. 161–70.

78 *brought relief to many:* Attested by Tacitus, *Annals* 13.12.

78 *"A handmaid for a daughter-in-law!":* Tacitus, *Annals* 13.13.

78 *"I made you emperor":* Dio 61.7.3.

78 *threatened to abdicate:* The time frame of this threat, reported by Suetonius (*Nero* 34.1), is not clear, but it seems to date from early in Nero's reign since his mother was still exerting powerful influence at the time it was made.

78 *his close friend Annaeus Serenus:* I am supposing that Griffin (*Nero,* pp. 447–48) is correct in her dating of Serenus' appointment to this post. Serenus, to whom Seneca addressed *De Constantia Sapientis* and *De Tranquillitate Animi,* was a dear friend whom Seneca bitterly mourned after his sudden death from accidental poisoning (*Letters* 63.14); see Pliny, *Natural History* 22.96.

80 *"It'll be a daughter of Germanicus":* Agrippina's words are quoted by Tacitus at *Annals* 13.14. Barrett (*Agrippina,* p. 240) says "the passage is hardly believable," but this seems to me a misunderstanding of Tacitus' method, which is to provide speeches—admittedly, in some cases, invented ones—that exemplify the cast of mind of his characters as he understood it from his sources. Indeed, Ronald Mellor (*Tacitus' Annals,* p. 167) quotes this precise speech and comments: "This rant has the ring of truth—a mother who feels she sacrificed all for her son only to be pushed aside."

80 *Britannicus had made plain:* Tacitus, *Annals* 13.15.

81 *a deadline in the literal sense:* The ancient accounts of Britannicus' death are unanimous that Nero was to blame. Tacitus (*Annals* 13.15–17), Dio (61.7.4), and Suetonius (*Nero* 33.3) are in this case joined by Josephus (*Jewish War* 2.250, *Jewish Antiquities* 20.153). The testimony of the sources is more univocal and has raised fewer questions among historians than that concerning the death of Claudius, but there is, as always in poisoning stories, room for doubt. Barrett (*Agrippina,* p. 172)

inclines toward the view that Britannicus died of an epileptic seizure and asserts, wrongly in my view, that "modern authorities are generally skeptical about the notion that Britannicus died from foul play." Levick (*Claudius*, p. 77) regards the poisonings of Britannicus and Claudius as equally unprovable. Griffin (*Nero*, p. 74, and *Seneca*, pp. 134–35) expresses doubts about the latter but accepts the former as historical fact.

81 *so agitated that he struck her:* Suetonius, *Nero* 33.3. Tacitus (*Annals* 13.15) has Nero threaten the tribune who was overseeing the operation and vow to have Locusta executed.

82 *"So I'm afraid of the Julian law":* Suetonius, *Nero* 33.3. Many laws were known as "Julian" because of their adoption under Julius Caesar or Augustus. It is not clear which one is referred to here; K. R. Bradley thinks that Suetonius, or his source, erred in the name. K. R. Bradley, *Suetonius' Life of Nero: An Historical Commentary* (Brussels, 1978), p. 199.

82 *Did Seneca help Nero:* That Seneca at least knew the "inside story" later in life is suggested by Tacitus, *Annals* 15.62, where Seneca adverts to the murder of Britannicus in his last hours. Griffin (*Seneca*, p. 135) also notes that the involvement of a Praetorian tribune in the plot (asserted by Tacitus, *Annals* 13.15.4–5) suggests that Burrus was a party. Wiedemann ("Tiberius to Nero," in *Cambridge Ancient History*, p. 10:245) asks, as though this were a natural question, "whether or not Seneca and Burrus were personally responsible" for Britannicus' death.

82 *the imperial family dined together:* The details here and in what follows are taken from Tacitus, *Annals* 13.16.

82 *"the need of seeing into the minds of others":* A. Wallace-Hadrill, "The Imperial Court," *Cambridge Ancient History*, p. 10.295.

84 *a kind of poisoning academy:* Unique information found at Suetonius, *Nero* 33.3. Locusta would survive into the reign of Galba, who had her put to death in a general purge of Nero's associates in A.D. 68 (Dio 63.3.4).

84 *got into the system of Titus:* Suetonius, *Titus* 2, is the sole source. It is not clear how Titus' meal could have been contaminated, if the poison was delivered in the manner Tacitus reports.

84 *darkened Britannicus' skin:* Unique information in Dio (61.7.4), and therefore open to graver doubts than the rest of the tale. Barrett (*Agrippina*, p. 172) asserts—probably seconding an offhand comment by Alexis Dawson, "Whatever Happened to Lady

Agrippina?" *Classical Journal* 64 (1969), p. 256 n. 2—that no poison known to the ancient world could have caused this effect, but I am not familiar with any thorough toxicological investigations.

85 *Her image was no longer shown:* The sequence of Agrippina's imagery on imperial coins is laid out by Barrett (*Agrippina*, pp. 226–27) and discussed by Rose (*Dynastic Commemoration*, p. 47) and Wood (*Imperial Women*, pp. 293–95).

85 *another outcast at court, her stepdaughter Octavia:* Tacitus, *Annals* 13.18.

85 *My fear forbids me: Octavia*, lines 66–71. Octavia is here comparing her own situation to that of the mythic heroine Electra, who lived in fear at the court of a murderous mother.

86 *disturbing report, of uncertain credibility:* Tacitus, *Annals* 13.17, attributed to anonymous primary sources.

87 *"Not stopping a wrong":* The line is spoken by Agamemnon, whom Seneca constructed as an embodiment of restrained monarchic power, in *Trojan Women* (line 291). Interpreters have raised the possibility that Agamemnon in this play is a spokesman for Seneca's own political ideals; see Elaine Fantham, *Seneca's Troades* (Princeton, 1982), 252.

87 *"There was no lack of those":* Tacitus, *Annals* 13.18. The sneering reference to "men who affected moral seriousness" has been taken as a hit at Seneca, for example by Erich Koestermann, *Cornelius Tacitus: Annalen* (Heidelberg, 1967), p. 3:268.

87 *On one level, the scene evokes:* See Tarrant, *Seneca's Thyestes*, p. 48 n. 164.

87 *an incurable moral illness:* See p. 104 in this book on *De Vita Beata*, where Seneca compares himself to a gout sufferer. In *Letters to Lucilius* 8.3, Seneca says he is suffering from skin lesions that will not heal.

CHAPTER 4: MATRICIDE (A.D. 55–59)

89 *"harshness sheathed, but mercy battle-ready":* De Clementia 1.1.4.

90 *death of Britannicus casts a long shadow:* Some scholars have even been tempted to revise the traditional dating of *De Clementia* to make it precede the death of Britannicus, and thereby exonerate Seneca from gross doublespeak; see Braund, *Seneca's De Clementia*, pp. 16–17, and Griffin, *Seneca*, pp. 407–11. The date is in fact rendered certain by Seneca's statement at 1.9.1 that Nero has recently passed his eighteenth birthday, which fell in December 55. Braund's own solution (p. 17) to

the problem of doublespeak—the claim that Nero in effect had a "pass" to commit murder within his family—is unconvincing, given that Seneca had made clear, in Augustus' speech in *Apocolocyntosis,* that he considered dynastic family murder an atrocity.

90 *"If only I were illiterate!": De Clementia* 2.1.2. Suetonius records much the same anecdote at *Nero* 10.2.

90 *Seneca's target audience:* "The law of this genre was to give advice only to those ready to accept it"—a group that excluded Nero himself, observes Paul Veyne in *Seneca: Life of a Stoic* (New York, 2003), p. 17.

91 *"We have all of us done wrong": De Clementia* 1.6.3.

91 *strikingly like Seneca's own:* "He is accusing himself . . . with sad distress," comments Elisabeth Henry on this passage, in *The Annals of Tacitus: A Study in the Writing of History* (Manchester, 1968), p. 224. Braund (*Seneca's De Clementia,* p. 237) comments on the particularly personal and emphatic tone of the sentence but understands its relevance in a different way.

91 *"He was never again the target": De Clementia* 1.9.11. The Cinna conspiracy and Augustus' pardon were also dealt with by Dio (55.14–22) and, much later, by Montaigne in *Essays* 1.24.

92 *He compares Nero to a* mind: *De Clementia* 1.3.5. The two texts that are often adduced as Seneca's models for this analogy, Aristotle's *Politics* (1254a34–b9) and Cicero's *Republic* (3.37), are not nearly as fully developed; it seems to me that Seneca should get more credit than he has for an original turn of thought.

93 *rapacious nighttime jaunts:* Tacitus, *Annals* 13.25; Suetonius, *Nero* 26; and Dio 61.8–9, all in close agreement. Pliny the Elder (*Natural History* 13.126) reports that Nero used a special remedy to heal his bruises and scrapes.

94 *cowed by the murder of Britannicus:* Analysis unique to Dio 61.7.5, though nothing in our other sources contradicts it.

94 *Marcus Otho and Claudius Senecio:* Named as Nero's closest friends by Tacitus (*Annals* 13.12), with the additional information that Otho came from a consular family while Senecio was a humble freedman's son. Otho was about five years older than Nero; Senecio's age is unknown.

94 *"Are you afraid of them?":* Quoted in Dio 61.4.5, as the remarks of court insiders generally.

94 *he took every measure taught by Terpnus:* Described in Suetonius, *Nero* 20.1, and Pliny the Elder, *Natural History* 34.166, 19.108. Edward Champlin's (*Nero*, pp. 52–83) discussion of Nero's artistic ambitions is highly revealing.

95 *a proposal to abolish all indirect taxes:* Tacitus (*Annals* 13.50) is our only source for this bizarre initiative. He specifies that Nero's *seniores* (text emended from the erroneous reading *senatores*), or elder counselors—a group that no doubt included Seneca— had to dissuade him.

95 *just how large is a matter of debate:* The issues are laid out admirably by Griffin (*Seneca*, pp. 67–128). The key question is whether to trust Dio's report (61.4.1–2) that in Nero's early years Seneca and Burrus were virtually in charge of the state. Griffin makes a persuasive case that Seneca's role in government was far less prominent than that. His contribution was "not proposals in the Senate or plans for financial reform, but personal influence on the emperor's public behavior and pronouncements" (p. 128).

96 *ordered Agrippina stripped of her bodyguard:* Tacitus, *Annals* 13.18; Suetonius, *Nero* 34.1. Tacitus specifies that the Germans had been stationed by Agrippina's side only recently, perhaps after Nero's accession.

96 *a conspicuous armed guard:* Tacitus, *Annals* 13.18. Agrippina was at this point living in the country estate of her grandmother Antonia.

97 *an old grudge against Agrippina:* As explained by Tacitus, *Annals* 13.19. Agrippina had reportedly driven off a suitor who was interested in marrying Julia.

97 *a new Praetorian prefect:* Tacitus (*Annals* 13.20) makes a distinction among his three named sources for the events of this night. Two of them had said nothing about Nero's mistrust of Burrus, while the third, Fabius Rusticus, gives intimate details about the effort to appoint a new prefect and Seneca's determination to stop it. Tacitus mistrusts Rusticus as a former protégé of Seneca's, and Griffin (*Seneca*, p. 88) thinks he was right to do so, but Barrett (*Agrippina*, p. 175) is less certain. There is nothing inherently implausible in the story, and if Rusticus had more motive than others to put Seneca in a favorable light, he also had greater access to Seneca's inside information.

99 *Faenius Rufus, a protégé of Agrippina:* Later to play an important, and unattractive, role in the Pisonian conspiracy; see pp. 187–89 in this book.

100 *bear a second son:* The fact that Agrippina had not had children with Claudius, or

with her second husband, Crispus Passienus, is remarkable. It seems that her own dynastic strategy, and later the plan she shared with Claudius, was to avoid creating a rival to Nero, if necessary by means of contraception and abortion. There is no reason to think she had become infertile.

100 *the highest constitutional office:* The question of the precise date of both Seneca's and Gallio's consulships is discussed by Griffin, *Seneca,* p. 73 n. 6. Both were suffect consuls, taking office as midterm replacements for the weightier *consules ordinarii.*

100 *estates in Egypt, Spain, and Campania:* The inventory of Seneca's probable properties has been compiled by Griffin, *Seneca,* pp. 286–94.

100 *famed for their size and magnificence:* Juvenal, *Satire* 10.16 (which is also the source of the term *praedives,* mentioned on p. 101 in this book).

100 *another property, a choice vineyard:* Attested by Pliny the Elder (*Natural History* 14.49), who says Seneca bought the property at huge expense but immediately improved it, so as to realize a quick profit.

101 *more than 180 gallons of wine to the acre:* The figure comes from a contemporary, Columella (*De Re Rustica* 3.3.3).

101 *Seneca invested in Britain:* Seneca nowhere mentions such British loans himself, but Griffin (see p. 132 in this book and note) and others do not doubt that there is some substance to Dio's claim (at 62.2.1), even if the amount seems exaggerated. According to Tacitus (*Annals* 13.42.7), Suillius Rufus, in the attack he leveled at Seneca in the Senate in 58, alleged rapacious lending in the provinces, without specifying which ones. See Barbara Levick, "Seneca and Money," in *Seneca uomo politico e l'età di Claudio e di Nerone,* ed. Arturo De Vivo and Elio Lo Cascio (Bari, 2003), pp. 223–24. Dio seems to make a further claim that Seneca pressed the money on borrowers against their will, but the Greek word that indicates this is emended by some editors to instead show that the British chiefs wanted the money.

102 *a harder, tougher regimen:* See Griffin, *Seneca,* pp. 294–314, and *"Imago Vitae Suae,"* pp. 55–58.

102 *"No one excelled this millionaire":* Griffin, *Seneca,* p. 286. The paradox is exemplified by a line Seneca quoted from a Cynic teacher he especially admired: "A man may despise the riches in his own pocket" (*Letters to Lucilius* 20.10). Griffin's greatest misgiving on this score, as expressed both in *Seneca* and *"Imago Vitae Suae,"* is that Seneca had orthodox Stoic justifications for his wealth, and used them on occasion, but elsewhere turned to Cynic-style rants against affluence. Paul Veyne's

attempts (*Seneca,* pp. 10–16) to get Seneca out of his moral paradox form a study in rationalization.

102 *"By what kind of wisdom":* Tacitus, *Annals* 13.42. Tacitus' inclusion of the long quotation, without explicit disavowal, shows that he harbored some doubts himself about how Seneca's deeds accorded with his words.

103 *"Even after denouncing tyranny":* The long list of charges is found at Dio 61.10. They stand in the correct chronological position to be connected to Suillius' speech, and some seem to echo the portion of that speech recorded by Tacitus, but others go far beyond it.

104 *"Why do you speak better":* The turn comes at the start of chap. 17, where Seneca introduces his critics abruptly: "So, if one of those who bark like dogs against philosophy says the kind of thing they always say . . ." The bitter tone of what follows has seemed to many scholars an ad hominem rebuttal, prompted by Suillius' speech, though this cannot be proven. Griffin (*Seneca,* pp. 308–9), in discussing the problem, takes a moderate position: "Seneca has not simply described what Suillius has said omitting his name; he has generalized, using Suillius' criticisms and others he has suffered at different times as a core." In her chronological table (pp. 396 and 399) she makes clear that the *De Vita Beata* must be dated after, though not necessarily soon after, the speech by Suillius.

104 *The questions go on and on:* One would give much to know to what degree these imagined questions reflect what was actually thought about, or even true of, Seneca's own lifestyle. Seneca often moves imperceptibly from a personal case to a hypothetical or general one, or back again, so one cannot infer that the "you" addressed here is always Seneca himself. Nonetheless little in the content of the questions is manifestly at odds with known circumstances of Seneca's life. Even when he mentions shedding tears at the death of a wife (*De Vita Beata* 17.1), it is conceivable that he refers to his own experience. (See the note to p. 52 above for the possibility that Seneca had lost his first wife.)

104 *it is strange that he does so:* The same phenomenon is seen in a later work, *De Beneficiis,* in which Seneca evokes the Cynic Demetrius as his mask, but then has Demetrius attack the very practices in which Seneca is known to have engaged (see pp. 132–33 in this book). Seneca's writings sometimes exhibit what a modern psychologist might call reaction formation: sources of anxiety in his life, or guilt over his own behavior, become embodied in his created personae.

105 *ability to pull imperial strings:* Griffin (*Seneca,* pp. 97, 247) gives credence to the argument, first raised by W. H. Alexander, (1952, 322), that Seneca was instrumental in arranging the prosecution and banishment of Suillius, a move she considers a form of "revenge."

105 *continued sleeping with Acte:* According to Tacitus (*Annals* 13.46), Poppaea referred to the continuing affair at the time that Nero first took an interest in her.

105 A haughty whore, bedecked: *Octavia,* lines 125–6. Ferri's commentary clarifies the metaphor: "The expression . . . describes Poppaea in terms of a victorious epic warrior" (*Octavia,* p. 162).

106 *distorting Poppaea into a caricature:* As discussed by Franz Holtrattner, *Poppaea Neronis potens: die Gestalt der Poppaea Sabina in den Nerobüchern des Tacitus* (Graz 1995).

106 *two different reports:* Tacitus, in *Histories* (1.13) and *Annals* (13.45–46). The version in the *Histories,* which makes Poppaea's marriage to Otho a sham contrived by Nero, is seconded by Suetonius (*Otho* 3), Dio (62.11.2), and Plutarch (*Galba* 19.106). That of the *Annals,* in which Otho is a true husband displaced by Nero, has generally been preferred by modern historians. See Griffin, *Nero,* p. 102, for example.

106 *Otho ended up far from Rome:* Suetonius' report (*Otho* 3) that Otho was at Baiae in 59, so as to host a dinner party for Nero and Agrippina, seems to be in error; Tacitus (*Annals* 13.46) specifies that he stayed in Lusitania until 69.

107 *"erotic kisses and endearments":* Tacitus, *Annals* 14.2. Tacitus gives considerable effort in this chapter to determining the story's veracity, and his tone shows he inclines toward belief.

107 *Suetonius endorsed this alternate version:* Suetonius, *Nero* 28, implies that Nero was prevented from consummating his desires. Suetonius in the same chapter cites a popular rumor that Nero emerged from the curtained litter of Agrippina with stained and rumpled clothing. This prompts an amusing comment from Wood (*Imperial Women,* p. 264) about the difficulty of having sex, incestuous or otherwise, in a moving litter. Champlin (*Nero,* p. 88) discredits the anecdote about the litter on other grounds but does not pass judgment on the incest story generally.

107 *Dio preserved a bizarre third variant:* Dio 62.11.2, adduced as a certainty after Dio has refused to comment on the veracity of the incest tale.

107 *The truth lies beyond our grasp:* No modern historian has to my knowledge taken a firm position on the incest tale; see for example Champlin, *Nero,* p. 88, and Barrett,

Agrippina, p. 183. Wood (*Imperial Women*, p. 264) is skeptical but says that only the two participants in the relationship could have known the truth. Griffin does not discuss it.

108 *He reported that Seneca used Acte:* Tacitus, *Annals* 14.2.

108 *a Greek freedman named Anicetus:* Tacitus (*Annals* 14.3) specifies that he was formerly one of Nero's tutors, making his elevation above Seneca in the episode that follows all the more pointed.

108 that the future will believe with difficulty: *Octavia*, lines 359–60.

109 *Tacitus wondered:* Tacitus, *Annals* 14.7.3, where Nero summons Seneca and Burrus, whom Tacitus describes as *incertum an et ante gnaros*—"perhaps previously informed [of the murder plot], perhaps not."

109 *Dio made Seneca chief instigator:* Dio 62.12.1: "Seneca too urged him on [in addition to Poppaea], as has been reported by many trustworthy authorities, whether because he wanted to silence the charges against himself, or because he wanted to lead Nero forward into unholy bloodshed so that he would be destroyed as soon as possible by both gods and men."

109 *perhaps even fortifying herself with antidotes:* So claim Tacitus (*Annals* 14.2) and Suetonius (*Nero* 34.2). Suetonius even asserts that Nero tried to poison Agrippina on three occasions, without success.

110 *"Why do we need to see":* Letters to Lucilius 51.12. Seneca neatly resolves the paradox of his having been to Baiae himself to witness these things: he begins by telling Lucilius that he left the resort town, presumably in disgust, the day after he got there (51.1).

110 *moored at a Baiae villa:* Tacitus writes confusedly about the movements of the ship, placing it first at Bauli and claiming that Agrippina was suspicious and declined to use it (*Annals* 14.4.5–6), then situating it at Baiae without explanation (14.4.7). The report of Suetonius (*Nero* 34) has the ship at Baiae all along, but Suetonius (*Otho* 3) also, improbably, states that Otho, the banished former husband of Poppaea, was the host at the final dinner party. Such inconsistencies cloud the picture but should not call the credibility of the whole tale into question, as Dawson ("Whatever Happened to Lady Agrippina?") would have it.

111 *Nero's kisses, as he put her on board:* For reasons that escape me, all three major sources include the single striking detail that Nero kissed his mother's *breasts* in farewell:

Tacitus, *Annals* 14.4.8; Dio, 62.13.2; Suetonius, *Nero* 34.2. This was in no way a customary or appropriate way for a son to bid farewell to a mother, even one who had become his incestuous lover.

113 *Nero's old guard had temporized:* Barrett's (*Agrippina,* p. 189) editorializing comment on Burrus' behavior applies equally well to Seneca: "He lacked the courage to object to the murder but also lacked the courage to follow the emperor's orders to carry it out."

114 *Dying and wretched, she makes one last request: Octavia,* lines 367–76. Tacitus (*Annals* 14.8.6) and Dio (62.13.5) give similar reports. The final words of Jocasta in Seneca's tragedy *Oedipus* have a strangely similar point, but it is not clear what the historical relationship is between the play and the accounts of Agrippina's death.

CHAPTER 5: MARITOCIDE (A.D. 59–62)

115 *peer vacantly into the darkness:* The scene is drawn with superb artistry by Tacitus (*Annals* 14.10) and confirmed by Dio (62.14.4).

116 *to view the corpse:* Tacitus (*Annals* 14.9.1) leaves the question open, but the sequence of his own narrative tells against it. Dio (62.14.2) and Suetonius (*Nero* 34.4) are certain he came, and Dio has him remark, as he studies her naked form, "I did not know I had so beautiful a mother."

116 *winning their acquiescence:* Seneca's authorship of the letter to the Senate is strongly implied by Tacitus (*Annals* 14.11.4) and is stated explicitly by Quintilian (8.5.18). But see the discussion by W. H. Alexander, "The Communiqué to the Senate on Agrippina's Death," *Classical Philology* 49 (1954): 94–97, which reaches the bizarre conclusion that Seneca was not the author of the letter, ancient testimony notwithstanding.

116 *a record of its content and structure:* Tacitus, *Annals* 14.10.10–11.3.

116 *arranging gifts and handouts:* A donative of silver for the Praetorians is attested by Dio (62.14.3).

117 *"I neither believe nor rejoice":* Quoted in Quintilian, *Institutio Oratoria* 8.5.18.

117 *a stiff-necked Stoic named Thrasea Paetus:* The timing of this departure is given slightly differently by Tacitus (*Annals* 14.12.2), who implies that it followed the voting of honors to Nero, and by Dio (62.15.2), who says explicitly that the walkout immediately followed the reading of the letter.

118 *"Farewell father, farewell mother"*: Datus is known only from this anecdote, recorded by Suetonius (*Nero* 39.3). Datus was apparently banished as a result of his indiscretion.

119 *One wag hung a leather sack:* Dio 62.16.1–2. Suetonius (*Nero* 39) gives an elaborate list of derogatory graffiti.

119 *not wishing to give substance to rumors:* Dio 62.16.3, closely seconded by Suetonius, *Nero* 39.

119 *the Ludi Maximi:* Description from Dio 62.17.2–18.3. A valuable chronology of Nero's games and spectacles is found in Champlin, *Nero*, pp. 69–75.

120 *"Please hear me graciously, masters":* The humility of this plea was not intended ironically, if we follow Champlin's (*Nero*, chap. 3) insightful discussion of Nero's artistic ambitions.

120 *stationed where he could be seen:* Dio 62.20.3. Tacitus (*Annals* 14.15.7) notes the participation of Burrus, "grieving but praising," but is silent on Seneca and his brother. It would be natural for Seneca to be coopted into the same role as Burrus at this event, and Tacitus shows at other points a desire to spare Seneca from humiliation, so Dio's report seems credible.

121 *the sage was enlisted to prompt Nero:* Dio 62.20.3.

121 *Seneca and Burrus had forbidden it:* Clearly implied by Tacitus at *Annals* 14.14.1 and 3, where he notes that Nero had yearned to race chariots for a long time and that at the current moment, Seneca and Burrus could no longer stand up to him.

122 *two years younger than Nero:* The facts of Lucan's life are known from two brief biographies, one by Suetonius and the other by Vacca (a medieval grammarian), and from a laudatory poem by Statius, *Silvae* 2.7.

122 *a summons to return to Rome:* No firm date is given for Lucan's recall, but the poet was already back in Rome for the Neronia of 60. See Griffin's discussion (*Nero*, pp. 157–58) for more detail.

123 *"There is no torment of the heart":* Consolation to Helvia 18.5. The "Marcus" referred to here is almost certainly Lucan; see Griffin, *Seneca*, p. 58. The boy was at this time three or four years old.

123 *a very fast political track:* Griffin, *Nero*, pp. 157–58. The five-year acceleration, previously used only for heirs to the throne, is so shocking that a few scholars have deemed it impossible. See Fred Ahl, *Lucan: An Introduction* (Ithaca, 1976), p. 347n.

123 *Lucan had begun work:* The chronology of the *Civil War* is a matter of some con-

troversy. Vacca's biography records that three books were circulated first, probably books 1 through 3, and that their publication preceded the souring of relations between Nero and Lucan, dated by most scholars to 62.

124 *some have read it as satire:* See Ahl, *Lucan,* pp. 47–48, and Stephen Hinds, "Generalizing About Ovid," in *The Imperial Muse,* ed. A. J. Boyle (Victoria, Australia, 1987), pp. 27–29. An eloquent defense of the passage's sincerity has been made by Michael Dewar, "Laying It On with a Trowel: The Proem to Lucan and Related Texts," *Classical Quarterly* 44 (1994): 199–211.

125 *removed his crown and awarded it:* This seems to be the inevitable inference that results from combining Suetonius' report (*Nero* 12.3), that the winners of poetic and rhetorical competitions at the Neronia gave their crowns to Nero, with that of Vacca (*Vita Lucani*), that Lucan was the winner in Roman poetry.

125 *other authors at his court:* Details from Tacitus, *Annals* 14.16. The first satire of Persius, an embittered rant against the well-fed and conventional poets who wrote to please, is generally regarded as a critique of Nero's court circle, penned by one who was not a member.

126 *mock naval battles:* Suetonius, *Nero* 12.1; Dio 61.9.5. For a discussion, see K. Coleman, "Launching into History: Aquatic Displays in the Early Empire," *Journal of Roman Studies* 83 (1993): 55–57.

126 *exotic creatures from far-off lands:* These grand games were described by Calpurnius Siculus, *Eclogue* 7, beginning at line 23. The description of "seals chased by bears" was first seen as a reference to polar bears by George Jennison, "Polar Bears at Rome: Calpurnius Siculus, *Ecl.* 7.65–66," *Classical Review* 36 (1922): 73, though the connection has been doubted. For discussion see G. B. Townsend, "Calpurnius Siculus and the *Munus Neronis,*" *Journal of Roman Studies* 70 (1980): 169–74.

126 *it would repeat every five years:* There is a notorious chronological problem here in that Nero may have intended the Neronia to recur every four years (Suetonius, *Nero* 12.3; Dio 62.21.1), yet the second iteration came in 65, without any notice in our sources of a delay. It could be that Suetonius or his source has misused the word *quinquennale*—which usually means "every four years" due to the Roman method of inclusive counting—to mean "every five years" instead. Those interested in the problem can consult J. D. P. Bolton, "Was the *Neronia* a Freak Festival?," *Classical Quarterly* 42 (1948): 82–90.

126 *supplied at his own expense:* In contrast to ordinary games, paid for privately by wealthy officials; see Tacitus, *Annals* 14.21.4.

126 *boundary lines were hard to draw:* "It is not improbable that by A.D. 68 the *aerarium* [a treasury of public funds] and the *fiscus* [the emperor's private estate] were, in practice, hardly distinguishable." So says C. H. V. Sutherland, "*Aerarium* and *Fiscus* During the Early Empire," *American Journal of Philology* 66 (1945): 166. Griffin (*Nero,* pp. 199–200) gives a more nuanced view but concurs that "a shortage in the *fiscus* was eventually liable to cause trouble in the *aerarium* too."

126 *by a reform enacted under his reign:* See Tacitus, *Annals* 13.29, and Griffin, *Nero,* pp. 56–57.

127 *give 10 million sesterces to a freedman:* Anecdote related by Dio 61.5.4.

127 *tried (with little success) to get most of it back:* See Suetonius, *Galba* 15; Tacitus, *Histories* 1.20.

127 *this kind of giving:* Tacitus, *Annals* 13.18.

128 *some of them touching closely:* The peculiar relevance of Seneca's own life to the theme of *De Beneficiis* has been discussed by Miriam Griffin in several contexts, including a 2012 book on *De Beneficiis* that I was not able to consult. But see "*De Beneficiis* and Roman Society," *Journal of Roman Studies* 93 (2003): 92–113; "Seneca as a Sociologist: *De Beneficiis,*" in De Vivo and Lo Cascio, *Seneca uomo politico,* especially 106–9; and the introduction she coauthored with Brad Inwood in their new translation, *Seneca: On Benefits* (Chicago, 2011).

129 *Boudicca, warrior-queen of the Iceni:* Various versions of her name are in current use, including *Boudica* and *Boadicea.* The form used here is that found in the best Tacitus manuscripts; the variant *Boadicea* apparently arose from the title of an eighteenth-century English poem.

129 *an opportune moment to strike:* The historical account that follows is taken largely from Tacitus, *Annals* 14.31–39.

129 *Temple of Divine Claudius:* The base of the temple today underlies a Norman castle in Colchester.

130 *the long speeches Dio assigns her:* At 62.3–6, Dio quotes an extremely long and detailed diatribe against all things Roman by the British queen, where Tacitus (*Annals* 14.35) gives her only a short speech.

132 *some modern historians credit his account:* In particular, Christoph M. Bulst, who

regards the report as exaggerated but "unlikely to be an invention"; see "The Revolt of Queen Boudicca in A.D. 60," *Historia* 10 (1961): 501. This seems to be essentially Miriam Griffin's position (*Seneca,* pp. 232 and 246; see also *Nero,* p. 226), for she rejects the idea that "Seneca alone caused the panic" but accepts that he did recall his British loans. On the other side of the argument, Dio's accusation against Seneca is entirely rejected by John C. Overbeck, "Tacitus and Dio on Seneca's Rebellion," *American Journal of Philology* 90 (1969): 140–41, and by Furneaux, *Annals of Tacitus.* John Wacher, "Britain: 43 B.C. to A.D. 69," in *Cambridge Ancient History,* pp. 10.508–9, does not mention Seneca in his discussion of the rebellion's causes.

132 *ingeniously linked it:* C. E. Stevens, "The Will of Q. Veranius," *Classical Review* 1 (1951), 4–7; endorsed by Bulst, "Revolt of Queen Boudicca," p. 501.

132 *prior to the rebellion:* Argued by Stevens, "Will of Q. Veranius" 4, on different grounds than mine (the fact that Tacitus gives no hint of it). In a long discussion, K. R. Bradley (*Suetonius' Life of Nero,* pp. 110–13) cites numerous attempts to date this report and himself opts for the year or so after Nero's accession. What is certain is that the oft-mentioned date of A.D. 61, or any date after the start of the rebellion, can be rejected. Nero committed sizable forces to quelling the revolt, and the loss of Roman life that it entailed made withdrawal unthinkable.

134 *he mentions Burrus only once:* See p. 90 in this book.

134 *a painful throat swelling:* Recounted by Tacitus, *Annals* 14.51. Tacitus admits to doubt about the poisoning theory that he said was held by the majority of sources. Dio (62.13.3) and Suetonius (*Nero* 35) are more certain on this score, as is McDermott ("Sextus Afranius Burrus," pp. 252–53).

134 *owner of Burrus' house:* See Tacitus, *Annals* 14.60.5, where Nero is able, shortly after this, to make a gift of Burrus' house to Octavia as part of a divorce settlement.

134 *the case of a wealthy aunt, Domitia:* Dio 62.17.1–2; Suetonius *Nero* 34.5. Tacitus says nothing of the death of Domitia to either confirm or refute these rumors of poisoning, but the words he chooses in describing the poisoning of Pallas—"by his long old age he was keeping back [from Nero] a huge fortune"—confirm that Nero sometimes could not wait for nature to take its course.

135 *Tigellinus demonized Seneca and other Stoics:* Tacitus, *Annals* 14.57.5. This is the first occasion (to judge by Tacitus' evidence) on which the Stoic school was branded a political faction adverse to the interests of the princeps, but that view was to develop strongly under Tigellinus' prefecture; see p. 164 in this book.

135 *Seneca's enemies roused themselves:* Tacitus (*Annals* 14.52) repeats their charges at some length. He castigates these men as *deteriores,* "the worse sort," but nonetheless (as he did earlier with Suillius Rufus) gives them unusual latitude to express themselves.

137 *"Sure, and be certain to give back":* Anecdote related by Dio 62.13.2. Dio's account implies that Nero poisoned Burrus in part to clear the way for divorcing Octavia.

139 *jolted the princeps into action:* It has often been wondered why Nero waited so long after the death of Agrippina, who had been his principal stumbling block, to divorce Octavia and marry Poppaea. The sequence of cause and effect in 62 is also a source of confusion: Did Nero feel free to divorce Octavia after the deaths of Plautus and Sulla? Or was it Poppaea's pregnancy that freed his hand, and the murders were only an expedient? What role did the death of Burrus play? We do not have an exact enough chronology of these events to be certain.

139 *Do as I order: Octavia,* lines 437–38, addressed to a character identified in the manuscripts only as "prefect." Ferri (*Octavia,* pp. 250–51) correctly surmises that this is an anonymous or "type" character, not to be identified either as Burrus or as one of his successors, Faenius Rufus or Tigellinus. For the view that it is Tigellinus, see P. Kragelund, "The Prefect's Dilemma and the Date of *Octavia,*" *Classical Quarterly* 38 (1988): 492–508.

140 *journey in only five days:* Not a record-setting speed for an ancient ship sailing under favorable winds but impressive nonetheless. See Lionel Casson, "Speed Under Sail of Ancient Ships," *Transactions of the American Philological Association* 82 (1951): 136–48. Details of the episode are from Tacitus, *Annals* 14.57.4.

140 *got wind of the coming attack:* The details are supplied by Tacitus, *Annals* 14.58–59.

140 *safeguard his wife and children:* Tacitus (*Annals* 14.59) gives the double motive. If Plautus meant to protect Pollitta, his actions were sadly in vain; Tacitus narrates her grim suicide three years later at *Annals* 16.10–11.

141 *a revolution was at hand:* The long speech is paraphrased by Tacitus at *Annals* 14.61.

141 *banishment to some comfortable place:* In fact, Anicetus ended up on Sardinia, as Tacitus (*Annals* 14.62.6) informs us, where he died a natural death.

142 *under house arrest in a sumptuous villa:* The ruins of what is today known as Villa Giulia (after Augustus' daughter Julia, who occupied it in the early first century A.D.) can be seen at the north end of modern Ventotene (ancient Pandateria).

142 *set in motion the events:* This is the interpretation of the line by Ferri (*Octavia,* pp. 401–2), though there are admitted obscurities and possible textual problems.

CHAPTER 6: HOLOCAUST (A.D. 62–64)

143 *poisoned for his estate:* Tacitus, *Annals* 14.65.1.

143 *Doryphorus, a special favorite:* Suetonius, *Nero* 29.

144 *"I've told you already":* Quoted in Dio 62.13.2.

144 *a strangely adverse effect:* The ancient sources are vague about the timing of the downturn in Nero's relations with Lucan, but all imply that artistic jealousy, not political
ideology, was its source; see Griffin, *Nero,* pp. 158–59. Vacca's biography specifies
that three books of *Civil War* had appeared before this downturn, probably meaning books 1, 2, and 3 (43–47).

145 *The "crime" took place:* Tacitus, *Annals* 14.48–49.

145 *picking up a chamber pot:* Retold by Seneca in *De Beneficiis* (3.26) as an example of
how any small joke or gesture could bring an indictment in the time of Tiberius.
The victim of this outrage, Paulus (not otherwise known), was saved when his
quick-thinking slave slipped the ring off his finger.

146 *The story is plausible:* Griffin (*Nero,* pp. 48–49) explains her reasons for concurring
with Tacitus' inference, though she also makes clear it was only an inference, not
based on primary sources.

146 *the birthdays of the tyrant-slayers:* Attested by Juvenal, *Satire* 5.36–37, as a rite that
Thrasea shared with his son-in-law, Helvidius Priscus.

147 *aided the prosecution:* Tacitus, *Annals* 13.33.3 and 16.21.3.

147 *one of his many snapshots:* Tacitus, *Annals* 15.23.6.

148 *the routine of a powerful statesman:* Tacitus, *Annals* 14.56.6.

148 *his most harrowing tragedy,* Thyestes: The problem of dating Seneca's tragedies has
been discussed in chapter 2. *Thyestes* is generally acknowledged to be a late play,
according to Fitch's metrical criteria, and its political themes have been felt to be
particularly appropriate to the early 60s. See Tarrant, *Seneca's Thyestes,* pp. 13 and
48. There are additionally individual lines of the play that seem to postdate the
late 50s. See Tarrant, *Seneca's Thyestes,* p. 182, and R. G. Nisbet, "The Dating of
Seneca's Tragedies, with Special Reference to *Thyestes,*" in Fitch, *Oxford Readings:
Seneca.*

148 *"among the decrepit":* Letters to Lucilius 26.1.

148 *Making the rounds of his estates:* The incident is related at *Letters to Lucilius* 12.1–2.

148 *following the emperor and the court through Italy:* Inferential, but in my view inescap-

able, in that Nero had denied Seneca's request in 62 to retire. Tacitus (*Annals* 14.56) indicates that Seneca curbed his political activity thereafter, but he could not have brought it to a halt without incurring Nero's enmity. The fact that Seneca had to take further steps toward withdrawal in 64 (see pp. 169–70 in this book) proves that up to that time he had remained partially engaged.

148 *so many other friends were dead:* Burrus' death in 62 was preceded by that of Annaeus Serenus, addressee of both *De Constantia Sapientis* and *De Tranquillitate Animi*. Another close friend, Aufidius Bassus, is described as near death in *Letter* 30, and the deaths of Cornelius Senecio and Tullius Marcelinus also occurred during the period when the *Letters* were being composed (101.1–3, 77.5–9).

149 *having undergone torture:* Seneca alludes to this painful episode in the preface to book 4 of *Natural Questions,* sections 15–17. The reason for Lucilius' persecution, as given there, was his friendship with Gaetulicus, an army officer who had plotted a rebellion against Caligula.

149 *a trip to a friend's vacation home:* The letter summarized here is number 53, written probably in 63. Seneca does not indicate whom he was visiting or why, or what had brought him to Baiae and vicinity, which is his location as well in *Letters* 51, 55, and 57. Elaine Fantham has speculated that he was joining the Roman court and Senate for its "spring break" April holiday, or August beach getaway, when he wrote these Campanian letters. See Fantham, ed., *Seneca: Selected Letters* (Oxford, 2010), p. xxii n22.

150 *how an author's style reflects his character:* The celebrated *Letter* 114.

151 *spinning himself:* Modern admirers of Seneca's *Letters,* whose ranks include the esteemed philosopher Michel Foucault, may be dismayed by my brief and skeptical treatment of them. I hasten to repeat the words of my introduction, that I am not undertaking a survey of Seneca's philosophic ideas, a task that in the case of the *Letters* would be lengthy and complex. My concern is with the points of contact between Seneca's literary and political careers. That the *Letters* do contain such points of contact is, I think, incontestable, given the following: (1) the *Letters* were written to be published and seen by a wide audience of contemporaries, including much of the Roman elite and Nero himself; (2) Seneca was not "in retirement" at the time he wrote the *Letters*, as is often asserted, but was striving to lower his political profile even while remaining at court, at Nero's insistence; (3) Seneca felt the need to appease or warn off Nero at this time, as shown by *Natural Questions,*

a work roughly concurrent with the *Letters* (see pp. 154–55 in this book); and (4) at least one letter in the collection (as discussed in this book, pp. 153–54) contains what appears unmistakably to be a coded communication directed at Nero, though readers can disagree (as I disagree with Paul Veyne below, note to p. 153) as to its message.

151   *"Philosophy is such a sacred thing":* Letters 55.4.

151   *he too deceives:* An extreme and, to my mind, absurd interpretive position holds that not even the most pointedly autobiographical statements in Seneca's *Letters* can be taken as "true" or be used to reconstruct Seneca's life, discussed for example by Catharine Edwards, "Self-scrutiny and Self-transformation in Seneca's Letters," in Fitch, *Oxford Readings: Seneca,* p. 85 and n. 4. That being said, there are statements in the *Letters* that one cannot take literally without creating absurdities. Did Seneca *really* move into rooms above a public bath simply to test his powers of concentration (*Letter* 56)? Or was it just a "thought experiment"? (I leave aside the issue of whether the *Letters* represent one side of an actual correspondence between Seneca and Lucilius; most scholars today agree it does not, though Seneca has gone to great lengths to create a convincing fiction.)

151   *the course of a typical day:* The opening section of *Letter* 83 is referred to. In *Letter* 76.1, Seneca similarly indicates that he has spent much of his day, for the previous five days, listening to philosophic discourse.

152   *"We are dying every day":* The precise words quoted here, *cotidie morimur* in Latin, are in fact from *Letter* 24.20.

153   *"Even while suffocating":* Letter 54.3.

153   *Two cases:* Letter 70.20–23.

153   *whether one should commit suicide:* Letter 70.8–13. Elaine Fantham (*Seneca: Selected Letters,* p. 109) notes the relevance of this letter to "the experience of Seneca and others at Nero's court."

153   *a mutual nonaggression pact:* The letter referred to is 73, about which Fantham (*Seneca: Selected Letters,* p. 116) comments: "It is as near as Seneca comes to asserting his loyalty to the treacherous emperor Nero." René Waltz first stressed the self-protective, deal-making aspect of this letter in *Vie de Sénèque* (Paris, 1909), p. 418, a view rejected by Griffin (*Seneca,* p. 360). More recently Paul Veyne (*Seneca,* pp. 160–63) has devoted an extensive discussion to *Letter* 73, which he correctly assesses as "an open letter intended for Nero" but, in my view, misreads and mis-

characterizes. Veyne skews his analysis by prefacing it with an anecdote, taken from Philostratus, "to recreate the climate of those years"—a climate of extreme autocratic repression, as he sees it. But the anecdote dates from a time after the Pisonian conspiracy, when the climate at Rome had changed considerably from what it was when Seneca was writing. In general, Veyne would like to see the *Letters to Lucilius* as oppositional literature, "keeping the torch of truth burning" in a dark time, and he compares them (p. 159) to the underground publications of modern East Bloc dissidents before perestroika, but this analogy, again, badly overstates the degree of repression in Nero's Rome at the time the *Letters* were written. "Until the conspiracy of Piso in 65 most senators were free from the terror that had hardly abated in the previous generation." P. A. Brunt, "Stoicism and the Principate," *Papers of the British School at Rome* 43 (Rome, 1975), p. 26.

154 *Natural Questions:* The two works are both dated by Miriam Griffin (*Seneca*, p. 396) to "after the retirement in 62." *Natural Questions* has segments that must fall earlier than summer 64, and others that must be later than February 63. The *Letters* have a "dramatic date" between winter 63 and autumn 64 and were probably published (at least in part) in late 64 or early 65. It is thus barely possible, but unlikely, that one work entirely preceded the other. Yet this is the thesis on which Paul Veyne (*Seneca*, p. 25) sharply distinguishes his assessment of Seneca's technique in the two works, claiming that "something happened around 63" to alter Seneca's mind-set.

154 *praises Nero for his poetry:* At *Natural Questions* 1.5.6, in a discussion of iridescence, Seneca quotes Nero's verse description of peacocks' necks, "the neck of Venus' dove glitters as it moves," and characterizes the line as "very beautifully turned."

154 *"a man passionately devoted to truth":* *Natural Questions* 6.8.1. Harry Hine has discussed the phrase extensively in "Rome, the Cosmos, and the Emperor in Seneca's *Natural Questions*," *Journal of Roman Studies* 96 (2006): 64–67, giving it a more generous interpretation than I have done. Hine would like to see Nero as genuinely possessing "some, perhaps modest . . . commitment to furthering knowledge of the natural world," but such commitment, in my view, was so modest as to be invisible.

155 *"an eternal charge against Alexander":* *Natural Questions* 6.23.2–3. The parallel between the situation of Seneca with respect to Nero, and that of Callisthenes with respect

to Alexander, seems to me inescapable, though it is downplayed by Hine ("Rome, the Cosmos," p. 64) and more recently by Gareth Williams, *The Cosmic Viewpoint: A Study of Seneca's "Natural Questions"* (Oxford, 2012), p. 254 and n. 151. My own reading falls into line with that of Italo Lana, *Lucio Anneo Seneca* (Turin, 1955), p. 55.

155 *62 or 63:* Seneca clearly dates the quake to 63, but Tacitus (*Annals* 15.22.2) a year earlier. Both dates have been defended by scholars. See Wallace-Hadrill, "Seneca and the Pompeian Earthquake," in De Vivo and Lo Cascio, *Seneca uomo politico.*

155 *Curious details: Natural Questions* 6.1.2–3 and 6.27–30.

157 *lost everything in the fire:* The name of a certain Quintus Aebutius Liberalis, a mid-rank military officer, has been found on two inscriptions in Dalmatia. See Griffin, *Seneca,* pp. 455–56. If this is the same man as Seneca's friend or even a close relation, then the falloff in the family's fortunes was indeed severe, for the post Quintus occupied did not befit a wealthy *eques.*

157 *"Exile, torture, disease, war, shipwreck": Letter* 91.8.

157 *"There won't be long until the destruction": Natural Questions* 30.1.5.

158 *"All boundaries will be sundered": Natural Questions* 1.29.8–9.

158 *ban state commendations:* Tacitus, *Annals* 15.20–22.

160 *"Some animals mix up their own footprints": Letters* 68.4.

160 *"It is difficult, if not impossible":* Griffin, *Seneca,* p. 334. Brunt ("Stoicism and the Principate," p. 19) says similarly, "Seneca's views on the propriety of a political career are self-contradictory."

161 *banquets that stretched from noon to midnight:* Suetonius, *Nero* 27.2; see also 22.3. 40.4.

162 *"I hate you, Nero":* Quoted in Dio 62.15.1.

163 *a rigorous diet heavily weighted with leeks:* Suetonius, *Nero* 20.1, and Pliny the Elder, *Natural History* 34.166.

163 *"for the safety of Nero":* Griffin, *Nero,* p. 102.

163 *he had found the theater of Neapolis:* See *Letter* 76.4, and the remarks of Griffin (*Seneca,* p. 360). I do not find it implausible, as Griffin does, that Seneca would have tempted the princeps' anger with such a remark. It is cleverly couched—Seneca indicates that flute competitions, not singing, were going on in the theater at that time—yet it is still self-exculpating enough to register with readers whose good

opinion mattered to the author. Here we again run into the problem of how many "secondary purposes" are present in Seneca's writings. See the note to p. xvii above.

165 *"the comet we saw for six months"*: Natural Questions 7.21.3.

165 *near the Circus Maximus:* The account of the great fire followed here is that of Tacitus, *Annals* 15.38–45, not significantly contradicted by either Suetonius or Dio (except in the matter of Nero's culpability—see next note).

167 *Was Nero far enough gone:* The question has bothered many historians. Tacitus (*Annals* 15.38.1), to his great credit, confessed his uncertainty on this point and recorded a disagreement among his sources. Dio (62.16.1), Suetonius (*Nero* 38), Pliny the Elder (*Natural History* 17.1.1), and the author of *Octavia* (lines 831–33) are all convinced of Nero's guilt. This matter involves the modern historian in so many imponderables—above all the question of motive, which in the case of a Nero is truly beyond reach of speculation—that I have avoided taking any position. But I do note that a recent and highly esteemed scholar, Edward Champlin (*Nero,* pp. 185–91), has argued strongly, by way of new and ingenious arguments, that Nero did indeed set the blaze.

168 *Christiani, and their founder Christus:* The dispute over the authenticity of *Annals* 15.44, the first mention by a non-Christian author of Christ or Christians, has been almost as heated as the question of Nero's arson. Already in 1907 Henry Furneaux inserted a long appendix on the topic into his edition of the *Annals* (pp. 2:416–27), and there have been many contributions to the debate since then. Most scholars are satisfied the passage is genuine.

169 *the Colossus Neronis:* Its height is variously given by Suetonius (*Nero* 38.1), Dio (66.15.1), and Pliny the Elder (*Natural History* 34.45). The colossus was reshaped after Nero's death (or perhaps was originally designed by Nero) to suggest the god Helius (Roman Sol), and was moved to a position in front of the Flavian amphitheater, which thereby acquired its modern name, the Colosseum. It is not known how or when the statue was destroyed, sometime in the Middle Ages, but no trace of it survives.

169 *Acratus, one of Nero's trusted freedmen, and Secundus Carrinas:* Named as Nero's agents by Tacitus (*Annals* 15.45.3), with a typically devastating thumbnail sketch of the latter.

170 *but on Nero's terms:* Seneca's surrender of his wealth during the period after the fire is

attested only by Dio (62.25.3) but perhaps also implied by Tacitus (*Annals* 15.64.6). Nero's refusal to grant retirement, and Seneca's subsequent feigning of illness, are found at *Annals* 15.45.5.

170 *no reason to doubt the information:* Tacitus (*Annals* 15.60.3) later refers to the report as though it were an established fact. Griffin (*Seneca,* p. 276, and "*Imago Vitae Suae,*" p. 48) withholds comment.

CHAPTER 7: SUICIDE (II) (A.D. 64–66)

172 *"That which is undergirded by truth":* De Clementia 1.1.5, a passage obviously addressed to Romans concerned about the youth of the new princeps.

172 *the failures weighed on him heavily:* A key passage is *Letters* 8.3, where Seneca describes himself as suffering from the moral equivalent of skin lesions and says he has found the right path of life—philosophy—only late and after much straying. At *Letters* 56.9, Seneca speaks of having withdrawn from a position of power that had been distasteful to begin with, after that position became untenable, but since he uses his maddeningly vague first-person plural, it is unclear whether he is referring to himself or constructing a hypothetical situation. See Edwards, "Self-scrutiny and Self-transformation," in Fitch, *Oxford Readings: Seneca,* p. 85.

172 *his own moral state:* In addition to the passage at 56.9 discussed in the previous note, where Seneca (or his hypothetical "we") admits to still feeling the pull of ambition, there is the less ambiguous evidence of *Letter* 75.14–17, where Seneca situates his "we"—this time clearly meaning either himself, or himself and Lucilius—among those moral strivers who "have got beyond many great faults but not all." Switching to the third person, Seneca describes the lot of a typical member of this class of strivers: "He has fled greed but still feels anger; he is no longer troubled by lust, but is still troubled by ambition" (14). Rolando Ferri (*Octavia,* p. 232), drawing a thumbnail sketch of Seneca from the facts of his political career, calls him "a wobbly *sapiens* vulnerable to sin and ambition," which would also be an apt description of the title character of *Thyestes.*

173 *almost certainly composed:* On the dating of *Thyestes,* see the note to p. 35 above.

174 *Why does Thyestes return to Argos:* Tarrant's (*Seneca's Thyestes,* pp. 148–49) commentary deals with this question in insightful ways: "From the outset . . . Seneca hints that Thyestes may be less than fully committed to the ideals he professes. . . . Sen-

eca [creates] a masterful portrait of a man who literally does not know his own mind." In discussing Thyestes' diatribe against wealth and power (lines 446–70), Tarrant (p.155) observes: "The gusto with which Thyestes enumerates the trappings of wealth seems a clear sign that he does not find this existence as distasteful as he claims."

175 *the disappearance of the sun:* Anticipated at lines 120–21, then described as a fait accompli in lines 776–88 and the choral ode that follows. This element of the story seems to have been developed by Seneca out of a minor piece of the mythic tradition, which held that Zeus had caused the sun to reverse course and set in the East to help Atreus drive Thyestes out of Argos. In Seneca's play, this reversal of the sun becomes a disappearance and assumes much larger thematic importance.

175 *Are we, out of all generations:* Thyestes, lines 875–80. Tarrant (*Seneca's Thyestes,* p. 215), noting the unusual shift to the first person plural, comments that "it is tempting to see a meaning in these lines that projects beyond the dramatic context."

176 *broke up one recitation:* Attested by Suetonius, *Vita Lucani*. The date is uncertain, but it must have preceded Nero's outright ban on Lucan's readings, a ban that Griffin (*Nero*, p. 158) is inclined to place at A.D. 64 despite the evidence of Dio (62.29.4) that it fell in 65.

177 *border on sedition:* The passages most often cited as glaring examples are 7:440–58, 640–46. Griffin (*Nero*, p. 159) has disputed the degree of oppositional inflation in later books but does not dispute that there is some; Ahl and Sullivan are more inclined to emphasize it.

177 *a bon mot that later became legendary:* Retold by Suetonius in *Vita Lucani*. As with all reported events in Lucan's life, this one is difficult to date, but clearly a time after the souring of relations with Nero is indicated, perhaps 64.

178 *too young to rule:* Tacitus (*Annals* 15.52.3) reports that Piso feared Silanus as a potential rival; that indicates there would indeed have been support for Silanus' accession. It is hard to explain then why the plot did not take shape around this man. Tacitus (*Annals* 16.7.4–16.9.5) adds to the mystery by making clear his great respect for Silanus' character.

178 *restoring the republic:* There was apparently some fear that the consul Atticus Vestinus might seize the moment of regicide to proclaim the return of freedom, though Tacitus (*Annals* 15.52.4–5), with his report, implies that such a move would have had only self-serving motives.

179 *hoped to enlist Seneca:* I follow the account of Tacitus here rather than Dio (62.24.1), who makes Seneca a ringleader of the conspiracy.

180 *arrival of this messenger:* That Seneca was aware of the plot I think is beyond question, given Lucan's participation, that of Epicharis (an intimate of Mela's), and the urgent communiqués from Piso. But that issue has often been confused with the separate matter of his collaboration, itself a matter of grave dispute. See Koestermann, *Tacitus: Annalen,* pp. 309–10, for a summary of opposing views. Griffin (*"Imago Vitae Suae,"* pp. 49–50), while strongly asserting Seneca's noninvolvement in the plot, has come close to acknowledging that he must nevertheless have had foreknowledge of it. This is important because if Seneca knew of the plot, he had the power to prevent it but did not, making him at least a passive supporter.

181 *elaborate pleasantry:* If it is accepted that Seneca was aware of the purpose of Piso's entreaty, then there can be little doubt that the words he used in his sign-off were intended to convey a covert message, though W. H. Alexander opined otherwise in "The *Enquête* on Seneca's Treason," *Classical Philology* 47 (1952): 1–6. Indeed, Koestermann (*Tacitus: Annalen,* p. 297) takes these words as evidence that Seneca was well aware of the plot in hand. Griffin (*"Imago Vitae Suae,"* pp. 49–50) agrees the words carry a covert meaning but interprets them, improbably in my view, as a "warning" to Piso "against taking risks."

181 *a story heard and recorded:* The plausibility of the report is perhaps increased by the fact that Seneca was old and had no children. Over the preceding century, the dynastic character of the principate had become its worst problem, such that Galba, three years hence, could claim as arguments for his own elevation to princeps that he was old and childless, and would of necessity choose a successor by adoption. Tacitus, *Histories* 1.16.

181 *nor are many modern historians:* Opinions have been expressed only by a few. Koestermann (*Tacitus: Annalen,* p. 4:309) is skeptical, and Veyne (*Seneca,* p. 168) even more so. Griffin (*"Imago Vitae Suae,"* p. 50) appears more equivocal, though in a private communication she has indicated to me that she also has grave doubts. More telling perhaps are the number of books and articles that do not deal with the report at all.

181 *Piso, with his charm and affability:* A portrait of Piso's character is preserved in *Laus Pisonis* (*Praise of Piso*), a Neronian-era poem of uncertain authorship (perhaps by

Lucan). Piso is portrayed in that work as a talented and convivial man who was adept at many performing arts and board games—hardly the type to lead a regicidal plot. Indeed, Piso vetoed the plan that would have most likely succeeded, an attack on Nero at Piso's own villa.

182 *went into high gear:* Unless otherwise noted, all that follows in this chapter has been taken from Tacitus' account of the Pisonian conspiracy, at the end of book 15 of *Annals.*

182 *A similar strategy:* According to the accounts of Plutarch and Suetonius, a senator named Tillius Cimber approached Julius Caesar with a petition for the recall of his brother. That allowed the other assassins to gather around in close proximity to their target.

186 *offering Nero's head as a gift:* A piquant detail from Suetonius' *Vita Lucani.*

187 *as inscrutable as ever:* Tacitus notes Seneca's arrival from Campania at this moment as though it were significant, but then warily says he doesn't know whether the timing was merely a coincidence or the result of foreknowledge. I agree with Koestermann (*Tacitus: Annalen,* p. 298) that foreknowledge is the far more likely explanation.

192 *Tacitus declined to specify:* Dio (62.5.2) says that Seneca gave his last literary efforts to an anti-Nero work and took steps to prevent it from falling into Nero's hands. Perhaps this was the same work Tacitus refers to, saying that it was so widely known in his own time that he has no need to restate its contents.

195 *Among the last to go:* The death of Thrasea Paetus is the final episode in the extant portion of Tacitus' *Annals* (16.21–35). Other deaths were required by Nero in the remaining two years of his reign, of course, but few were putatively connected to the Piso conspiracy.

196 *Arulenus Rusticus:* Tacitus, *Annals* 16.26.6–8. For Rusticus' later history, see p. 206 in this book.

197 *the stage of Pompey's Theater:* Details of what follows are taken from Tacitus, *Annals* 16.4–5, and Suetonius, *Nero* 4 and 23.

198 *commoners who did not clap loudly enough:* This abusive treatment is described by Tacitus (*Annals* 16.5) as a feature of the second Neronia; Suetonius (*Nero* 23), however, appears to situate them on Nero's first tour of Greece in 66–67. Dio (62.15.3) reports that in Nero's later years, spectators at his singing performances would pretend to faint in order to get safely out of the theater.

EPILOGUE: EUTHANASIA (A.D. 68 AND AFTER)

199 *"No matter how many you kill":* Reported by Dio (62.18.3) as part of the aftermath of Agrippina's murder, with the claim that the adage actually caused Nero to restrain his impulses.

199 *Nero's stepson Rufrius Crispinus:* Suetonius, *Nero* 35.

200 *Nero had poison:* Details of the episode leading up to Nero's death are taken from the extraordinary account of Suetonius, *Nero* 47–49.

203 *"Too late," he said:* The famous phrase *qualis artifex pereo,* "What an artist dies with me," are often described as Nero's last words, but in fact Suetonius, who records them, instead says that Nero muttered them repeatedly as he oversaw preparations for disposal of his corpse, an hour or two before his death.

204 *"in everyone's hands":* Quintilian's disquisition on Seneca's style and influence can be found at *Institutio Oratoria* 10.1.125–31.

204 *"I see the groves":* See Marcello Gigante, "Seneca tragico da Pompei all'Egitto," *Studi italiani di filologia classica* 19 (2001): 89–104.

204 *most agree it should be deattributed:* The questioning of the attribution to Seneca began with Petrarch, according to Ferri (*Octavia,* p. 6 n. 15). Senecan authorship was defended in print in recent times by Berthe Marti, "Seneca's *Apocolocyntosis* and *Octavia*: A Diptych," *American Journal of Philology* 73 (1952): 24–36, and one or two other scholars have since then admitted to at least thinking the attribution possible.

205 princeps eruditorum, *"princeps of the wise":* Pliny, *Natural History* 14.51, with discussion by Griffin, *Seneca,* p. 434.

206 *Helvidius tried to get revenge:* Tacitus, *Histories* 4.6.

206 *dared Vespasian:* As reported by Epictetus, who was quite possibly an eyewitness, in *Discourses* 1.2.19–24. For the evolution of the conflict between Stoics and princeps in the Flavian period, see Brunt, "Stoicism and the Principate," pp. 7–35.

Bibliography

Abel, Karlhans. *Bauformen in Senecas Dialogen*. Heidelberg, 1967.

Ahl, Fred. *Lucan: An Introduction*. Ithaca, 1976.

Alexander, W. H. "Seneca's *Ad Polybium*: A Reappraisal." *Transactions of the Royal Society of Canada* 37 (1943): 33–55.

———. "The *Enquête* on Seneca's Treason." *Classical Philology* 47 (1952): 1–6.

———. "The Tacitean '*non liquet*' on Seneca." *University of California Publications in Classical Philology* 14 (1952): 265–386.

———. "The Communiqué to the Senate on Agrippina's Death." *Classical Philology* 49 (1954): 94–97,

Asmis, Elizabeth. "Seneca on Fortune and the Kingdom of God." In *Seneca and the Self*. Edited by Shadi Bartsch and David Wray. Cambridge, 2009.

Aveline, John. "The Death of Claudius." *Historia* 53 (2004): 453–75.

Barnes, T. D. "The Composition of Cassius Dio's *Roman History*." *Phoenix* 38 (1984): 240–55.

Barrett, Anthony A. *Caligula: The Corruption of Power*. London, 1989.

———. *Agrippina: Sex, Power, and Politics in the Early Empire*. New Haven, Conn., 1996.

Barton, Tamsyn. "The *Inventio* of Nero: Suetonius." In *Reflections of Nero: Culture, History, and Representation*. Edited by Jás Elsner and Jamie Masters. Chapel Hill, N.C., 1994.

Bartsch, Shadi. *Ideology in Cold Blood: A Reading of Lucan's "Civil War."* Cambridge, Mass., 1997.

———. "Senecan Metaphor and Stoic Self-instruction." In *Seneca and the Self.* Edited by Shadi Bartsch and David Wray. Cambridge, 2009.

Bartsch, Shadi, and David Wray, eds. *Seneca and the Self.* Cambridge, 2009.

Bauman, Richard A. *Women and Politics in Ancient Rome.* London, 1992.

Bellincioni, Maria. *Potere ed etica in Seneca: Clementia e voluntas amica.* Brescia, 1984.

Berry, D. H., and Andrew Erskine, eds. *Form and Function in Roman Oratory.* Cambridge and New York, 2010.

Bishop, John. *Nero: The Man and the Legend.* New York, 1964.

Bolton, J. D. P. "Was the *Neronia* a Freak Festival?": *Classical Quarterly* 42 (1948): 82–90.

Bowman, Alan K., Edward Champlin, and Andrew Lintott, eds. *The Cambridge Ancient History,* vol. 10, *The Augustan Empire: 43 B.C. to A.D. 69.* Cambridge, 1996.

Bowersock, Glen W. "Seneca's Greek." In *Seneca uomo politico e l'età di Claudio e di Nerone.* Edited by Arturo De Vivo and Elio Lo Cascio. Bari, 2003.

Boyle, A. J. *Tragic Seneca: An Essay in the Theatrical Tradition.* New York, 1997.

Boyle, A. J., ed. *Seneca's Phaedra: Introduction, Text, Translation and Notes.* Liverpool and Wolfeboro, 1987.

———. *Octavia: Attributed to Seneca.* New York, 2008.

Bradley, K. R. *Suetonius' Life of Nero: An Historical Commentary.* Brussels, 1978.

Branigan, Keith, and P. J. Fowler. *The Roman West Country.* North Pomfret and North Vancouver, 1976.

Braund, Susanna, ed. *Seneca, De Clementia.* Oxford, 2009.

Brunt, P. A. "Stoicism and the Principate," *Papers of the British School at Rome,* vol. 43. Rome, 1975.

Bulst, Christoph M. "The Revolt of Queen Boudicca in A.D. 60: Roman Politics and the Iceni." *Historia: Zeitschrift für alte Geschichte* 10, no. 4 (1961): 496–509.

Cairns, Francis, and Elaine Fantham, eds. *Caesar Against Liberty? Perspectives on His Autocracy.* Cambridge, 2003.

Cairns, Francis, and Malcolm Heath, eds. *Papers of the Leeds International Latin Seminar: Sixth Volume.* Leeds, 1990.

Casson, Lionel. "Speed Under Sail of Ancient Ships." *Transactions of the American Philological Association* 82 (1951): 136–48.

Champlin, Edward. *Nero.* Cambridge, Mass., 2003.

———. "Nero, Apollo and the Poets." *Phoenix* 57 (2003): 276–83.

Cizek, Eugen. *Néron.* Paris, 1982.

Clarke, G. W. "Seneca the Younger Under Caligula." *Latomus* 24 (1965): 62–69.

Codoner, Carmen. "La expression del poder en Seneca." In *Seneca uomo politico e l'età di Claudio e di Nerone*. Edited by Arturo De Vivo and Elio Lo Cascio. Bari, 2003.

Coffey, Michael, and Roland Mayer, eds. *Seneca: Phaedra*. Cambridge, 1990.

Coleman, K. "Launching into History: Aquatic Displays in the Early Empire." *Journal of Roman Studies* 83 (1993): 55–57.

Cooper, John M., and J. F. Procopé, eds. *Seneca: Moral and Political Essays*. Cambridge, 1995.

Corbier, Mireille. "Male Power and Legitimacy Through Women: The *Domus Augusta* Under the Julio-Claudians." In *Women in Antiquity: New Assessments*. Edited by Richard Hawley and Barbara Levick. London and New York, 1995.

Costa, C. D. N. *Seneca*. Boston and London, 1974.

———. *Seneca: 17 Letters*. Warminster, 1988.

Currie, H. MacL. "The Purpose of the *Apocolocyntosis*." *Acta Classica* 31 (1962): 91–97.

Dando-Collins, Stephen. *The Great Fire of Rome: The Fall of the Emperor Nero and His City*. Cambridge, 2010.

D'Anna, Giovanni. "Seneca uomo politico nel giudizio do Tacito." In *Seneca uomo politico e l'età di Claudio e di Nerone*. Edited by Arturo De Vivo and Elio Lo Cascio. Bari, 2003.

Dawson, Alexis. "Whatever Happened to Lady Agrippina?" *Classical Journal* 64 (1969): 253–67.

De Vivo, Arturo. "Premessa." In *Seneca uomo politico e l'età di Claudio e di Nerone*. Edited by Arturo De Vivo and Elio Lo Cascio. Bari, 2003.

De Vivo, Arturo, and Elio Lo Cascio, eds. *Seneca uomo politico e l'età di Claudio e di Nerone*. Bari, 2003.

Dewar, Michael. "Laying It On with a Trowel: The Proem to Lucan and Related Texts." *Classical Quarterly* 44 (1994): 199–211.

Dingel, Joachim. *Senecas Epigramme und andere Gedichte aus der "Anthologia Latina": Ausgabe mit Übersetzung und Kommentar*. Heidelberg, 2007.

D'Ippolito, Frederico. "Etica e stato in età giulio-claudia." In *Seneca uomo politico e l'età di Claudio e di Nerone*. Edited by Arturo De Vivo and Elio Lo Cascio. Bari, 2003.

Dominik, William J. "The Style Is the Man: Seneca, Tacitus and Quintilian's Canon." In *Roman Eloquence: Rhetoric in Society and Literature*. Edited by William J. Dominik. New York, 1997.

Dominik, William J., ed. *Roman Eloquence: Rhetoric in Society and Literature.* New York, 1997.

Eden, P. T., ed. *Seneca: Apocolocyntosis.* Cambridge, 1984.

Edwards, Catharine. *Death in Ancient Rome.* New Haven, Conn., 2007.

———. "Self-scrutiny and Self-transformation in Seneca's Letters." In *Oxford Readings in Classical Studies: Seneca.* Edited by John G. Fitch. Oxford, 2008.

———. "Free Yourself! Slavery, Freedom and the Self in Seneca's *Letters.*" In *Seneca and the Self.* Edited by Shadi Bartsch and David Wray. Cambridge, 2009.

Elsner, Jás, and Jamie Masters, eds. *Reflections of Nero: Culture, History, and Representation.* Chapel Hill, N.C., 1994.

Fantham, Elaine. *Seneca's Troades: A Literary Introduction.* Princeton, 1982.

———. "Dialogues of Displacement: Seneca's Consolations to Helvia and Polybius." In *Writing Exile: The Discourse of Displacement in Greco-Roman Antiquity and Beyond.* Edited by Jan Felix Gaertner. Boston, 2007.

Fantham, Elaine, ed. *Lucan: De Bello Civili.* Cambridge, 1992.

———. *Seneca: Selected Letters.* Oxford, 2010.

Ferri, Rollando, ed. *Octavia: A Play Attributed to Seneca.* Cambridge, 2003.

Fitch, John G., "Sense-pauses and Relative Dating in Seneca, Sophocles and Shakespeare." *American Journal of Philology* 102 (1981): 289–307.

Fitch, John G., ed. *Oxford Readings in Classical Studies: Seneca.* Oxford, 2008.

Fuhrmann, Manfred. *Seneca und Kaiser Nero: Eine Biographie.* Berlin, 1997.

Furneaux, Henry, ed. *The Annals of Tacitus.* 2 vols. London, 1896–1907.

Gabba, Emilio. "Conclusioni." In *Seneca uomo politico e l'età di Claudio e di Nerone.* Edited by Arturo De Vivo and Elio Lo Cascio. Bari, 2003.

Gahan, John J. "Seneca, Ovid, and Exile." *Classical World* 78 (1985): 145–47.

Gallivan, Paul A. "Suetonius and Chronology in the 'De Vita Neronis.'" *Historia: Zeitschrift für alte Geschichte* 23, no. 3 (1974): 297–318.

Gigante, Marcello. "Seneca tragico da Pompei all'Egitto." *Studi italiani di filologia classica* 19 (2001): 89–104.

Ginsburg, Judith. *Representing Agrippina: Constructions of Female Power in the Early Roman Empire.* New York, 2006.

Goar, R. J. *The Legend of Cato Uticensis from the First Century* B.C. *to the Fifth Century* A.D. Brussels, 1987.

Grewe, Klaus. *Licht am Ende des Tunnels: Planung und Trassierung im antiken Tunnelbau.* Mainz am Rhein, 1998.

Griffin, Miriam T. "*De Brevitate Vitae.*" *Journal of Roman Studies* 52 (1962): 104–13.

———. *Seneca: A Philosopher in Politics.* Oxford, 1976.

———. *Nero: The End of a Dynasty.* London, 1984.

———. "Philosophy, Cato, and Roman Suicide." *Greece and Rome* 33 (1986): 64–77 and 192–202.

———. "Seneca as a Sociologist: *De Beneficiis.*" In *Seneca uomo politico e l'età di Claudio e di Nerone.* Edited by Arturo De Vivo and Elio Lo Cascio. Bari, 2003.

———. "*De Beneficiis* and Roman Society." *Journal of Roman Studies* 93 (2003): 92–113.

———. "*Imago Vitae Suae.*" In *Oxford Readings in Classical Studies: Seneca.* Edited by John Fitch. Oxford, 2008.

Griffin, Miriam T., and Brad Inwood, trans. *Lucius Annaeus Seneca: On Benefits.* Chicago, 2011.

Grimal, Pierre. *Sénèque et la prose latine.* Geneva, 1991.

———. *Sénèque: ou, la conscience de l'empire.* Paris, 1991.

Habinek, Thomas N. "An Aristocracy of Virtue: Seneca on the Beginnings of Wisdom." *Yale Classical Studies* 29 (1992): 187–203.

Henry, Denis, and B. Walker, "Tacitus and Seneca." *Greece and Rome* 10, no. 2 (1963): 98–110.

Henry, Elisabeth. *The Annals of Tacitus: A Study in the Writing of History.* Manchester, 1968.

Herrmann, Horst. *Nero.* Berlin, 2005.

Hiesinger, Ulrich W. "The Portraits of Nero." *American Journal of Archaeology* 79 (1975): 113–24.

Hill, Timothy. *Ambitiosa Mors: Suicide and Self in Roman Thought and Literature.* New York, 2004.

Hinds, Stephen. "Generalizing About Ovid." In *The Imperial Muse.* Edited by A. J. Boyle. Victoria, Australia, 1987.

Hine, Harry M. "Rome, the Cosmos, and the Emperor in Seneca's *Natural Questions.*" *Journal of Roman Studies* 92 (2002): 42–72.

Hine, Harry M., ed. *Seneca: Medea.* Warminster, 2000.

Holland, Richard. *Nero: The Man Behind the Myth.* Gloucestershire, 2000.

Holtrattner, Franz. *Poppaea Neronis potens: die Gestalt der Poppaea Sabina in den Nerobüchern des Tacitus.* Graz, 1995.

Impara, Paolo. *Seneca: Filosofia e potere.* Rome, 1994.

Inwood, Brad. "Seneca in His Philosophical Milieu." *Harvard Studies in Classical Philology* 97 (1995): 63–76.

———. *Reading Seneca: Stoic Philosophy at Rome.* New York, 2005.

Inwood, Brad, ed. and trans. *Seneca: Selected Philosophical Letters.* New York, 2007.

Jennison, George. "Polar Bears at Rome: Calpurnius Siculus, *Ecl.* 7.65–66." *Classical Review* 36 (1922): 73.

Jones, Christopher P. "Oratoria di Nerone." In *Seneca uomo politico e l'età di Claudio e di Nerone.* Edited by Arturo De Vivo and Elio Lo Cascio. Bari, 2003.

Kamp, H. W. "Seneca's Appearance." *Classical Weekly* 29 (1935): 49–51.

Kaster, Robert A., and Martha C. Nussbaum, trans. *Lucius Annaeus Seneca: Anger, Mercy, Revenge.* Chicago, 2010.

Ker, James. "Seneca, Man of Many Genres." In *Seeing Seneca Whole: Perspectives on Philosophy, Poetry and Politics.* Edited by Katharina Volk and Gareth D. Williams. Boston, 2006.

———. *The Deaths of Seneca.* New York, 2009.

———. "Seneca on Self-examination: Re-reading *On Anger* 3.36." In *Seneca and the Self.* Edited by Shadi Bartsch and David Wray. Cambridge, 2009.

Ker, James, Ronnie Ancona, and Laurie Haight Keenan, eds. *A Seneca Reader: Selections from Prose and Tragedy.* Mundelein, Ill., 2011.

Koestermann, Erich. *Cornelius Tacitus: Annalen.* Heidelberg, 1968.

Kohn, Thomas D. "Who Wrote Seneca's Plays?" *Classical World* 96 (2003): 271–80.

Kragelund, P. "The Prefect's Dilemma and the Date of *Octavia.*" *Classical Quarterly* 38 (1988): 492–508.

Lana, Italo. *Lucio Anneo Seneca.* Turin, 1955.

Lawall, Gilbert. "Seneca's *Medea*: The Elusive Triumph of Civilization." In *Arktouros: Hellenistic Studies Presented to B. M. W. Knox.* Edited by G. W. Bowersock. New York, 1979.

Lefèvre, Eckard. "Die politische Bedeutung von Senecas *Phaedra.*" *Wiener Studien* 103 (1990): 109–22.

Leigh, Matthew. *Lucan: Spectacle and Engagement.* Oxford, 1997.

Leveau, Philippe. "Mentalité économique et grands travaux. Le drainage du lac Fucin: Aux origines d'un modèle." *Annales ESC* 48, no. 1 (1993): 3–16.

Levick, Barbara. *Claudius.* London, 1990.

———. "Seneca and Money." In *Seneca uomo politico e l'età di Claudio e di Nerone.* Edited by Arturo De Vivo and Elio Lo Cascio. Bari, 2003.

L'Hoir, Francesca Santoro. "Tacitus and Women's Usurpation of Power." *Classical World* 88, no. 1 (1994): 5–25.

Lissner, Ivar. *The Caesars: Might and Madness.* New York, 1958.

Long, A. A. "The Stoics on World Conflagration and Eternal Recurrence." *Southern Journal of Philosophy* 23 (1985): 13–33.

Löwenstein, Hubertus Prinz zu. *Seneca: Kaiser ohne Purpur, Philosoph, Staatsmann, und Verschwörer.* Munich, 1975.

Luce, T. J., and A. J. Woodman. *Tacitus and the Tacitean Tradition.* Princeton, 1993.

Malaspina, Ermanno. "La teoria politica del *De clementia*: Un inevitabile fallimento." In *Seneca uomo politico e l'età di Claudio e di Nerone.* Edited by Arturo De Vivo and Elio Lo Cascio. Bari, 2003.

Malitz, Jürgen. *Nero.* Translated by Allison Brown. Malden, Mass., 2005.

Manning, C. E. *On Seneca's Ad Marciam.* Leiden, 1981.

Marti, Berthe. "Seneca's *Apocolocyntosis* and *Octavia*: A Diptych." *American Journal of Philology* 73 (1952): 24–36.

Masters, Jamie. "Deceiving the Reader: The Political Mission of Lucan's *Bellum Civile*." In *Reflections of Nero: Culture, History, and Representation.* Edited by Jás Elsner and Jamie Masters. Chapel Hill, N.C., 1994.

Mazzoli, Giancarlo. "Seneca de ira e de clementia: La politica negli specchi della morale." In *Seneca uomo politico e l'età di Claudio e di Nerone.* Edited by Arturo De Vivo and Elio Lo Cascio. Bari, 2003.

McAlindon, D. "Senatorial Opposition to Claudius and Nero," *American Journal of Philology* 77 (1956): 113–32.

McDermott, W. C. "Sextus Afranius Burrus." *Latomus 8* (1949): 229–54.

Mellor, Ronald. *Tacitus' Annals (Oxford Approaches to Classical Literature).* New York, 2010.

Millar, Fergus. *The Emperor in the Roman World.* London, 1977.

Momigliano, Arnaldo. "Note sulla leggenda del cristianesimo di Seneca." *Rivista storica italiana* 62 (1950): 325–44.

Mommsen, Theodor. *A History of Rome Under the Emperors.* New York, 1992.

Morford, Mark P. O. *The Poet Lucan: Studies in Rhetorical Epic.* Oxford, 1967.

———. "The Training of Three Roman Emperors." *Phoenix* 22 (1968): 57–72.

Motto, Anna Lydia. "The Idea of Progress in Senecan Thought." *Classical Journal* 79, no. 3 (1984): 225–40.

———. *Further Essays on Seneca.* Frankfurt, 2001.

Motto, Anna Lydia, and John R. Clark. *Seneca: A Critical Bibliography, 1900–1980, Scholarship on His Life, Thought, Prose, and Influence.* Amsterdam, 1989.

———. *Essays on Seneca.* Frankfurt, 1993.

Murphy-O'Connor, Jerome. *Paul: A Critical Life.* Oxford, 1996.

Nisbet, R. G. M. "The Dating of Seneca's Tragedies, with Special References to *Thyestes*." In *Papers of the Leeds International Latin Seminar: Sixth Volume.* Edited by Francis Cairns and Malcolm Heath. Leeds, 1990.

Nussbaum, Martha. *Therapy of Desire: Theory and Practice in Hellenistic Ethics.* Princeton, 1994.

———. "Stoic Laughter: A Reading of Seneca's *Apocolocyntosis*." In *Seneca and the Self.* Edited by Shadi Bartsch and David Wray. Cambridge, 2009.

Ogden, Daniel, ed. *The Hellenistic World: New Perspectives.* London, 2002.

O'Gorman, Ellen. *Irony and Misreading in the Annals of Tacitus.* Cambridge, 2000.

Osgood, Josiah. *Claudius Caesar: Image and Power in the Early Roman Empire.* Cambridge, 2011.

Overbeck, John C. "Tacitus and Dio on Seneca's Rebellion." *American Journal of Philology* 90 (1969): 129–45.

Pack, R. W. "Seneca's Evidence in the Deaths of Claudius and Narcissus." *Classical Weekly* 36 (1953): 150–51.

Palagi, Laura Bocciolini. *Epistolario apocrifo di Seneca e San Paolo.* Florence, 1985.

Pecchiura, P. *La figura di Catone Uticense nella letteratura latina.* Turin, 1965.

Plass, Paul. *The Game of Death in Ancient Rome: Arena Sport and Political Suicide.* Madison, Wis., 1995.

Prévost, M. H. *Les adoptions politiques à Rome.* Paris, 1949.

Radius, Emilio. *La vita di Nerone.* Milan, 1963.

Reynolds, Leighton D., ed. *L. Annaei Senecae: Dialogorum, Libri Duodecim.* Oxford, 1977.

———. *Texts and Transmission: A Survey of the Latin Classics.* Oxford, 1983.

Roller, Matthew B. *Constructing Autocracy: Aristocrats and Emperors in Julio-Claudian Rome.* Princeton, 2001.

Romm, James. "New World and *Novos Orbes:* Seneca in the Renaissance Debate over Ancient Knowledge of the Americas." In *The Classical Tradition and the Americas.* Edited by Wolfgang Haase and Meyer Reinhold. Berlin, 1993.

Rose, Charles Brian. *Dynastic Commemoration and Imperial Portraiture in the Julio-Claudian Period.* Cambridge, 1997.

Rosenmeyer, Thomas. *Senecan Drama and Stoic Cosmology.* Berkeley and Los Angeles, 1989.

Rubiés, Jon-Paul. "Nero in Tacitus and Nero in Tacitism: The Historian's Craft." In *Reflections of Nero: Culture, History, and Representation.* Edited by Jás Elsner and Jamie Masters. Chapel Hill, N.C., 1994.

Rudich, Vasily. *Political Dissidence Under Nero: The Price of Dissimulation.* London and New York, 1993.

———. *Dissidence and Literature Under Nero: The Price of Rhetoricization.* London and New York, 1997.

Schiavone, Aldo. "Anni difficili. Giuristi e principi nella crisi del primo secolo." In *Seneca uomo politico e l'età di Claudio e di Nerone.* Edited by Arturo De Vivo and Elio Lo Cascio. Bari, 2003.

Schiesaro, Alessandro. "Seneca's *Thyestes* and the Morality of Tragic *Furor.*" In *Reflections of Nero: Culture, History, and Representation.* Edited by Jás Elsner and Jamie Masters. Chapel Hill, N.C., 1994.

Seidensticker, Bernd, ed. *Seneca "Thyestes."* Frankfurt, 2002.

Shotter, David. *Nero Caesar Augustus: Emperor of Rome.* Harlow, 2008.

Smallwood, E. Mary. *Documents Illustrating the Principates of Gaius Claudius and Nero.* Cambridge, 1967.

Sorenson, Villy. *Seneca: The Humanist at the Court of Nero.* Edinburgh and Chicago, 1984.

Squillante, Marisa. "Il tempo della politica." In *Seneca uomo politico e l'età di Claudio e di Nerone.* Edited by Arturo De Vivo and Elio Lo Cascio. Bari, 2003.

Staley, Gregory A. *Seneca and the Idea of Tragedy.* Oxford and New York, 2010.

Stevens, C. E. "The Will of Q. Veranius." *Classical Review* 1 (1951): 4–7.

Stewart, Zeph. "Sejanus, Gaetulicus, and Seneca." *American Journal of Philology* 74 (1953): 70-85.

Strem, George G. *The Life and Teaching of Lucius Annaeus Seneca.* New York, 1981.

Sullivan, J. P. *Literature and Politics in the Age of Nero.* Ithaca and London, 1985.

Sutherland, C. H. V. "*Aerarium* and *Fiscus* During the Early Empire." *American Journal of Philology* 66 (1945): 151–70.

———. *Coinage in Roman Imperial Policy: 31 B.C.–A.D. 68.* London, 1951.

Syme, Ronald. *Tacitus.* Oxford, 1958.

Taoka, Yasuko. "Quintilian, Seneca, *Imitatio:* Re-reading *Instutio Oratoria* 10.1.125–31." *Arethusa* 44 (2011): 123–37.

Tarrant, Richard J., ed. *Seneca's Thyestes.* Atlanta, 1985.

Too, Yun Lee. "Educating Nero: A Reading of Seneca's *Moral Epistles.*" In *Reflections of Nero: Culture, History, and Representation.* Edited by Jás Elsner and Jamie Masters. Chapel Hill, N.C., 1994.

Townsend, G. B. "Calpurnius Siculus and the *Munus Neronis.*" *Journal of Roman Studies* 70 (1980): 169–74.

Tresch, Jolanda. *Die Nerobücher in den Annalen des Tacitus: Tradition und Leistung.* Heidelberg, 1965.

Trillitzsch, Winfried. *Seneca im Literarischen Urteil der Antike.* Amsterdam, 1971.

Trillmich, Walter. *Familienpropaganda der Kaiser Caligula und Claudius: Agrippina Minor und Antonia Augusta auf Münzen.* Berlin, 1978.

Vandenberg, Philipp. *Nero: Kaiser und Gott, Künstler und Narr.* Munich, 1981.

Veyne, Paul. *Seneca: The Life of a Stoic.* New York, 2003.

Volk, Katharina, and Gareth D. Williams, eds. *Seeing Seneca Whole: Perspectives on Philosophy, Poetry and Politics.* Boston, 2006.

Vottero, Dionigi. *Lucio Anneo Seneca: I frammenti.* Bologna, 1998.

Wacher, John. "Britain: 43 B.C. to A.D. 69." In *The Cambridge Ancient History,* vol. 10, *The Augustan Empire: 43 B.C. to A.D. 69.* Edited by Alan K. Bowman, Edward Champlin, and Andrew Lintott. Cambridge, 1996.

Wallace-Hadrill, Andrew. "The Imperial Court." In *The Cambridge Ancient History,* vol. 10, *The Augustan Empire: 43 B.C. to A.D. 69.* Edited by Alan K. Bowman, Edward Champlin, and Andrew Lintott. Cambridge, 1996.

———. "Seneca and the Pompeian Earthquake." In *Seneca uomo politico e l'età di Claudio e di Nerone.* Edited by Arturo De Vivo and Elio Lo Cascio. Bari, 2003.

Waltz, René. *Vie de Sénèque.* Paris, 1909.

Warmington, B. H. *Nero: Reality and Legend.* London, 1969.

———. *Suetonius: Nero.* London, 1977.

Wiedemann, T. E. J. "Tiberius to Nero." In *The Cambridge Ancient History,* vol. 10, *The Augustan Empire: 43 B.C. to A.D. 69.* Edited by Alan K. Bowman, Edward Champlin, and Andrew Lintott. Cambridge, 1996.

Williams, Gareth. "Nero, Seneca and Stoicism in the *Octavia.*" In *Reflections of Nero: Culture, History, and Representation.* Edited by Jás Elsner and Jamie Masters. Chapel Hill, N.C., 1994.

———. *The Cosmic Viewpoint: A Study of Seneca's "Natural Questions."* Oxford, 2012.

Williams, Gareth, ed. *Seneca: De Otio, De Brevitate Vitae.* Cambridge, 2003.

Winters, Jeffrey. *Oligarchy.* Cambridge, 2011.

Wood, Susan. *Imperial Women: A Study in Public Images, 40 B.C.–A.D. 68.* Leiden, 1999.

Woodman, A. J. *Tacitus Reviewed.* Oxford and New York, 1998.

———. "*Aliena facundia*: Seneca in Tacitus." In *Form and Function in Roman Oratory.* Edited by D. H. Berry and Andrew Erskine. Cambridge and New York, 2010.

Index

A NOTE ON THE TYPE

This book was set in Adobe Garamond. Designed for the Adobe Corporation by Robert Slimbach, the fonts are based on types first cut by Claude Garamond (c. 1480–1561). Garamond was a pupil of Geoffroy Tory and is believed to have followed the Venetian models, although he introduced a number of important differences, and it is to him that we owe the letter we now know as "old style." He gave to his letters a certain elegance and feeling of movement that won their creator an immediate reputation and the patronage of Francis I of France.

Composed by North Market Street Graphics,
Lancaster, Pennsylvania

Printed and bound by Berryville Graphics,
Berryville, Virginia

Designed by Soonyoung Kwon